SERVING NEW IMMIGRANT COMMUNITIES IN THE LIBRARY

SERVING NEW IMMIGRANT COMMUNITIES IN THE LIBRARY

Sondra Cuban

Foreword by Kathleen de la Peña McCook

U N L I M I T E D

A Member of the Greenwood Publishing Group

Westport, Connecticut • London

Library of Congress Cataloging-in-Publication Data

Cuban, Sondra.
    Serving new immigrant communities in the library / Sondra Cuban.
      p. cm.
    Includes bibliographical references and index.
    ISBN-13: 978-1-59158-297-7 (alk. paper)
    ISBN-10: 1-59158-297-0 (alk. paper)
    1. Libraries and immigrants—United States. I. Title.
    Z711.8C83 2007
    027.6'3—dc22   2006036843

British Library Cataloguing in Publication Data is available.

Library of Congress Catalog Card Number: 2006036843
ISBN: 978-1-59158-297-7

First published in 2007

Libraries Unlimited, 88 Post Road West, Westport, CT 06881
A Member of the Greenwood Publishing Group, Inc.
www.lu.com

Printed in the United States of America

The paper used in this book complies with the
Permanent Paper Standard issued by the National
Information Standards Organization (Z39.48–1984).

10   9   8   7   6   5   4   3   2   1

To my grandparents with loving memories:
Anne and Maurice Smith and Morris and Fanny Cuban

Contents

Foreword

The essayists in *Letters of Transit*, André Aciman, Eva Hoffman, Bharati Mukherjee, Edward W. Said, and Charles Simic, all spoke at the New York Public Library on different aspects of nomadism, immigration, exile and loss. The sponsorship of the series by a library long known for its commitment to serving people new to the United States exemplifies a model of cultural sensitivity. In *Serving New Immigrant Communities in the Library* Sondra Cuban challenges librarians throughout the United States to make similar commitments.

In her clear, straightforward narrative Cuban outlines the changing demographics of the United States, with new immigrants coming from a variety of countries—Mexico, India, the Philippines and China among them. Cuban's assessment coincides with intense national focus on immigration. On May 1, 2006, hundreds of thousands of immigrants demonstrated to influence Congress to allow those in the United States illegally to pursue citizenship; bills were presented in some states to punish employers who hire illegal immigrants; members of the House of Representatives called for 700 miles of fence to be built along the Mexico border; President Bush increased border patrols; deportations increased; and public debate was acrimonious and passionate.

As Cuban points out, citizens' attitudes toward immigrants tend to be negative or celebratory. Librarians can use the public sphere to explore citizens' responses to new immigrants by helping them face their attitudes with objectivity and information. Negative attitudes toward immigrants have recently been pulled together in Patrick J. Buchanan's

State of Emergency. A culturally competent librarian could sponsor a discussion of Buchanan's book juxtaposed with Richard Rodriguez's *Brown: The Last Discovery of America* or Owen Fiss's *A Community of Equals: The Constitutional Protection of New Americans.* By encouraging community discourse, anxieties based on ignorance or appeals to fear such as Buchanan's can be countered. General community discussion involving librarians can help to establish a baseline of philosophical intent that is grounded in respect for human dignity. Sondra Cuban emphasizes the need for cultural competence as a central value essential from the first day of study throughout a librarian's life and career.

The core of *Serving New Immigrant Communities in the Library* is a series of well-defined stages on which to develop a foundation for service. These include identification and understanding of the immigrants in a given community. As Cuban points out emphatically there is no single template that characterizes new immigrants. Even groups that seem similar—the Spanish-speaking, for example—may be from nations thousands of miles apart with extraordinarily different customs and sensibilities.

As a teacher of new librarians I am often surprised at the insularity of even well-meaning U.S. citizens. I recently taught a course on "Librarians and Human Rights" which included both students with roots in French-speaking Haiti and the Spanish-speaking Dominican Republic. I found that the U.S. students did not have common understanding of the colonial pasts of the two nations that share one island. Haiti's history as the first independent Black republic (1804) and the heroism of Toussaint L'ouverture was known to most, but not so the fact that Haiti ruled the Dominican Republic for nearly a quarter of a century until its independence in 1844. If a librarian in Miami-Dade County, Florida was to prepare a public program that appealed to the 36,000 people from the Dominican Republic and the 71,000 people from Haiti that reside in her service area, it would be essential to recognize the very different linguistic, cultural, and political differences among those whose families were from the same island. Similar challenges face librarians that want to be inclusive in providing access for people new to the United States. A service plan should be sensitive to the cultural and historical aspects of the lives of those to whom the library reaches out.

Community needs assessments require a greater and refined understanding of demographics if these assessments are to be effective in helping to craft programs that will appeal to new immigrants. It is especially important to differentiate by county of origin rather than language alone. Review of census data should help librarians tailor assessment tools to language *and* culture of community residents. If possible, multiple language instruments should be employed, but certainly connection to community agencies that serve immigrants is essential. An ambitious example serving the 60,000 Hmong people of St. Paul, Minnesota, demonstrates the kind of assessment process that Cuban recommends (Johnson 2001). However, librarians have seen quite recently (summer 2006) in Gwinnett County, Georgia that board members denied the right of librarians to purchase materials in Spanish (Eberhart 2006). National negative publicity caused them to overturn this decision, but the board's inclination to diminish services to immigrants is an indicator of the complexity of community assessment issues.

Once a community understands the totality of its residents' needs and culture and decides that service to all is truly the library's mission, a plan can be put into place to implement services. Cuban identifies multicultural resources. She also ties service delivery to the creation of culturally sensitive policies. Her exploration of the concept that resources alone do not activate service is a fresh approach to serving new immigrant communities. She is persistent in underscoring the need for librarians to adopt attitudes that facilitate use. Simple acquisition of materials is not enough.

In a larger sense Sondra Cuban is helping to form a new style of service that considers access to education and information as a human right (McCook and Phenix 2007). By recognizing that so many new immigrants come from the informal sector of their countries of origin and become part of the informal sector in the United States, it is imperative that intervention take place, especially for women and children. Access to the library and its resources can enable new immigrants to move from a marginalized status to participation in the full society.

Each new immigrant has a different story, but in the United States so many arrive from marginal economic circumstances that it is safe to point out that librarians can provide a spectrum of service and support. We can provide basic essentials such as literacy or ESOL resources to help new immigrants function in society. We can hold programs that help with cultural competence. We can develop opportunities to meet and discuss books from their former homes to alleviate strangeness. We can do so many things that will help in practical ways as well as in emotional and intellectual ways.

Above all, as Sondra Cuban shows with such lucidity, we must recognize the humanity in each new immigrant. I read Mahi Binebine's ironically named novel, *Welcome to Paradise,* last year. Although it is the story of immigrants trying to travel to Europe from Africa across the Strait of Gibraltar, it is also the story of all new immigrants.

The world went on turning. No one bothered about us, it was as if we didn't exist, as if we'd never been born. So come on, honestly, what did it matter if we were devoured here, or somewhere else or on the open seas? (p. 178)

In *Serving New Immigrant Communities in the Library* Sondra Cuban shows librarians how we must be concerned about these new immigrants, how we must help them to know they exist, and how we must ensure they are not devoured by an uncaring society but given the tools with which to flourish in their new homes. The dignity and respect that are each person's due as guaranteed by the *Universal Declaration of Human Rights* will be the framework that will guide librarians to be advocates for these new members of our communities.

Kathleen de la Peña McCook

ADDITIONAL RESOURCES

Aciman, Andre. *Letters of Transit: Reflections on Exile and Memory.* New York: New Press, 2000.

Alba, Richard, and Victor Nee. *Remaking the American Mainstream: Assimilation and Contemporary Immigration.* Cambridge, MA: Harvard University Press, 2005.

Binebine, Mahi. *Welcome to Paradise.* London: Granta, 2003.

Buchanan, Patrick J. *State of Emergency: The Third World Invasion and Conquest of America.* New York: St. Martin's Press, 2006.

Davis, Mike. *Planet of Slums.* London: Verso, 2006.

Eberhart, George. "Gwinnett County Board Fires Director." *American Libraries* 37 (August 2006).

Fiss, Owen. *A Community of Equals: The Constitutional Protection of New Americans.* Boston: Beacon Press, 1999.

Johnson, Carol P., and others. "Collaboration Generates Synergy: Saint Paul Public Library, the College of St. Catherine, and the 'Family Place' Program." *Reference and User Services Quarterly* 41 (Fall 2001).

McCook, Kathleen de la Peña and Katharine Phenix. "Public Librarians and Human Rights." *Public Library Quarterly* (forthcoming, 2007).

Rodriguez, Richard. *Brown: The Last Discovery of America.* New York: Penguin, 2003.

Acknowledgments

I would like to thank all of the public librarians and public library advocates I talked to who are committed to making libraries more culturally diverse and accommodating for new immigrant communities. These are Kathleen de la Peña McCook, Anne Helmholz, Maru Villalpando, Deborah Jacobs, Shelley Quezada, Maureen O'Connor, Satia Orange, Dale Lipschultz, Hediana Utarti, Tracie Hall, Steve Sumerford, Gale Greenlee, Robin Osborne, Yolanda Cuesta, Yazmin Mehdi, and Emily Wong. There are countless other tireless workers in library land whom I did not get a chance to talk to, but whose work with new immigrants is very important to their communities.

I would also like to thank all of the library learners and patrons I talked to in my study of persistence (who remain anonymous) about their experiences in library literacy programs and about their lives, as well as the directors and staff of these programs. The data from the persistence study were supported by the many adult literacy educators with whom I worked: Kathy Endaya, Norma Jones, Leslie McGinnis, Resonja Willoughby, Mari Noguchi, Gale Greenlee, Steve Sumerford, Lou Sua, Bruce Carmel, Michael Semple, Anita Citron, Sherlette Lee, Barbara Martinez, Terry Sheehan, Decklan Fox, and Ken English. This study would not have happened without the help of the learners and these dedicated professionals. The Hilo Public Library and Hawai'i's public library system were also gracious, and I thank them for their assistance and support during the time I lived in Hilo as well as the leaders of the

Hawai'i public library system and the University of Hawai'i library staff. Finally, the staff of the Seattle Public Library was tremendously helpful.

For the book, I thank my editor, Barbara Ittner, who believed in my work and helped to get this in shape for publication.

My friends in adult literacy and ESOL were invaluable for supporting me in the writing of this book: Steve Reder, Lorna Rivera, Rachel Martin, Clare Strawn, Alisa Belzer, Klaudia Rivera, Elsa Auerbach, and Carolyn Clarke. At Harvard, I thank my colleagues and friends who also supported me: Liz Molle, Rebecca Garland, Robin Waterman, Dominique Chlup, Lauren Wedam, and Ellie Drago-Severson, as well as visiting professor and colleague Nelly Stromquist, who took a special interest. Lastly, I have been lucky to have worked with Deborah Brandt, whose ideas on sponsorship took my work to the next level.

My Seattle Book Club friends, especially Catherine Cantrell and Patti McLaughlin sustained me through the writing of this book as did Pam Taylor, Bob Peña, and Jeffrey Anderson at Seattle University. At Lancaster, a very special thanks to my mentor, Mary Hamilton, and also to David Barton and Corinne Fowler for their wonderful support during the writing of this book and to all of the Literacy Research Centre staff for their inspiration.

Thanks also to my family and my oldest, dearest friends for showing interest, helping me persist, and believing in me: Ozias Goodwin, Larry and Barbara Cuban, Janice Cuban, Cielle Cuban, Betty Hayes, Aviva Samet, Kimberly Coleman, Angela Giacomini, Katharina Heyer, and Hediana Utarti.

INTRODUCTION
Serving New Immigrant Communities

THE NEED FOR LIBRARY SERVICES FOR
NEW IMMIGRANT COMMUNITIES

They let you know you're not alone, and that's what they're here for. And believe you me, if you come here tired, when you leave here you feel like a million dollars, because you feel like you learned something. (Simone)[1]

"If immigration is to be a success," one librarian stated, "institutions like libraries have to make it work" (Larsen, Jacobs, and Vlimmeren 2004: 4). For generations, librarians have faced the great challenge of meeting the needs and interests of their changing ethnic communities. However, today's immigrants contend with different societal issues than did those in the past, and they test library services in new ways. Although "migration is not a new story," observes library diversity specialist Tracie Hall, "it is written larger than before—on a wider scale everywhere" (Hall 2005).

How so? The creation of new and more sophisticated demands in literacy, education, and workforce qualifications has raised the ante for survival for new immigrant communities, challenging libraries to adapt to complex pressures. Consider Simone. She is a Jamaican food-service worker who attends a library-based literacy program in preparation to get her GED diploma. This diploma is a necessary tool for the new economy and one that her library has decided is critical to help provide.

Simone represents the one out of every thirty-five persons—over 3 percent of the global population—who is an international migrant. The United States leads the world as one of the top destination countries for immigrants. Since the late 1990s, sending countries include Mexico, the Philippines, Vietnam, the Dominican Republic, and China.[2]

Top Ten Countries of Legal Immigrants in the United States (listed in descending order according to number of people coming from these countries)[3]
Mexico
India
Philippines
China
El Salvador
Dominican Republic
Vietnam
Colombia
Guatemala
Russia

Who are the new immigrants and how are they different from previous generations of immigrants? Although no hard and fast definition exists, it is instructive to look back a few decades.

Essentially, the new immigration started in the mid-1960s, when the civil rights movement was in high gear and the United States passed the Hart-Cellar Act. This important bill abolished the old quota systems that gave preferential treatment to Europeans over immigrants from other countries. It also set in place criteria such as family ties and needed skills that made it easier for people to enter the country, and it increased the overall quota of immigrants.[4]

The New Immigrants

After the passage of this law in 1965, immigration rates grew faster—especially in the 1990s, a decade that reached the highest point in immigration in nearly a century (Jones 2004).[5] Many librarians consider the last ten to fifteen years to be a defining period of the "new immigrants" (Cuesta 2005; Osborne 2005). And the pattern continues.[6] Due to the forces of globalization and world conflict, nearly every year many legal immigrants enter the United States to join their family members, to work, and to increase their standard of living.

Undocumented immigrants, temporary residents, and refugees also enter, and more women than ever are on the move in search of work in what has been referred to as "the feminization of migration."[7] Upward of 750,000 legal immigrants arrive in the United States each year, as well as an estimated 450,000 to 500,000 illegal immigrants.

Currently, around 32.5 million foreign-born people reside in the United States, representing approximately 11 to 12 percent of the total population. Most of these immigrants come from one of the ten major countries; and they settle in areas where their friends and families live or recommend—in twenty-seven of the largest urban areas of the United States (Alfred 2001; Bernstein 2005; Jones 2004; Lieschoff 2004; Lobo and Salvo 2004; Milam 2003; Waldinger 2001).

Criteria for Finding Good Statistics on Immigration

Many websites claim to have statistics on immigration that seem to be from official authorities. These sources may be entitled "Center of . . . " but take a closer look:

- Look at the source—is it official? (Is it the census? the *2004 Yearbook of Immigration Statistics*?)
- Look at the language—is there a clear bias against immigration? Does the text include terms such as "terrorist" or phrases such as "ruining America"?
- If it is a national think tank on immigration, see what other websites say about it—what is its political viewpoint?
- Ask what websites your colleagues use to gain answers to immigration FAQs.
- Remember that certain sources have access only to legal immigration figures, whereas illegal immigration figures are only estimates. Related to this, "illegal" is a political term. When a person has his or her documents taken away, that person can become "illegal," so be careful in your use of this term.

At the cusp of the twenty-first century, the one in five Americans who were born abroad or who are children of parents born abroad are now considered the "emerging majorities" rather than "minorities" (Quezada 1992). Mostly from Asia and Latin America—especially from Mexico— the new immigrant communities are changing the ethnic landscape of both urban and rural communities, especially in states such as California, New York, Florida, Illinois, and Iowa; and their numbers have dramatically increased in just the last ten years (Abboud 2001; Jones 2004; Sparks 2001; Suarez-Orozco 2001a, 2001b; Waldinger 2001; *2002 Yearbook of Immigration Statistics*).

> **Where Do New Immigrants Live?**
> Of all new immigrants, 60 percent live in six states: California, New York, Texas, Florida, New Jersey, and Illinois. California has the highest percent of immigrants. But the fast-growing states are in "non-traditional" regions in the South and Midwest. To illustrate, Georgia's immigrant population grew by almost 39 percent in only five years.[8]

The American Southwest and West have experienced tremendous ethnic shifts, and multilingual/ethnic groups dominate many cities, such as Miami. Gateway cities, such as New York and Los Angeles, are still home to many immigrant groups; but within the last decade, the fastest-growing destination cities and states have been places such as Greensboro, North Carolina; Atlanta, Georgia; and Las Vegas, Nevada (Sykes 1994; Waldinger 2001, 2004).

This accelerated immigration rate has also altered the lingua franca of the United States. More than 35 million adults in the United States are native speakers of languages other than English; and this trend is expected to continue, especially for Spanish. There are 41.3 million Hispanics in the United States, and in some places, such as Los Angeles, more than half of the population is Hispanic. Latino populations expand at a faster rate than non-Hispanic populations and account for over half of the overall population growth.

Some major linguistic groups in the United States come from Mexico, the Philippines, India, China, Vietnam, Korea, Cuba, and El Salvador (Alire and Archibeque 1998; Associated Press 2005; Jacoby 2004a, 2004b; Lieschoff 2004; Quezada 1992). Of course, new immigrant communities speak multiple languages, with some places such as Queens boasting as many as seventy-seven multilingual groups. It has even been predicted that by 2010, English-speaking and non-English-speaking first-generation and second-generation black immigrants (with one foreign-born parent) will reach 4.3 million—12 percent of the total U.S. black population (Rong and Brown 2001).

Compared to the native-born population, immigrants arriving in the United States are disproportionately poor and have lower levels of education and opportunities (Suarez-Orozco 2001a, 2001b). In addition, having limited English proficiency (LEP) means lower earnings—62 percent of low-wage workers are considered to be LEP.[9] These factors—especially few educational opportunities—create new demands on institutions such as libraries to help immigrants better function within the greater society and ultimately reach social and economic parity. Such dramatic changes in population and ethnicity have had a ripple effect on libraries, and in becoming increasingly aware of this phenomenon, library leaders have expressed concern about being "adrift in a sea of change" (Carlson et al. 1990). Put simply, society is calling on libraries to serve a more diverse clientele, and therefore libraries should map their populations by language and ethnicity. Yet this is rarely being done (Carton 1993; Milam 2003).

Immigrants and the Library

In spite of the fact that library services do not always adequately meet the tremendous needs of new immigrant populations, immigrants use libraries. One librarian aptly refers to her library as a "mini United Nations" (Paulson 2004). An ALA national study showed that over a period of twelve months, 58 percent of the Hispanic population and 72 percent of the Asian/Pacific Islander population used libraries.[10]

Why do immigrants come to the library? What do they expect or need? How do they use the library? Immigrants (and low-income groups) want and expect different practices, services, and programs. New immigrant groups want educational services and they often perceive the public library system as enabling them to move up the socioeconomic ladder. The particular language spoken in the home and the presence of school-aged children often determines immigrants' amount of library use (Benton Foundation 1996; D'Elia 1993; Luevano-Molina 2001; NCES 2002).

As part of its historic mission, the American public library system plays key roles in helping immigrants adapt to their new lives by providing relevant information, materials, referrals, and programs that enable them to feel less "alone." The ALA 1997/98 policy campaign of President Barbara Ford, "Global reach, local touch," has attempted to respond to immigrants' needs and to recognize the roles of the public library and of public librarians in what is commonly referred to as "the global village."

One immigrant library user confessed to feeling out of touch with his new culture: "Being an immigrant, I had to deal with many cultural conflicts. Libraries provided solace and wisdom and experiences from many past generations of immigrants. I learned that the issues I faced were not unique."[11] This need for belonging is especially urgent during a time in which social and human services for immigrants have plummeted, and immigration laws have become even more stringent. In fact, the public library system may be one of a few "safe" institutions to which immigrants can turn. Libraries have an opportunity to increase immigrants' and refugees' self-determination and opportunities in communities. In turn, immigrants can provide libraries with many different kinds of support and sponsorship (Benton Foundation 1996; Elturk 2003; Jones 2004; Larsen, Jacobs, and Vlimmeren 2004; Shriver 2002).

Exemplary libraries have worked hard to reach out to immigrant populations and their different needs. Immigrants often say that these library staff members are like "family" because everyone is welcoming and concerned; and the staff may even speak their language. For immigrants, these libraries are accommodating social centers.

One Mexican community college student said, "Here I feel like I am part of a family. I am in the library meeting with people, or reading, or practicing."[12] In such libraries, immigrants experience a type of familiarity that is accepting of their cultures—an attitude that is unfortunately too often absent from other institutions.

Of her library experience one Guyanese woman exclaimed, "I feel light, like you come in and you talk to one another, and you feel nice—when I come out I feel like I forget my problem at home."

Other immigrants come to the library strictly to get materials, such as books and tapes for themselves and their children, and to use the computers. One Salvadoran single mother comes to the library with her son every Saturday, her one day off work each week. She states, "We read a book. We go downstairs. He likes the computer. So, he plays on the cartoonnetwork.com and I play with him or we read a book. We get books, movies, and things like that."

Another woman, a German professor who lives in Hawai'i, brings her one-year-old to the public library in order to instill the values of reading she grew up with in her country. Still others turn to the library for self-directed English learning.

A refugee from Rwanda studying for his TOEFL exam said, "My interest was the library, you know? It's evident that we like to read books, and that was my first question: 'Where is the library?' And I had that—I thirsted to improve my English . . . I think the way to improve my English will be to go to the library and try to read as much as I can. So, that's why I try to ask about the library."

Other immigrants come to the library for its one-on-one or small-group ESOL and literacy programs. One young Puerto-Rican man, a high-school dropout in New York, had never spent time in a library, but ultimately came to one because of its literacy services. He said, "I have never been to a library in New York City. . . . I was only staying home, hanging out with my friends. So I wasn't thinking about school. Now I decided because I said to myself, that's it. I can't take it no more.

So I decided to come here. It's all right. The staff here, they are nice . . . I am learning something here. How to use the computer. I'm writing now. My reading is getting better. I am getting to read like hard books."

As you can see, new immigrant adults come to the library for many reasons:

- To read
- To improve English
- To use computers
- To form community affiliation
- For their own reading enjoyment and that of their children

These learning opportunities are often unavailable in other institutions (such as community colleges), which charge fees, operate during limited weekday hours, require registration and proof of immigration status, and demand certain behavior and academic standards. Those institutions also require higher literacy skills (defined by federal compliance standards) as part of their entry requirements.

In contrast, libraries frequently serve as models for creating important "learning communities" that are adaptable and flexible, and help immigrants acculturate by offering multiple learning, literacy, and language opportunities, as well as comprehensive life-skill development.[13] In this sense, libraries compensate for the formality, rigidity, and scarcity of other institutions and resources.

Anti-Immigrant Sentiments

> We are a nation of immigrants that created foreigners.
> (Larsen, Jacobs, and Vlimmermen 2004: 23)

Let's face it. Other forces and beliefs often go against the acculturating efforts of the library system. Like other public institutions, libraries are not immune to larger societal forces. Although the public library mission has been to educate immigrants, and new immigrant groups such as Asians and Hispanics (especially Mexicans) have a high regard for public libraries, anti-immigrant movements have been building since the 1970s and are affecting libraries today (Escatiola 2001; Monroe 1986; Trejo 2001; Zhang 2001).

Some native-born community members resent the fact that their libraries focus on new immigrant communities, whose needs they may allude to as "foreignizing" influences. They lodge complaints about having to spend their tax dollars on non-English materials or on hosting programs for "aliens." A mayor in California, for example, was quoted as saying, "If they [librarians] want patrons to read foreign-language books and periodicals, they can go purchase books on their own," and, "This is the United States of America" (Trejo 2001: 115). Opponents of immigration generally believe that the purpose of libraries is to Americanize and assimilate immigrant communities, with an English-only agenda, rather than to acculturate or to pursue "selective acculturation," a process in which institutions support immigrants in taking many different paths (Portes 2004).

Public and private "think tanks" have studied these tensions and trends in the relations between immigrants and native born. But they can be biased. One agency (Center for Immigration Studies 2005) believes that public institutions such as libraries and schools are not assimilating immigrants as well as they should because the "culture at large is skeptical, even hostile, to patriotism and . . . technology enables immigrants to maintain strong psychological and physical ties to their countries of origin."

Some community members accuse libraries that accommodate immigrants of doing so only because they "boost door counts." In other reports, social conservatives blame immigrants—particularly post-1965 immigrants—for social problems ranging from overcrowding, consumption of valuable resources, and environmental degradation to crime and teen pregnancies; rather than viewing immigrants as a source of economic growth, national wealth, and cultural regeneration (Bischoff 2001; Escatiola 2001; Middle American News 2005).

Indeed, public opinion in the United States is divided on whether immigration is a positive or negative force. Although members of the public appear to be more welcoming now than they were just after 9/11, they are generally negative about immigrants' cultural impact. Some 62 percent of nonimmigrants say that the United States should have "basic American culture and values" and not be a "country made up of many cultures and values that change as people come here" (Orlando 2005).

Of utmost concern to many Americans is the volatile issue of illegal immigration. Some 63 percent of nonimmigrant taxpayers express that too much is spent on education and health care for immigrants, and 54 percent say that "the wrong kinds of people" are coming to the United States. These polls reveal a "let them stay but get tough policy" with limited regulations on labor, such as guest worker programs.[14]

Protests by immigrant communities across the nation erupted in April and May 2006 against punitive legislation making it a felony to be in the United States illegally, authorizing the building of a wall along the Mexico-U.S. border, and assessing penalties. Just prior to these protests, a *Time* poll of about 1,000 Americans showed these results: eighty-two percent felt that the government is not doing enough to keep illegal immigrants out; 75 percent felt illegal immigrants should not receive public services such as health care; and over 50 percent felt that the children of illegal immigrants should be denied a public education (Tumulty 2006). The general consensus is that these twenty-first-century new Americans from developing countries are less educated and less able to assimilate than previous immigrant groups. These attitudes are often also linked to negative attitudes Americans have about public services. In 2001, respondents to a *New York Times* poll expressed feelings of social and political alienation, and voiced isolationist sentiments about foreign policy (Bischoff 2001; Escatiola 2001).

Unhelpful Scripts

"Scripts" in the public discourse that either celebrate or denigrate new immigrant groups fuel sentiments about immigrants and polarize the population.[15] The anti-immigrant script can be seen in the mainstream news media, which inflame fears with depictions of immigration as an "invasion." The media claim that all immigrants are illegal and illegitimate, responsible for destroying a "good" homogeneous culture (Orlando 2005; Rao 2005).

Research and information fueling the immigration debate can be biased, with estimates of illegal immigrants ranging from 7 to 11 million (Jones 2004: 185). There is also the problem of quantifying assimilation (Berger n.d.; Jacoby 2004a, 2004b; Jones 2004: 185). Then the *Hernstein and Murray IQ Report* (1994) focuses on whites as more intelligent than others. New immigrants cannot ignore the thinly disguised expressions of racism all around them given the fact they are probably not Caucasian, unlike previous immigrants whom society considered more acceptable and viewed with less suspicion (Jeng 2001; Portes 2004).

Laws can also create anti-immigrant sentiments. Post-9/11 legislation reinforces the view of immigration as intrusion. The Patriot Act monitors communications, and its access to personal information expands the government's investigative authority. Stricter welfare reform excludes immigrants from many public services. English-only laws, such as

California's Proposition 187 (known as "save our state" legislation), and anti–affirmative action bills, such as Proposition 209, limit opportunities for immigrants. The Homeland Security Act and other changes in immigration law focus on security identification, limit citizenship applications, triple border controls, impose quotas on refugees, and expand guest worker programs to allow people to enter the United States solely for the purpose of work.[16]

Many human rights groups consider these laws to be exploitative of new immigrant groups, who are often casualties in workplaces that have hazardous conditions. According to a 2005 Human Rights Watch Report (*Beacon Hill News* 2005b: 5), "Federal laws and policies on immigrant workers are a mass of contradictions and incentives to violate their rights." All these significant measures demonstrate and reinforce alarmist views about immigration, while creating fear among immigrants about using institutions that could turn and betray them; for example, the profiling of immigrants from Muslim countries (Escatiola 2001; Jones 2004). One immigrant library patron in a library literacy program felt hypervigilant about her future; she cautioned that "anything could happen in this country."

The celebratory perspective, on the other hand, tends to romanticize the experiences of new immigrants, rather than taking into account the realities of their lives, struggles, and needs. When polled, for example, immigrants believe they are hardworking and that they are being unfairly discriminated against (Orlando 2005). These immigrants do not want to be romanticized by the public and the media, but only recognized as contributing to society. Certainly, complexity needs to be brought back into the picture. In one major study on multilingual gatekeepers in libraries, researcher Cheryl Metoyer-Duran (1993a) found that people's perceptions of their ethnic groups are complicated and defy simple categorization.

The library community as a whole has countered these trends through its resolutions on intellectual freedom and the U.S. Patriot Act, through the creation of the American Library Association (ALA) Office and Committee for Diversity and Intellectual Freedom, and through the Presidential Initiative on Minorities. For example, ALA has focused on identifying discrimination practices and on developing a "curriculum on readiness for the 21st century librarian."

In addition, in 2004 the ALA Office of Literacy and Outreach Services (OLOS) developed a guiding framework for library diversity issues. It includes partnering options in communities, creating a new mission statement that includes new Americans, ensuring that equity of access is reflected in practice, and developing collections and materials based on relevant needs and interests. But these measures do not go far enough.

Librarians must walk a fine line between these tensions and sometimes take unpopular stands in order to serve a socially excluded constituency with increasingly important needs. Immigrants do not yet have a full voice in our society (Waldinger 2001).

Tracie Hall claims that because much of the diversity work in librarianship is "ubiquitous, rhetorical, and accidental," it needs to be systematically and carefully implemented for it to take hold and be effective (Hall 2005). Diversity work starts in library schools and continues as graduates become practitioners. Library schools and public libraries must work together to increase the number of minorities being educated and working in libraries. This is essential for attracting a diverse clientele. It is also imperative from the beginning to create sensitivity among librarians to respond in a culturally competent way to the new immigrant communities that are increasingly using the library system.

A CULTURALLY RESPONSIVE APPROACH TOWARD NEW IMMIGRANT COMMUNITIES

Educator Sonia Nieto describes culture as "the ever changing values, tradition, social and political relationships and worldview created and shared by a group of people bound together by a combination of factors that can include a common history, geographic location, language, social class, and/or religion, [and which] are transformed by those who share them" (Mullins 2001: 3). Identified as "culturally diverse" institutions, libraries respond and adapt to their constituents' needs by being "cultural brokers," acutely aware of differences within the community (Paulson 2004; Sykes 2001). Yet libraries can and should provide meaningful services over and beyond typical "cultural tourism"—a token celebratory aspect of diversity and considered a supplemental rather than integral part of library culture. Although, for symbolic purposes, celebrating holidays of different cultural groups is important, librarians must respond to these groups' everyday needs in a dynamic, continuous, and nonsuperficial way. This deep level of cultural awareness empowers different cultural groups, helps to reduce anti-immigrant prejudice, and integrates content into all aspects of the library system (Quezada 1991).

Librarianship needs a multicultural education perspective (Banks and Banks 2004). At its best, multicultural education penetrates the very fabric of an institution, transforming social practices for the sake of social change. An advocacy approach in libraries allows different ethnic groups to use the library system to fulfill their needs and to confront mainstream society's discriminatory practices.

Keep in mind that new immigrants are not passive participants in existing social structures; instead, they actively interpret the meaning of their socialization and adaptation by engaging in activities that attempt to empower them within their ethnic communities (Giroux 1992; Ogbu 1983; Rong and Brown 2001; Sleeter and Grant 1987). For this reason, the librarian's role with new immigrant groups must be relational and interactive. Through a "socio-cultural approach to planning" (Sparks 2001), libraries can emphasize the tools, contexts, strategies, and practices of new immigrant users, focusing on complex factors of cultural differences in learning and meaning embedded in everyday life. By implementing this approach, libraries are supporting new immigrant communities to "read the word and the world" (Freire 1987).

Sponsoring New Immigrant Communities

Serving new immigrant communities well does not mean simply acting as an informational hub to connect immigrants with existing services. It entails going beyond by not only deeply responding to immigrant communities by preserving and building on their cultures but also serving as a bridge to mainstream society. This book explores the idea of responding to cultural diversity through sponsorship. According to educator Deborah Brandt (2001: 19–20), sponsors are

Powerful figures who bankroll events or smooth the way for initiates. Usually richer, more knowledgeable and more entrenched than the sponsored, sponsors nevertheless enter reciprocal relationships with those they underwrite. They lend their resources, credibility to the sponsored but also stand to gain benefits from their success, whether by direct repayment, or indirectly by association.

In policy, although not always in practice, libraries historically have sponsored new immigrant communities to increase their social and cultural capital. They do this by providing a pathway for immigrants to connect with other agencies and settle into their new communities, along with providing resources that assist in their transition and in meeting the real demands they face in mainstream society. Libraries serve as sponsors to help immigrants navigate and adjust to their new worlds. Librarians recognize the political implications of their roles and position themselves at the side of immigrants. In this context, individual librarians act as mediators. This role, according to Tracie Hall (2005), "is critically important—if librarians are out of touch, that will problematize the library as a cultural institution."

A HISTORICAL SKETCH OF LIBRARY SERVICES TO IMMIGRANTS

Today's immigrants, like earlier immigrant groups, perceive the American public library as a helper and a "passport to a better life." In cities such as New York and Boston, generations of immigrants have flocked to libraries for materials and services. New immigrants, some of whom never had access to libraries in their own countries, often first become aware of the library as an important resource even before they arrive in the United States. One new immigrant who could not get into a community college program in Queens due to the strict entry requirements, instead came immediately to the library and later reported, "Somebody is always there to help you out in some way."

An appreciative Jamaican woman in the Bronx said of the Centers for Reading and Writing (at the New York Public Library):

Working on the computer is like—it's an education. It's reading, and no matter what we have or what we do today, reading is the future . . . anyone who can get the opportunity any time to put their hand on a computer, or a library to read something, their life will be great. Yes.

This Jamaican woman is writing her story in a literacy program, thereby adding to the rich narratives of all of the immigrants who came before her. For example, in the nineteenth century the immigrant author Mary Antin, who wrote, "as I move about at will in the wide spaces of this splendid palace [the Boston Public Library] whose shadow covers acres. . . . It is not I that belong to the past, but the past that belongs to me" (Antin 1969: 36). Through programs such as the one the Jamaican woman is in, the library sponsors stories of marginalized people and thus makes their lives visible on shelves.

Libraries have assisted immigrants—from Eastern European Jews in the twentieth century to Jamaicans in this century—in telling their stories, becoming citizens, and networking with social service agencies and schools. Libraries have provided books and literacy services to build knowledge and for Americanization. The early immigrant groups did not so much intend to become culturally assimilated as to seize opportunities to become part of the American dream (Thernstrom 2004)—what author Mary Antin referred to as "the promised land." She, as an early twentieth-century Russian immigrant author, nostalgically referred to the library as a "kingdom in the slum" (1969: 337). Simone, the Jamaican woman (cited earlier), in *this* century says that the library makes her feel like "a million dollars." Like both of these women, countless other immigrants have relied on this enduring, secular, and free institution for adult community-based education necessary for their cultural adjustment, and even for preservation of their own cultures. Indeed, the American public library and immigrants for generations have been reciprocating sponsors—of immigrants' needs and of the library's cultural resources.

Historically, both barriers and incremental gains have marked the relationship between libraries and immigrant groups. This relationship continued to be paradoxical into the late twentieth century (Jones 2004), varying from Anglo-conformity at one end of the spectrum to sympathetic cultural pluralism at the other. At the Anglo-conformity end, such social reformers as John Foster Carr emphasized "melting-pot assimilation"; and librarians followed along with their Americanization efforts (Jones 1991, 1999; Wiegand 1998). Libraries' "high culture" collections were an important tool in this quest, according to John J. Arnold (1919), vice president of the National Bank of Chicago:

To spend an evening with a group of our foreign born in the study of literature or music without a doubt brings the conviction that here is the most fertile ground for the sowing of the seed of Americanization. We must aim to develop the normal man, which includes his physical, mental and spiritual nature. (18–19)

On the other end of the spectrum (sympathetic cultural pluralism), such library leaders as Ernestine Rose early in the twentieth century emphasized librarians' active roles in engaging with new immigrants in a substantive manner to help their process of acculturation. Libraries' services were to include foreign collections, comfortable environments that allowed for the varied dress codes and manners of different cultures, community needs assessments, librarian assistants who spoke different languages, personalized contacts, and a stimulation to read as well as gather practical information for day-to-day living.

In the early twentieth century, librarians actively marketed the library to new immigrants with leaflets and flyers; and they promoted their foreign collections for their intrinsic value. The enthusiasm and advocacy of such librarians led them to be labeled as "sovereign alchemists."

Their whole purpose was to assist new immigrants in becoming citizens while simultaneously endorsing their languages and cultures (Dain 1975; Fain 1992; Jones 1999).

Of course, librarians were not the only sponsors of new immigrants; older generations of immigrants were, too. Historical analyses have shown that ethnic groups used libraries for cultural preservation and that wealthier immigrants acculturated newer immigrants through library collections and assistance. This interethnic support may have served as the most significant buffer of all to new immigrant groups who experienced discrimination socially and politically through quota systems, literacy requirements, and citizenship tests (Beck 1992; Birge 1981; Cook 1977; Dain 1975; Fain 1992; Jeng 2001).

At that time, many laws had a racial bias in favor of Anglo-Europeans. For example, the first immigration laws in 1790 favored "free white persons"; and as of the late nineteenth century naturalization of Chinese and Japanese immigrants had been severely limited for decades (Jeng 2001; Lee and Sheared 2003).

What Has Changed?

Librarians have had to contend with important new characteristics of immigration in the post-1965 era. Immigration, now dominated by populations from non-European countries, as indicated earlier, brings up many language learning and education issues (Suarez-Orozco 2001a, 2001b). This trend poses challenging issues for the types of services and advocacy libraries can offer.

Many of the post-1965 library immigrant services grew out of progressive ideology from the nineteenth century (the sympathetic cultural pluralism discussed earlier) and the civil rights movement of the 1960s. Librarians served minority populations, called "the disadvantaged," in the context of an "opportunity library" (Lipsman 1972; Martin 1967). Librarians viewed this as a collective effort—and as part of their social responsibility—to empower communities, with the outreach campaign slogan of "People Make It Happen" (Coleman 1983; Hanna 1978). The Civil Rights Act of 1964 and the Immigration Reform Act of 1965 reinforced the national War on Poverty campaign and promoted libraries as elevating the "public good" and fostering democratic ideals (Thernstrom 2004).

Seldom did the rhetoric of social responsibility, however, match reality in some areas of outreach services, such as literacy education. Indeed, librarians showed considerable ambivalence about delivering literacy services. Although in theory social responsibility and professional ethics were a nice fit, in actual practice most librarians did not regard that joint agenda as their main professional role (Lipsman 1972; McDonald 1966; Nauratil 1985).

Plummer Jones's framework (2004) for understanding post-1965 immigrant library services and their development from the 1970s to the present reveals the paradox that has historically characterized the relationship between libraries, librarians, and immigrant groups. Here is a summary of Jones's framework.

The 1970s: Cultural Awareness

Jones (2004) characterizes this decade as one that focused intensely on ethnic awareness of new immigrant groups. Many Southeast Asian refugees (e.g., Vietnamese, Cambodian) came to the West Coast; and the East Coast saw an increase in Caribbean populations, such as Jamaicans and Dominicans. Libraries responded with model cities projects, neighborhood information centers, and other information and referral (I & R) services. Perhaps the biggest development was the Queens Borough Public Library's New Americans Program in 1977, with its focus being to "expand library services to immigrants whose primary language is not English and to attract newcomers to the library and assist them in adjusting to their new surroundings through acquisition of appropriate materials and creation of special training programs, workshops and services while fostering an appreciation for their unique cultural makeup" (Gitner and Chan 2001: 122).

The 1980s: A Multicultural Purpose

In the 1980s, public libraries began to recognize their need to do more than add special projects for burgeoning ethnic communities; they also needed to institutionalize these efforts to address fully the needs and expectations of immigrants through all library policies, programs, and services. Libraries drew up policies for encompassing ethnic diversity. Various task forces emerged in the ALA both to promote multicultural and multilingual services as necessary and to assert the need to understand ethnic minorities in order to develop more positive attitudes toward services for them.

California's library system, a major attraction for new immigrant communities, responded to the state's intense population growth with a 1988 initiative for a statewide conference to focus on racial and ethnic minorities. Following this, a government-sponsored White House Conference on Library and Information Services in Washington, D.C., made recommendations for multicultural and multilingual services (Cohen 2001).

These efforts had limited effects, however, under the conservative Reagan administration, which placed new restrictions on the number of refugees and immigrants who could enter the United States; and reduced federal funding for immigrant public services in general (Jones 2004; Lee and Sheared 2003). While more Southeast Asian, Irish, and Soviet immigrants and refugees, as well as Mexican, Filipino, Chinese, Korean, and Vietnamese groups, thronged into the country during this period, thousands of Central Americans—mainly Salvadorans fleeing from civil war—were deported. A movement to reduce undocumented immigration emerged at this time; and the Immigration Reform and Control Act of 1986 instituted new prohibitions on their employment.

The 1990s: Responding to the Growth and Mobility of New Immigrant Communities

Jones characterizes this decade as one of growth and conflict. With the rise of globalization and the economic boom, the U.S. population grew and changed more rapidly than at any previous time. More immigrants entered the country between 1990 and 1997 than during the entire 1980s. The growth in population during the 1990s to over 280 million, including 14 million immigrants, was reinforced by the NAFTA agreement that opened U.S. borders with Canada and Mexico. At the same time, a new nativist movement developed, focusing intensely on the issue of illegal immigration (in 1990 and 1995), with measures such as Proposition 187, "save our state," in California. Fewer immigrants applied for citizenship during this time, mobility between countries increased, and bilingual education was reduced (Jeng 2001).

Libraries devoted a smaller proportion of library budgets to minorities relative to their growth in population nationally, and immigrant services also declined. With the shift from the Library Services and Construction Act (LSCA) to the Library Services and Technology Act (LSTA), in 1996, projects were distributed according to a population-based formula and administered through states. Ultimately, this had the effect of inhibiting services—North Carolina's Foreign Language Center was closed down, for example—and they became increasingly limited to certain areas. One study found that although 50 percent of library literacy programs served immigrants, only 9 percent of such programs

were doing this through the more broadly based lifelong learning services (NCES 2002).

However, some growth in programs for new immigrants occurred
during the 1990s in specialized services for Spanish-speaking adults and
their families: for example, the United States–Mexico Cooperative Library
Education program, the Center for the Study of Books in Spanish for
Children, and the Trejo Foster Foundation. Immigrant subgroups also
grew in the 1990s, and efforts to recruit librarians from different ethnic
groups increased. The Spectrum Initiative was one notable program;
and REFORMA (the Association to Promote Library and Information
Services to Latinos and the Spanish Speaking) focused its initiatives on
multilingual populations. Clearly, research into the needs both of ethnic
librarians and of the populations they represented was called for, but
libraries did not collect data systematically (Padilla 1991: 158). Until
research is done properly, myths about the twenty-first century's new immigrant communities will persist as barriers to libraries' genuine sponsorship of cultural diversity. As this decade is still forming itself within the era
of globalization and mass migration, libraries can become key players.

UNDERSTANDING IMMIGRANT POPULATIONS: MYTHS AND REALITIES

Consider some common myths about new immigrant communities
with regard to how people talk, relate, eat, work, and live their lives.
Where did these views originate? Most people's perceptions about new
immigrant groups come from a variety of places: media, school, family,
friends, workplaces, and the streets, as well as firsthand experiences.
One of the most difficult myths to debunk is the belief that people from
the same ethnic group are all the same. Let's say you have a conversation
with someone from a different ethnic group than your own, and you
do not continue to engage with this person or anybody else from that
group. You may begin unconsciously to believe that all people from this
group think and act the same way. You carry this mythic idea around
with you, and it impacts the way you respond. The same goes for countries. Not all people from the same country speak the same language or
are from the same ethnic group. With little education or exposure, these
myths can easily develop into stereotypes. Librarians must be in touch
with the diversity of new immigrants, both as groups and as individuals.
Therefore, it is vital not to neatly package and label an immigrant group
as having one particular characteristic.

We receive the first generation stranger not with an open embrace but with mockery, with jokes and slurs and sweatshop wages, with inferior schools in the inner cities, and with harangues about "assimilation" with simpleton or savage representations on our movie and TV screens. Most of us who are Americans now were immigrants before, but a generation or two removed from the fact, we regard the "wretched refuse" with embarrassment (Martinez 2004: 7).

Differences Among New Immigrants

Different immigrant groups bring with them a multiplicity of characteristics and resources; and they construct their experiences in their adopted land in different ways. In order to make your library services relevant in practice as well as in theory, you must acknowledge and understand these differences. Let's turn to a more detailed examination of new immigrants and their characteristics.

Only one other decade (1900–1910), when over 8 million immigrants entered the United States, has witnessed similar rates of immigration as now. But two important differences exist between present-day immigration and the immigration of the early twentieth century: today's ethnic diversity among immigrants and a more polarized social-class demographic pattern (Jacoby 2004b; Lee and Sheared 2003; Sparks 2001; Suarez-Orozco 2001a, 2001b). This is known as the "hourglass" syndrome, with the most educated and wealthy at one extreme, and the least educated and most poor at the other extreme (Jacoby 2004b; Suarez-Orozco 2001a, 2001b). Here are five important considerations for libraries with respect to new immigrant groups:

1. The reasons for immigration
2. Occupational status and social class
3. Nationality and race
4. Gender
5. Generational factors

These factors create distinct pathways that new immigrants follow in their adjustment to the United States.

The Reasons for Immigration

Is immigration voluntary or nonvoluntary? Are individuals immigrating for a better quality of material life, or do they come as refugees from life-threatening circumstances (Alfred 2001)? Perhaps both.

Within your community, find out what countries people are coming from and why. Where do the new immigrants come from? An educated northern or southern Asian professional who immigrates with savings and firm plans to develop a family business, or to work in a well-paying industry, experiences life in the United States very differently from a refugee from Southeast Asia who has spent years in refugee camps and has little education or savings. Educated and prospering immigrants can be considered upwardly mobile "transnationals," straddling the cultures of their home countries and the United States, sending money home, visiting, and sponsoring family through financial means (Alfred 2001). In contrast, many refugees dare not return to their countries, even to visit, for fear of persecution; and it is much harder for them to become financial sponsors of relatives still in their home countries. In terms of library services, the first group might want financial information on starting a business, whereas the second would need basic survival information.

Occupational Status and Social Class

Labor migrants, professional immigrants, and entrepreneurial immigrants each have distinct needs (Alfred 2001), as well as different social mobility routes. The labor migrant encounters limitations because "unlike the low-skilled factory jobs of yesterday, the kinds of jobs typically available to low-skilled immigrants today do not hold much realistic promise for upward mobility. These immigrants tend to settle in areas of deep poverty and racial segregation" (Suarez-Orozco 2001a, 2001b: 350). For example, labor migrants in the early twentieth century were likely working in manufacturing plants, where they might rise to supervisory status or have the opportunity to learn English on the job, which could empower them to transfer to other businesses. However, today's labor migrants tend to be involved in agriculture and service industries, where they are often stuck. Labor migrants enter the United States legally through Family Reunification Bills and through other channels. They may come to the United States to "resolve their financial problems at home, and then return, when they are able" (*Beacon Hill News* 2005a). These "bidirectional" arrangements serve the needs of individuals and the interests of the country that accepts them (Alfred 2001).

Professional immigrants, on the other hand, are given preference by the U.S. government. With more advanced degrees, they are drawn to the knowledge-intensive sectors of the economy; they intend to thrive, rather than just survive (Suarez-Orozco 2001b). However, they still may suffer from racial discrimination, just as the labor migrants do. Entrepreneurial immigrants must show proof of sufficient funds in order to enter the United States. They typically have a single purpose—to establish a business within a specific period of time (usually two years); and they contribute to the U.S. economy through work or investment. Many of the people in this group have management experience and have owned businesses in their native countries—Korea, Italy, Iran, Pakistan, Canada, Russia, and Japan (Alfred 2001). However, even these immigrants may experience racial discrimination and a downward economic spiral in this country. For example, highly qualified Chinese and Taiwanese may be barred from promotions to managerial status just because they are not white (Alfred 2001). This brings up race issues.

Nationality and Race

In the process of acculturation, immigrants of all kinds—voluntary or not, legal or undocumented—find that nationality and race play an important role in their ability to succeed. The most important factors are skin color (sometimes also hair) and language (Lee and Sheared 2003). In the past, Jews, Irish, Italians (Gans 2004), and the Portuguese in Hawai'i were all considered "people of color"; but they eventually assumed the status of whites once they dominated the middle class. Unfortunately, this has not been the case for blacks (Gans 2004), who were taken to this country against their wills and still struggle with racism and oppression today. In fact, Asians and Hispanics have achieved more "residential assimilation" than have African Americans (Steinberg 2004). Such prejudices may become adopted and internalized among new immigrants; for example, they, too, may start to discriminate against African Americans (Gans 2004).

Mainstream Americans' labels for immigrant groups—such as the "model minority" label often applied to all Asians (Trejo 2001; Zhang 2001; Zhou 2004)—increase racial prejudices by creating various illusions. Examples are that racial discrimination does not exist, that only "hard work" counts, that immigrants need no legal protections, and that no subgroups exist.

Mexican-Americans, for example, have even been called "permanent foreigners" although there is a Latino middle class (Rodriguez 2004), a growing consumer sector, a rising rate of intermarriage with Caucasians, and a broadening of what it means to be Latino.[17] Despite all these visible trends, mainstream Americans all too often possess a prejudiced and separatist attitude toward Mexican immigrants, assuming that they and other Latino immigrants constitute a single group (Alire and Archibeque 1998).

Gender

On the global level, half of all immigrants are women.[18] Women often deal with a double layer of discrimination in their home countries and in the receiving culture between their traditional roles and their new roles. One study (Rockhill 1990) found that Mexican immigrant women wanted to learn English and receive an education in order to acculturate and have a social identity. Because these aims conflicted with their domestic roles, their husbands regarded their newfound education with suspicion and resentment.

Another study (Zhou 2004) of immigrant Chinese women with little English found that they took lower paying jobs in Chinatown because those employers were flexible about the women's domestic commitments. As a result, these women were able to socialize with other Chinese women, exchange information, support their children's academic progress, and help one another. In addition, they gained valuable information about acculturation from middle-class Chinese people who visited or did business with them. Strong ethnic community empowered these women.

In contrast, stressful and isolating circumstances—domestic violence, war-induced trauma, poor health coverage, and the demands of caregiving (Adkins, Birman, and Sample 1999; Cumming 1992; Isserlis 2000; Singleton 2002)—all too often compromise the health of women immigrants and refugees in general. They also prevent women from achieving their goals in their new country.

Generational Factors

Older generations of immigrant communities (those in the United States early in the post-1965 boom period or before) are a critical force in brokering ethnic power (Beck 1992; Metoyer-Duran 1993a). Over time, a number of immigrants have leveraged their dual-citizenship electoral rights and their earning power (Suarez-Orozco 2001a, 2001b). For example, second-generation immigrants tend to earn more than the first generation (Jacoby 2004a).

However, both newer and older generations of immigrants contend with cultural challenges, such as the preservation and use of their languages in the United States, sometimes referred to as a "graveyard of languages" (Jacoby 2004a: 24). Poverty does not help. Second-generation children who were born abroad, or whose parents were originally from another country, and who attend overcrowded inner-city schools, may scorn mainstream success (Suarez-Orozco 2001b). Yet one study has pointed to a "post-ethnic" generation of children who at school generally speak English, but at home speak their native language, as well as vernaculars such as Spanglish.

In creating a service plan for new immigrants, it is vital to build on the realities of new immigrant communities, which contrast starkly to popular myths. And remember, that librarians are in a position to educate the public as well as support immigrants in their endeavors to improve their lives.

Before You Start, Consider These Questions

1. What are your attitudes toward, and experiences of, providing services to new immigrant communities?
2. What myths do you believe about new immigrant communities, and how do you think they affect services in the library?
3. Who are the "new immigrants" in your community, and how are they being served—or not—by your library?
4. How much do you know about immigration trends, and what types of knowledge can help you to fill in the gaps?

ENDNOTES

1. "Simone" is a pseudonym for a learner in the Center for Reading and Writing, Fordham Library, of the New York Public Library. The author interviewed her for a study on persistence (from 1999 to 2003); the study has appeared in a jointly published work: Porter, Cuban, and Comings 2005.

2. For more statistics on immigration on an international level, see the following sources: Antonia G. Moreno, "Public Libraries and Immigrant Populations in Spain." Presentation at the IFLA Satellite Meeting, Utrecht, The Netherlands, August 11, 2003. See http://www.sitegenerator.bibliotheek.nl/iflautrecht/img/docs/Moreno%20spain%20def.ppt. See also James Smith and Barry Edmonston, eds., *The New Americans: Economic, Demographic and Fiscal Effects of Immigration* (Washington, D.C.: National Academies Press, 1997) at http://darwin.nap.edu/books/0309063566/html/28.html. For national statistics of new immigrants, one of the best official sources is the *2004 Yearbook of Immigration Statistics* at http://www.uscis.gov/graphics/shared/statistics/yearbook/index.htm; see also the 2002 version to compare: *2002 Yearbook of Immigration Statistics*.

For a population growth story, see http://www.cbsnews.com/stories/2006/05/12/politics/main1615051.shtml. Be aware of the many websites (and the sources they use) to be able to discuss immigration in relation to population growth.

3. Statistic is from the Migration Policy Institute, *Immigration Facts* no. 9 (October 2004). See http://www.migrationpolicy.org/Factsheet_102904.pdf. For more information on immigrant mobility from a historical perspective, see Waldinger 2001, 2004.

4. The world statistics are drawn from Moreno, "Public Libraries and Immigrant Populations in Spain." See also UNPAC, *Women and the Economy*, Winnepeg, Manitoba, Canada. See http://www.unpac.ca/economy/introglob.html.

5. The census of 2000 shows that the national foreign-born population increased at a faster rate in the 1990s, by 57 percent, to over 31 million in 2000, accounting for 11 percent of the U.S. population, up from 8 percent in 1990; reported in Lobo and Salvo 2004. See also Waldinger 2001.

6. See Bernstein 2005. She has reported on a study showing a decline in legal immigration in conjunction with a rise in illegal immigration, especially from Mexico, since 2000.

7. For more information on the feminization of migration, see UNPAC, *Women and the Economy*; and Barbara Ehrenreich and Arlie Hochschild, *Global Woman: Nannies, Maids And Sex Workers in the New Economy* (New York: Henry Holt, 2002). For information on immigrants as second language learners, see Lieschoff 2004.

8. See Migration Policy Institute, *Immigration Facts* no. 9. (October 2004); see also Rob Paral. "The Growth and Reach of Immigration," Immigration Policy Brief, August 16, 2006 (as well as other articles on different subjects) of the American Immigration Law Foundation. See http://www.ailf.org/ipc/policybrief/policybrief_2006_81606.shtml.

9. See National Immigration Law Center, *Facts About Immigration,* 2004. For more statistics on immigration, literacy, education levels, and the labor market, see a Mass Inc. policy document: Comings, Sum, and Uvin 2001. See also Suarez-Orozco 2001b for an excellent perspective on socioeconomic disparities of new immigrants; and http://gseweb.harvard.edu/~hepg/fa01msuar.htm.

10. See *ALA Fact Sheet* no. 6, [From "Using Public Libraries: What Makes a Difference?" in *American Libraries*, November 1997], American Library Association, 2005. See http://www.ala.org/ala/alalibrary/libraryfactsheet/alalibraryfactsheet6.htm.

11. This anecdote is from Jack Su, Champaign, Illinois. Other anecdotes from library patrons appeared at the end of an American Library Association website article entitled "Libraries: Global Reach. Local Touch" (1997), which is now defunct.

12. This college student and the subsequent anecdotes, except for the German professor, were taken from the author's interview notes for the persistence study (Porter, Cuban, and Comings 2005).

13. For more information on learning communities, see Jean Lave and Etienne Wenger, *Situated Learning: Legitimate Peripheral Participation* (Cambridge, England: Cambridge University Press, 1991).

14. For more information on these issues, see an article, Orlando 2005; and a report, Tumulty 2006.

15. Suarez-Orozco is quoted in an American Education Research Association paper by Stanton Wortham, Elaine Allard, and Katherine Mortimer, "Chronicles of Change: Models of Mexican Immigrant Identity in Suburban Community Narratives," presentation at the American Educational Research Association, San Francisco, 2006.

16. See Martinez 2004; Luevano-Molina 2001; and Escatiola 2001. The 9/11 factor has reduced refugee entry by 72 percent in 2002, according to Alfred 2001/02; the *Yearbook of Immigration Statistics* also reports a decline in refugees for the third consecutive year in 2002, representing low levels since the late 1970s. The numbers of legal immigrants have also declined according to a study reported by Bernstein 2005: 1; policies that were proposed in 2005 by the Bush administration would allow illegal immigrants to apply for guest worker status for a limited time period. For this and more, see Bacon 2005.

17. See Jacoby 2004a, 2004b; She reports on corporate ethnic markets and that Latino buying power grew heavily in the last decade. Hispanic America claims the eleventh highest GDP in the world.

18. Moreno, "Public Libraries and Immigrant Populations in Spain."

CHAPTER 1
Knowing and Planning for New Immigrants' Needs

Immigrants have substantial informational and practical needs for help with adjusting to life in a new country. Due to differences in language, culture, and other factors such as access, however, new immigrants are a difficult population to study. As a result, little research has examined their predilections from an information behavior perspective.[1]

It may seem obvious that libraries can be bridges to community resources for new immigrant communities (Hall 2005; Sisco and Whitson 1990). But exactly what are those needs, and which ones should be given priority? This chapter will show how to lay the groundwork for your plan to serve new immigrants' needs and to become an information mediator with this population. Of course, librarians' roles as information mediators to new immigrant communities are part of a long history, and a brief look at it follows.

A BRIEF HISTORY OF THE LIBRARY AS INFORMATION MEDIATOR

A century ago, librarians in immigrant centers in New York saw the library as a "meeting place." In 1917, Ernestine Rose wrote, "It is the one institution . . . where all beliefs, creeds, ages, and races may meet. You are free as air; you may come, you may go; you will not be proselytized if

you stay . . . perhaps the freedom and helpfulness of the libraries result
in more natural social contacts than any conscious activity" (1917: 12).
At this time, because they were unfamiliar with their new constituents,
librarians actively reached out to local community groups and assessed
needs by walking the streets, visiting people's homes, going to lectures,
getting training, and using informants who advised them on what their
new communities wanted from the library. Staff members might greet
immigrants in their own languages (Gottfried 2001). Further, libraries
conducted lectures, theatrical productions, and readings by immigrant
authors accompanied by receptions. Indeed, from field trips to museums to mothers' clubs to parties and gardening, libraries created space
to accommodate immigrants' needs and interests (Gotffried 2001; Rose
1917). One user commented, "You have the Jewish spirit in this room.
We feel it as Jews! And yet you are Christians!" (Rose 1917: 23). This
willingness to learn through informal types of assessments continues
today, as librarians still walk neighborhoods with community members,
keeping their "ear to the streets" (Hall 2005).

By the 1930s, the library began to take on a role as a community educator for adults (Birge 1981), but it was not until the 1960s that libraries
started to experiment with this role for low-income and minority populations. During this decade, libraries sought to provide new immigrant
communities with different types of information services—for their
survival, for their social activism against discrimination, and for their
citizenship applications (Durrance 1984; Owens 1983, 1987). Terms
such as "community librarianship" (Martin 1967) meant that libraries
intervened socially in communities, as instruments of social change.
Part of this agenda was to "de-institutionalize" the library to enable it
to become more accessible and fit with other core agencies (such as
human services and schools). The library system became a multiser-
vice, one-stop center with identities ranging from a community activity
center, to an independent learning center, to a popular materials library
(Nelson 2001: 62).

During this period, librarians primarily focused on learning community
members' needs through "community-based research," whose heyday in
the education field was in the 1960s and 1970s (Strand et al. 2003). Also
at this time community needs assessments came into vogue. Library
leader Helen Lyman asserted that libraries were in a good position to
conduct community assessments because of their importance in communities and their capability in necessary research skills. In Lyman's
view it was vital that librarians develop ethnic awareness and meet new
immigrants' current needs and preferences, such as for materials in their

own language and from their own cultures. She developed a community analysis checklist for this purpose and defined various steps in the process: identifying key people (called stakeholders) already interested, targeting a sector of society, and then developing a proposal to initiate new programs. Of course, the whole process required some flexibility because of inevitable changes in structuring and collaboration, as well as organizational (i.e., curricular) reform (Lyman 1973, 1977a, 1977b).

The efforts of librarians in the early twentieth century were a direct response to the influx of immigrants that came into the United States. In the years following, after the wave of immigration subsided, other concerns and roles took priority in libraries. For example, the library as a repository of information became a popular trend. Today this situation is similar to that of the early twentieth century, with a burgeoning and diverse immigrant community. Many of the ideas dating from thirty or even a hundred years ago are valid today, going by different names such as "community profiling," "environmental scanning," and "community asset mapping." These and other methods focus on strengths in communities rather than deficiencies, and they seek to use them to the immigrants' advantage. Most importantly, in practicing these methods, librarians get to know their communities so deeply that they become advocates. Librarians, according to library historians, "must know the community, must study its component parts, its industries, its recreations, its connections with the rest of the world" (Plummer Jones in Vang n.d.: 3). Chapter Two discusses these strategies and presents both practical and meaningful ways to tap into—and plan for—the needs of new immigrants. But first, let's take a closer look at what information needs are and how they apply to good practice.

INFORMATION "NEEDS": WHAT THEY ARE AND HOW THEY APPLY TO NEW IMMIGRANT COMMUNITIES

Information needs analysis can help you build understanding of how community members define their needs, under what conditions they express their needs, and the barriers that prevent access to achieving needs (Dervin 1977, 1980; Kulthau 1991; Zweizig 1976). Our communities are changing rapidly, so this is not a one-time effort. Needs analysis must be conducted on a regular basis. Furthermore, in an era in which new immigrants readily relocate, it is not uncommon for librarians to find themselves abruptly in the midst of a new community whose needs they do not know. A library in Queens had to turn swiftly to addressing the needs of a Croatian community, for example (Abboud 2002). Consider the many barriers to library use that immigrants face (Pateman 2003).

1. *Institutional barriers* are punitive rules and complicated procedures in libraries that make it difficult for new immigrants to use them, such as fine systems and identification requirements.
2. *Personal and social barriers* are ways of interacting that do not take into account the cultures of new immigrant communities; for example, telling patrons who are translating to one another to hush.
3. *Environmental barriers* are problems in the community that make it difficult for new immigrants to physically access the library, such as poor transportation systems.
4. *Perceptional barriers* involve new immigrants' lack of knowledge about the library or not believing that libraries can actually address their needs, for example, in locating housing or finding a job.

The Hardest Barrier to Reduce

Let's take a closer look at perceptual barriers, which can be the most difficult ones to address. One librarian observed:

When faced with a move, a learner used the internet to research available housing, obtain quotes from movers, and use Mapquest to pinpoint locations. (Weaver 2001: 145)

Consider this: What if new immigrants in a community must move, and they need information but do not know that this service exists at the library? Librarians must do research about what new immigrants know and do not know about the library.

Through conducting research on new immigrant communities, you can identify these barriers and discover what new immigrants need from the library. It may not be easy for the library to switch gears and play the role of listener and questioner; checking out people is a much different process from checking out books (Seager 1993). Yet it is vital to know about cultural differences and what information people need in order to bridge the culture gap between the library and the community. Chapter Two addresses the particulars of how to assess community needs.

Planning for the information needs and barriers that you identify is the key to success. In designing your strategic plan, you will need to take into account all of the different factors that could affect new immigrants' use of the library, such as gender, age, education levels, and other cultural issues (see Introduction). Ask, observe, and immerse yourself in new immigrant communities, seeing these community members as resources for the library: as advocates, board members, employees, volunteers, and, most importantly, as planning members. Creating a strategic plan that includes all of the library's stakeholders should be the first action step.

A STRATEGIC SERVICE PLAN FOR NEW IMMIGRANT NEEDS

Before starting the process of actively planning to meet new immigrants' information needs, identify those needs. Then think strategically and develop an approach that is systematic and brings the right people to the table.

An Inclusive and Well-Organized Plan

New immigrants should know the library's policy direction and the rationale for this, and their views should be incorporated into a consensus on vision and purpose. New immigrant communities, librarians, and other community members are responsible for this process. Take steps that fit with cultural norms, proceed within a reasonable time frame, and make sure goals and objectives are all commensurate with available resources. The overall planning process involves the following four important elements:[2]

- Articulating a community vision for serving new immigrants
- Scanning the community and identifying its needs
- Scanning library services to determine how to address new immigrant community needs
- Writing a cumulative vision statement to be implemented at the library

Articulating Your Community Vision for Serving New Immigrants

This important step positions the library as both an established member of the community and an integral player in community building. It also draws new immigrant community members into a process of dialoging about the future of their community. A community vision focuses on the gap between the current and future status of the community, and on how goals can be fulfilled within a given time span (for example, ten years).

To be meaningful to all members of the community, this vision should identify any known needs and barriers that exist as well as any that will be researched. Finally, the vision must place a premium on process, operating according to democratic principles in order to hear voices in an open forum. Form committees that include librarians, city officials, and community gatekeepers (representing different ethnic groups) to develop and discuss this vision, and name a diversity of library stakeholders representing different perspectives. Base the size of the committee on the number of perspectives that represent the community you want at the table. Likewise, meeting times need to be flexible and regular enough so as to ensure continuous involvement of as many participants as possible. Because the goal is to go step by step through the plan, the meetings should maintain both continuity and diversity.

Back up the vision with a plan to research new immigrant communities' needs. This research should follow steps for what is commonly referred to as a needs analysis (Sparhawk and Schickling 1994). First, consider the kinds of information needed for making informed recommendations and to ensure the representation of a broad range of stakeholders (for example, bringing together many different new immigrant communities and focusing on their needs through community dialogues). Second, assess the specific types of data to be collected (new immigrants' use of library services) and how to collect and analyze the data effectively (see Chapter Two). Finally, create a general vision statement that defines the commitment to achieving the vision, similar to a mission statement. It does not have to be definitive at this point and can be considered a draft. Here is a sample draft vision statement of a hypothetical library:

The Green Library is committed to being responsive, culturally sensitive, and a center to both current and future generations of new immigrants. We plan to learn about new immigrants' needs and resources in our community, and build on them through ongoing committee work, research, and dialogue. First and foremost, the library will take into account and address the needs and barriers of new immigrants. Presently the main needs and barriers are housing and job segregation; poor transportation systems; and little knowledge about the available services in the library—all of which limit new immigrants' opportunities. We aim to address these major needs and establish this vision within a five-year time period. This vision represents diverse perspectives of the library's key stakeholders. [State the names and whom they represent.]

Scanning the Community and Identifying Its Needs

The next step is to assess your community's needs by defining its current conditions (socioeconomic and others). This undertaking should be a collaborative process, to ensure recognition of all demographic conditions and factors and a consensus about their importance. Form several loose committees (different from or the same as the vision committee members) consisting of knowledgeable library stakeholders (including new immigrant representatives, library staff and board members, as well as city council members). These committees report on strengths and weaknesses of community resources, discuss opportunities for new growth, and define threats such as laws that inhibit freedom of speech. A listing of general community needs (based on current conditions) can then evolve from these reports, which then connects to the barriers found. The list might look like this:

- Quality transportation systems
- Better housing conditions
- Free Internet access
- More and better jobs

The New Americans Program in Queens provides a good example of a quality needs assessment. Faced with the challenge of how the established community could take advantage of the language resources of new immigrant communities, the library conducted a process of ongoing community assessment with different strategies (such as probing questions) and participants (Gitner and Chan 2001). Through these efforts the library staff pieced together a picture of neighborhood needs and target populations.

The Seattle Public Library undertook a similar endeavor in 2002 when its director formed a community task force to learn about the needs of two Seattle populations: the Vietnamese and the Spanish speaking. Although the decision to focus on these communities was not formalized, various factors provided the basis: (1) the greater knowledge that the library had of these groups; (2) the groups were visible, growing populations in Seattle; and (3) the library had available collections in their languages and a perceived ability to serve them well through future programming.

Early in the process, the Seattle task force sought to learn about best practices, so its members visited model library systems in the country such as the Queens Borough Public Library. In 2003–2004, they conducted focus groups of community gatekeepers (leaders in the community) and surveys (of library user walk-ins and people at community festivals). These reports identified programming needs, and then nineteen programs were designed for these communities that were consistent with the needs of immigrants and affected their use of the library (Mehdi 2005). Examples were job workshops, computer classes, story discussions, and writing seminars. The task force also discovered the importance of perceptual barriers (such as immigrants' knowledge of library resources) and social and personal barriers (needing personal attention) for library use.

Your committee first should ask basic questions about new immigrant communities' information needs:

- What familiar sources are useful for immigrants to turn to, how are they used, and why?
- In what situations is some information for immigrants considered better than others?
- For what problems is information used by some ethnic groups but not by others?

In addition, determine the responsiveness of certain communities to working together with libraries. If they are responsive, what types of communications would they prefer to use in this dialogue and in what languages? (Wagner 2004). What would be the best forum for communication: face-to-face meetings or newsletters or phone calls? As committee members dialogue about these issues with community stakeholders, a continuous conversation begins.

To learn even more about these questions, and especially about new phenomena in communities, the library can do some "environmental scanning" (discussed in more detail in Chapter Two). This is a kind of "radar to scan the world systematically and signal the new, the unexpected, the major and the minor," lending "strategic intelligence" to organizations (Morrison 1992). Environmental scanning involves gathering demographic information from your community to highlight critical environmental factors affecting the communities under study.

This crucial process should be a "natural" for librarians who have research skills and can use those skills to identify the demands of their communities and new issues that face them. Then the library can understand trends in new immigrant communities and their needs. It is important to scan for social, technological, political, economic, and environmental factors: to seek signs of change in communities, look for signals of potential events on the horizon (for example, imminent wars;

technological advances), search for experts' forecasts, examine indirect effects, and write abstracts that help communicate what is known about the trends and patterns (Morrison 1992).

Environmental Scan Factors	Name and Amount	Potential Events (future)	Expert Forecast
Social (schools, associations)			
Technological (amount of technology)			
Political (what group yields power)			
Economic (income levels)			
Environmental (pollution factors)			

Record information in these categories in spreadsheets or tables such as this to easily see the totality. After doing research, your committee should have this important information about these clearly identified factors. This general list should flag issues deserving of closer examination. Articulate how these issues affect the community (potential events on horizon, for example) by writing a brief report stating what these trends indicate about the community's current and future status. Decide how often to conduct scanning, taking into account the rapidity of demographic changes, as well as the availability of resources and time. You may want to consult knowledgeable resources to equip yourself and your staff in scanning techniques. (See Selected Bibliography, as well as ALA's list of library consultants on its main website, http://www.ala.org.)

Scanning Library Services to Determine How to Address New Immigrant Community Needs

The next step is to review, scan, and audit current library services to define what and how your library can best contribute to the community vision and new immigrants' needs, beyond simply gathering data. Before beginning this process, reflect on the library staff's general attitudes, experiences, and openness to learning. After all, "the first step in cultural competency is in acknowledging the fact that we don't know enough about other cultures" (Elturk 2004: 1). Knowledgeable library staff or library-based consultants can give self-reflection or antidiscrimination workshops that enable participants to reflect on their cultural assumptions and dialogue with one another about them.

Assess your library's past and present relations with new immigrant communities, as well as the gap between the present and (likely) future levels of diversity. This process helps to build a case that, even as budgets are stretched tight, librarians can readily answer the question of why resources are going to serve "these people" (Larsen, Jacobs, and Vlimmeren 2004: 21). Engage in a questioning process on all aspects of diversity—the library collections, mission statements, languages spoken, cooperation with other institutions, the existence or absence of respectful rules and regulations, and the degree of cultural sensitivity and incorporation of multicultural perspectives. What is the library's current level of multicultural education? For this, a multicultural education checklist (which includes the aforementioned issues) can assist in developing good questions, as well as training in multicultural education, which library-based and education consultants can give.

Your Multicultural Education (ME) Checklist
This is a useful *starting point* for assessing multicultural education (ME) in your library. But follow through with trainings and readings on ME.

1. Are all staff and community members aware of multicultural education?
2. Are all staff, including the administration, as well as community members willing to learn more about ME?
3. What is the current level of ME in your library? How can it be improved for new immigrants? What skills and resources can be drawn on to improve it?
4. Are all staff and community members willing to make changes to create a multicultural education library? Are they willing to change library mission statements, collections, services and programs, climate, collaborations, and policies to reflect an ME perspective? (Banks and Banks 2004; Cuesta 2004)

Also ask general questions for reflecting and assessing new immigrants' cultural needs and whether they are being addressed as part of the library's multicultural education. A literacy roundtable in North Carolina (NCLA) sponsored a program (ALA OLOS meeting 2004) focused around a basic question: "What's happening in ESOL at your library?" It also surveyed all North Carolina public libraries to determine the level of ESOL services and reported those results.

Overcoming Transportation Barriers

Hundreds were on the waiting list for Redwood City's Project READ, a library literacy program. In addition, ESOL learners (mostly women) had trouble getting to the main library because either they could not drive or else public transportation services were inconvenient and/or too costly. Therefore, the library arranged for new immigrants to have off-site, one-on-one tutoring in their homes or in small groups in nearby local schools. This arrangement dispensed with the logistical problems for the ESOL learners and increased the literacy program's effectiveness and reach. This innovative strategy can be clearly stated in the library's vision statement and serves as a model.

Writing a Cumulative Vision Statement That Can Be Implemented at Your Library

After finishing your needs assessment, return to the original vision statement and flesh out the details. For this, the library may want to form a single committee to make the process more manageable. But you can pilot it on the other committees, as well as other library systems, to get their feedback and strengthen it. For this vision statement, committee members will more definitively state the following: how, and to what degree, the library can meet various needs of its immigrant communities; or else what types of collaborations with other agencies could enhance services or fulfill these needs in some other way.

For example, committee members may discover that better transportation is a major need of a new immigrant community. The library might not be the best institution to provide for this need directly, but it certainly can deal with the need indirectly. The committee might articulate this by stating, for example, that the library can provide information and referral for alternative transportation, advocacy for better public transportation, collaboration with other agencies such as schools, and improved outreach through bookmobiles.

To write your cumulative vision statement, return to the original, draft vision statement and add in all of the needs and barriers of the community that you have identified (not just the main ones), as well as the resources and limitations of your library. Together, these elements make your vision statement relevant and practical. Then the far-reaching mission—that is, the library's desire to develop and maintain strong relationships with its new immigrant communities and be a bridge for them within the community—can actually be implemented. Consider your cumulative vision statement as a tool that will help the library grow according to the needs of new immigrants, as they change. Your vision statement also will guide policies (to be discussed in Chapter Five), ensuring that practices reflect library values. This vision statement should be a substantive document, at least two to three pages; contain all of your research; and reveal, through a well-written narrative, how to use it to create a high-quality service plan for the library and the community. The body of it will contain the following:[3]

1. *A summary.* This includes the scope, content, mission of library, major issues and needs in the community, and key strategies for improving relations and services for new immigrant communities.
2. *Organizational history with new immigrants.* This is a description of the library's services with new immigrant communities, its accomplishments, and its problems. It also outlines the direction the library has moved in over the years with new immigrants and includes a description of the strategic planning process.
3. *Core statements about needs and barriers.* This section includes three to four bulleted sentences about the importance of the library in addressing new immigrants' needs and barriers. It also covers your research about the needs and barriers of new immigrants to library use.
4. *Goals and strategies.* This section contains a list of current and future strategies that move toward the goals of providing better services, as well as a timetable for these services (see Chapter Five for goals and Chapter Six for services).
5. *Names of committee members.* These should be visible, so that the report reveals everyone involved.

These sections are not mandatory and you can modify them. Be creative in writing this vision statement, as there is no cookie cutter formula. It should be meaningful and clearly tell the story of how your library has come to place value on establishing good working relations with new immigrant communities, and what it will do to ensure that this happens.

Your research and service plan not only will uncover unmet needs and opportunities for extending library service but also will reveal hidden assets in your community—in other organizations and in new immigrant communities.

Now that you have learned about the purpose of strategic planning for new immigrants' needs, as well as the key components of a service plan, let's take a closer look in Chapter Two at some of the basic methods for knowing about new immigrants' needs.

ADDITIONAL RESOURCE

McNamara, Carter. *Environmental Scanning*. 1999. Downloaded from the web on May 9, 2006. http://www.managementhelp.org/plan_dec/str_plan/drvnforc. htm.

ENDNOTES

1. See Institute of Museum Studies, *Immigrants' Use of New American and Adult Learner Programs in Queens, NY* (2000–2003). http://ibec.ischool.washington. edu/ibecCat.aspx?subCat=•%20Immigrant%20Learning&cat=Projects.

2. I draw on Nelson 2001, p. 79 in particular, and on pp. 166–69. It recommends a process whereby the library identifies needs, states how it provides for them, and targets audiences and service aspects as well as resource allocations to consider facilities, technology, and objectives (people served, how well the service met the needs of people served, and total units of service delivered). See also Pat Wagner, "Marketing as if Your Library Depends on It—and It Does." A SEMLS, May 28, 2003. See http://www.njstatelib.org/LDB/Trustees/Trustee_ Institute/Marketing%20Wagner.pdf. Kathleen de la Peña McCook, "Rocks in the Whirlpool." paper (Chicago: American Library Association, May 2002); and Kathleen de la Peña McCook and Maria A. Jones, "Cultural Heritage Institutions and Community Building," *Reference and User Services Quarterly* 41, no. 2 (Summer 2002): 326–29.

3. See Carter McNamara, *Authenticity Consulting*, 1999. http://www. managementhelp.org/plan_dec/str_plan/stmnts.htm#anchor521412.

CHAPTER 2
How to Assess Community Needs and Assets

Assessing new immigrants' needs can involve qualitative and quantitative methods of data collection and analysis, such as gathering demographic data, being an observer, as well as conducting interviews, focus groups, and surveys. This research can be done through the library alone, within library networks, by professional library-based consultants, or as a collaborative effort between community groups and government organizations. Alternating among these research modes over a period of time ensures accumulating a diverse knowledge base about new immigrant communities. This information can then be inserted into your strategic planning process, as described in Chapter One.

Know when and how to use these methods. Moreover, any type of data collection that is conducted among new immigrants should be participatory and respect differing cultural mores in order to avoid being insensitive and intrusive (Shriver 2002). These considerations are essential, especially if you know little about the community being studied.

Research DOs

- Do spend time during the research to listen carefully, clarify, question, and reflect on what you read, see, and hear while engaged in this process.
- Do let go of your assumptions; catch yourself from jumping to quick conclusions or forming premature judgments based on impressions.

- Do record your findings in a journal, and share your thoughts with a colleague. Dialogue about differences between your culture and new immigrants' cultures.
- Do read small and large press newspapers about new immigrants; and the issues they face in the nation and in your community, as well as laws and trends that are considered to be racist, exclusive, and problematic for new immigrant communities.
- Do follow up with informants, and ask their opinions about data gathered from the media. Use this information in designing your focus groups, interviews, and surveys. Read continuously to become aware of what is happening around your library. This will assist in your environmental scanning process.

Research DON'Ts
- Don't jump in and try to fix a problem on first hearing about it. Go back to your service plan (described in Chapter One), and dialogue about the problem with committee members, because you may need to make adjustments or even major changes that better accommodate new immigrant communities.
- Don't ask just one person or use only one source to answer your questions about needs and barriers. Don't use just one method, or you will get limited information. Instead, use several approaches in sync with one other and to offset their weaknesses. To seek out diversity, conduct multiple interviews, surveys, or focus groups at different times and days.

With each of the following methods, consider how much time you and the library staff have available for research, what resources exist for outside consultants, whether translators are needed, whether available instruments and databases can hold information, what types of data can be measured, and how measuring can be done (Gupta 1999). In addition, discern which methods would yield certain types of information; for example, focus groups and surveys might be better than in-depth interviews in order to get broad-based information about library hours.

GATHERING DEMOGRAPHIC INFORMATION

Although it may appear daunting, arming your library with hard evidence can help secure the necessary resources and funding for designing culturally relevant services, ones that are not based on limited perceptions (Shriver 2002). This evidence can include everything from basic information (race, ethnicity, age, and the like) to social information (education level, languages spoken, employment status, degree of technological familiarity, and income) to the contextual trend factors of environmental scanning (social, technological, political, economic, and environmental factors). For this reason, if your library system has ample resources, you may choose to hire a demographer that studies known trends and can quickly and systematically track changes in your community. This process, otherwise called environmental scanning (discussed in Chapter One), can also yield information about some interesting new trends.

The Cleveland Public Library system scanned the community to collect important information about the media people use, and learned more about the population the library was trying to attract. The researchers discovered that the city had several newspapers and radio and TV stations in Spanish. (Pulver and Clark 2004)

Beyond identifying trends—established or new—scanning provides evidence for changing community conditions and information on gaps. Numbers (percentages) on income levels, levels of education, and number of languages spoken in the home, as well as other sociodemographic variables, can be gathered for descriptive presentations or (in more advanced statistical analyses) for predicting trends on new immigrant communities.

Make an effort to consult multiple types of data sources, because some data sources may undercount certain ethnic groups (Alire and Archibeque 1998). Also, make sure your data are current. Use the resources of community leaders, who will act as informants, as well as data collected from telephone books, walking door to door and conducting surveys, the census, and school data. City planning departments, churches and synagogues, other community agencies, and county-level sources have timely data. Statistical tables showing representation of certain groups can be used, and software such as Geographic Information Systems (GIS), used by some library systems, is very useful (Gitner and Chan 2001). These statistical tables can also be converted to reports and maps that depict neighborhoods and library usage in a comparative fashion. The most commonly used source for general sociodemographic information is *American Demographics* (Crain Communications, Inc., 1979–present). This source contains new information on different ethnic groups' social practices, for example, their online usage (Hall 2005).

Making New Immigrants the Focus

Your library may already collect, value, and use demographic data. What library staff might not realize, however, is that methods need to change when new immigrants are the focus. Libraries should modify methods of data collection in accordance with major factors in new immigrants' lives such as language, phone access, high mobility and frequent address changes, as well as the degree of trust and rapport between new immigrants and library researchers. Moreover, cultural identity should be precise, which is a problem with census data; for example, the term "Latino" is too broad. An increasing number of multiracial populations ("other categories" on census forms) also exists, and their identities—and needs—must be recognized to be sure that your study is culturally sensitive and relevant (Alire and Archibeque 1998).

Perhaps most importantly, keep in mind that many undocumented new immigrants may not understand the purpose of a survey; they may be uncomfortable answering questions accurately because of their risk of being discovered and deported. It is important, therefore, to recognize limitations when collecting and analyzing demographic information.

In addition, some agencies may be reluctant—or else prohibited by law—to share information about their clients because of issues or laws. For example, HIPAA, the Health Insurance Portability and Accountability Act of 1996, contains privacy standards that inhibit agencies, such as social services, from disclosing health-related information on clients without their permission. Most libraries currently do not collect patron data on language use or national origin (Milam 2003). Because of the Patriot Act, libraries may not feel comfortable holding valuable information that could be used against their patrons. In two cases where libraries developed a sophisticated, grant-funded database in their literacy programs, containing much information about immigrant users, they felt uneasy about retaining those records due to the library's concern. It is critical to recognize these issues and limitations when collecting and analyzing sociodemographic information.

Let's look at some other ways to gather demographic information that are not well documented, but that can reveal your community's hidden resources. These methods include *community profiling*, or *asset mapping*, and *windshield surveys*. Information gatherers often use community profiles to make a case about a phenomenon in reports or grants. These profiles look like case studies and highlight a particular community's assets, which may not be well known. Windshield surveys are drive-by snapshots of a particular situation in a community. Researchers use them for learning about sudden changes in a community, for elaborating on findings of research, for directing the subject of new research, or as new data to make a case at community or library meetings.

Community Profiling

Community profiling differs from environmental scanning in that it goes further to identify and explain a population's local resources, conditions, and activities, in order to reveal its gaps, barriers, and various needs. This occurs by recording case studies. The best types of community profiles use diverse types of data from a variety of both quantitative and qualitative sources.

Those working on a community profile may use descriptive data (numbers in the form of percentages) to build an initial baseline picture of a particular community. Then, by providing anecdotes from interviews or surveys about people's experiences, they can combine qualitative data with those numbers in order make a case for greater compatibility between services and populations, for bridging learning gaps, and for increasing the population's assets.

A checklist or form can assist in the process of beginning this community profile (Alire and Archibeque 1998; Nelson 2001). The form should contain the community's dimensions and which are considered to be its resources or assets. Auditing a community's assets takes into account people, physical structures, natural resources, informal organizations, businesses, and cultural information. It starts with what is present in the community and concentrates on agenda building and community renewal. The profile can consist of general asset categories (Beaulieu 2002; Kerka 2003a; McKnight and Kretzmann, 1993; Melcher et al. 1998):

Community Profile Checklist of Assets
1. Individuals in the community (skills, talents, expertise)
2. Institutions (numbers and types, including schools, colleges)
3. Federal and state agencies (the number of departments and their type) and physical attributes (lakes, rivers)
4. Cultural resources (museums, associations)
5. Organizations (small and large businesses)
6. Other

Because you may not know where to look for information for these categories of assets, your first step might be to brainstorm all of the information you already know about the community (its geographic boundaries, associations, special talents, cultural information). Make a free-form list, and subsume it under the categories in the preceding checklist of assets. Then, start gathering sociodemographic information to help fill in the gaps in your list. You may want to do this through some of the techniques mentioned previously (telephone books, community leaders as informants, census data), in addition to asking a knowledgeable colleague or as a collaborative committee activity.

Create or reproduce a visual depiction (a modified map) to reflect a whole picture of your community. Draw it or find one on the Internet or in local books. The categories that you created will become reference points on your map. The idea of the map is to display clearly the resources of particular new immigrant communities that your library has chosen to focus on, and to make a detailed case showing areas of strengths and needs that build on the library vision.

An Easy Way to Do a Community Asset Map
1. Go to an Internet map site and locate a map of your community.
2. Paste it into a Word document.
3. Identify important landmarks in the community that are popular resources for new immigrants.
4. Label them with different icons that represent them visually (trees for a park).
5. Under the map, make a key code and describe what they are and what resources they offer new immigrants.

A more sophisticated community asset map provides not only a picture and a short description about resources and what they offer but also a written narrative about them. Let's look closer at major categories of community assets:

- Cultural resources (i.e., ethnic associations)
- Institutions (i.e., schools, colleges, hospitals)
- Organizations (i.e., YMCA, YWCA)

These categories constitute the social and cultural capital of communities, and they are important concerns for your library as you get to know new immigrant communities and discover their needs, barriers, and assets. For a highly developed profile, blow up your map (or create additional targeted maps) to specify the community's cultural, institutional, and organizational resources that the library can draw on. Write about how these resources came to exist, whom they serve, and why. Be able to identify how they interrelate and compensate for or strengthen one another. To further elaborate the narrative, focus on the library's role (how it can help build these resources). This involves cultural, social, and community relationship mapping. What are these?

Cultural asset mapping documents the long-term customs, behaviors, and activities that have meaning in a community; and it outlines what can be done to protect and conserve traditions and resources. After you highlight on your map various religious or other cultural organizations, and their functions in this community, write in-depth about their advantages and disadvantages for new immigrant communities and how the library can build on these to strengthen them as resources.

Public, or *social, capital mapping* involves social gatherings and meeting spaces. For this, highlight social meeting halls that exist in the community, who uses them, and why. Then, write about how, when, and why new immigrant communities use the spaces, and the role of the library in strengthening this resource.

Another variety, *community relationship mapping,* focuses on identifying relationships in the community that have organizational linkages and those that are promising for collaborative projects (McKnight and Kretzmann 1993; Melcher et al. 1998). For this, consult a community leader to find out where people or organizations go for information in the community (a local store or hair salon, for example) and their uses of this information. Highlight these important informal informational hubs on your map, and write about them. You can use quotes from community leaders about their meanings. Write about how the library can play a role in strengthening community relationships. You may also want to make a video depicting these relationships.

The whole process of designing a community profile (with checklists, maps, and narratives) is best done in collaboration with community gatekeepers, to develop genuinely community-based profiles identified by— and rooted in—the local knowledge base (Strand et al. 2003). The profile will also help you to argue your case for acquiring more resources for this community and the library and in building familiar relationships.

A recent asset-based study of Chicago Public Library's branches, called *The Engaged Library* (Kretzmann and Rans 2005) for the Urban Libraries Council, found the following: libraries that have strong community connections position themselves in the center of their communities, know who is in their communities, say "yes" to new ideas that fall within their mission, and discover unique traits of their communities to create opportunities to support the community.

Windshield Surveys

The term "windshield" in this context refers to the vision through a car windshield when driving through a neighborhood or community. But windshield surveys also can be taken from a bus. In fact, taking a bus allows you to write or type as you move, and you can ask fellow passengers questions. The survey is what you see as you ride through a community. Windshield surveys are like community profiles, except that they are highly subjective, intensive, and qualitative descriptions. They can give quick and ready answers to basic questions or confirm information heard from colleagues or patrons. The surveys seek to answer questions about a number of important issues affecting new immigrants (see checklist).

Windshield Survey Checklist (describe the following)
- The places where people currently hang out
- The areas that have recently become poorer or wealthier
- The current use of the land
- The number of vacant buildings in a given area
- Where new establishments exist and how they are used
- How law enforcement is operating in a given community
- The placement of new bus stops and routes and how accessible they are to mental health and care facilities as well as recreation facilities
- Where businesses are located relative to where people live
- Which kinds of businesses seem to be lacking
- What types of media people use
- Which (if any) public access channels are available
- What other facilities for technology access exist
- How old the houses are and where new housing is slated to be built
- The conditions of the roads
- How far apart schools, homes, and businesses are from one another
- Other things seen on the drive or bus ride

This information is derived from direct observations. Community members can accompany you on your ride. In addition, casually interviewing people you pass by about the information in the checklist will help confirm information derived from observation and other demographic sources. Although driving by a community helps in obtaining useful, timely information to share in meetings, there is no substitute for spending time in a community to really know what is happening.

THE ETHNOGRAPHIC APPROACH:
BEING A PARTICIPANT OBSERVER

Even though it is possible to gauge a basic picture that can be used for case reports and informational meetings from community profiling and windshield surveys, and these methods corroborate findings of books and official research reports, they are done from a distance. In many other cases, getting a "close-up" view of a new immigrant community and people's livelihoods would be much more informative. Doing this requires "being" in a community—experiencing it as a participant and interacting with community members. Often called an *ethnographic approach* to collecting information, it involves both formal and informal meetings with community members, as individuals and in groups. This approach can help you to develop long-term, comfortable relationships with new immigrant communities through firsthand involvement in community issues. It also offers opportunities to destroy stereotypes or misperceptions that you or the library staff may have had of a certain group (McKnight and Kretzmann 1993; Melcher et al. 1998).

Being an Active Participant

To really get to know a new immigrant community, it helps to literally walk the streets (Hall 2005; Larsen, Jacobs, and Vlimmeren 2003), which is especially vital for librarians or outreach specialists to do if they are not part of the community. One librarian said she would get up at 6:00 a.m. and walk with other community members, which afforded the opportunity to discuss issues that matter to community members and to get to know them. Rotating between streets and neighborhoods, as well as between people to walk with and times to walk, is essential in order to get many different viewpoints. This type of informal contact helps you to be seen as a participant "in" the community who cares. It also can encourage people to further their informal contact when they arrive at the library and see a familiar face,which is especially important for new immigrants.

Going to neighborhood meetings (ones sponsored by community organizations or councils) helps you to understand needs as they change from a firsthand perspective. This type of outreach also offers opportunities for community members to interact informally with librarians on a nonprofessional basis. As a librarian, you should seriously consider attending these meetings regularly, to demonstrate and ensure your full commitment and to get involved rather than being a surveyor (Elturk 2004; Hall 2005). It enables you to actively listen to what people want and to find out who would be good to work with. The process may include making "cold calls" to initiate contacts and find out about the meetings (O'Connor 2004). Begin the call by saying who you are and about your intentions. Someone who knows the community well could call on your behalf and introduce you.

A further step in this direction is to participate in community organizations and discussions, and become personally immersed as a community activist. Observe, listen, and ask about appropriate ways that you can engage with the community to assert its goals. You may want to become active in immigrant rights groups, which could entail a range of activities from protesting on the street (as with the April and May 2006 demonstrations) to writing letters of support or doing research for them, in addition to referring activists to other sources and organizing with other activist librarians.[1] Of course, this depends on your level of commitment to these issues, your role in your library (for example, an outreach librarian) as well as the library's role in the community, and its willingness to become an advocate. If your library policies inhibit your involvement in immigrant rights issues, find out why, and connect with other organizations, as well as other library agencies, such as ALA, to try and change them. In this way, the community comes to see you, as well as your library, as its advocate. Although many libraries may not demand that librarians live in the immediate neighborhood, this requirement would be useful for getting to know the community where one works and becoming an advocate (Hall 2005). Oakland, California, offers a good example. In contrast with the city's evening and weekend absence of professionals, the library's literacy program made an effort to recruit staff who (in a period of intense gentrification) lived there and understood the clients and their needs.

Being an Observer

Some less action-oriented approaches for ethnographers include recording simple observations that account for the ways, whether traditional or changing, people behave and interact in certain contexts. This approach may be especially effective within special programs in the library (such as in ESOL groups) or in community organizations whose participants have agreed to be observed (with signed or verbal permission). Observing also helps document reading practices, technology usage, and other types of communication modes (such as text messaging) that new immigrant groups most frequently use.

With this approach, observe types of activities and their frequency, and log the amount of time taken to document their performance

(Gupta 1999). With permission from participants, the use of videos, photographs, secondary observations (by people such as tutors), and computer tracking systems, as well as tape recordings, counting devices, and field notes, also helps. For note taking, use a template form to track similar phenomena among different people, and state when, where, and how the observation took place. This accounts for biases and particular contexts. Using observational techniques in conjunction with interviews can account for what people do in contrast to what they say, as well as for unexplained patterns in data reports.

Sample Observation Form (it is best if you design it!)
Location: The Big Community Center
Time: 4:40 p.m.
What I am observing: Teenagers talking on their phones and listening to music from a stereo. I am sitting near the front.
Who is there: Three girls, two boys
Notes: They are listening to music I am not familiar with. Some of it sounds like it is in Spanish. They are text messaging on their phones about the music and taking photos of one another. They are speaking Spanglish.

INTERVIEWS AND FOCUS GROUPS

Interviews, like observations, are good ethnographic research techniques for gathering detailed information from new immigrants, which helps you to understand cultural issues. Interviews and observations complement one another in keeping track of what people say and do. On the other hand, you may choose interviewing as the main method to find out what people believe or their perceptions. Phone interviews, especially in a new immigrant's first language, are convenient for those who cannot come to the library, and allow for small, practical pieces of information to be obtained; face-to-face interviews require more time and preparation but can yield deep-rooted knowledge about new immigrants' cultures. Both kinds of interviews allow for personal interaction and can help you develop rapport and relationships.

However, before conducting the interview, it is important to build some rapport. Advanced preparation—finding and training an informant or contact person—is recommended. Interviews can be structured (using protocols, questionnaires, or scripts) or unstructured (creating a conversation or encouraging a lively discussion or set of reflections by initially asking loosely formed questions). Whatever the type of interview or format, follow some good general guidelines (Alire and Archibeque 1998; Gupta 1999; Seidman 1991; Spradley 1979). Face-to-face meetings require considerable preparation before, during, and after the interview.

Before the Interviews

Before interviewing, collect background information (such as the sociodemographic data mentioned previously); contact informants for setting up an interview or to get names of interviewees; contact your interviewee; and find a convenient place to meet. Finding informants may be the most effective means to finding a good interviewee, and community leaders can usually assist in this process. They may be local media contacts (for example, with a Spanish-language radio station), which can be found through a listing of community resources as well as local information sources (Alire and Archibeque 1998). Another good resource is local ethnic newspapers (Shriver 2002). Ask your informants whether they can translate, should that be necessary. If so, set up arrangements in advance, and the interviewee should know about the intermediary.

In selecting interviewees, be sure to achieve representation of a broad cross section of the group(s) being studied and to select "authentic resources" that have a stake in decision making (Elturk 2003). For example, in studying teenagers of a particular ethnic group, your interviewees should be male and female, from different geographic areas of the community, of different ages, and of varying educational levels. Interviewees can be paid for their time or offered some other type of compensation such as a prize; teenagers might appreciate a popular CD, for example. Tell the person why he or she is being interviewed, explain the purpose of the interview, demonstrate sincere interest in the interviewee, get permission to take notes or to use any type of audio or video device, and send a reminder about the interview ahead of time (Gupta 1999).

Designing the Interview

When designing the protocol, create a form with plenty of space to write basic (contact) information from the interviewee and about the interview (date, time, location, and duration). Ensure that the questions match the purpose of the interview, sequence them well, and be watchful of any type of controversial or culturally offensive types of questions and their possible effects. Be careful to word the questions appropriately and avoid asking overly abstract ones such as "Tell me about your culture."

Basic Contact Information Checklist for Your Interview Form
(this one is mass media usage)

Name of interviewee (first, middle, last):

Contact informant:

Date: Location: Time:

Phone: (cell)   email:

Age: Ethnicity: Country of birth:

Language(s):   Educational level:

How long living in community: Arrival date:

Occupation(s):

Family member(s):

Library use (how often, what):

Tell me about what kinds of media you prefer to use (TV, radio, computer, books, film, magazines, phone).

When do you use (each one selected) and for what purpose?

Before conducting the interview, test the questions' accuracy and validity with an informant or with colleagues who are familiar with the cultural norms of a particular new immigrant group. Practice your entire interview on a colleague who can give honest feedback. Decide where your interview will be conducted. At the library? At a community center? In the interviewee's home? Over the telephone? Choose a safe, convenient place that is comfortable for you and the interviewee.

Interview Delivery

Before the interview, check out the meeting place to make sure you know the exact location. Be certain that the facility has a quiet and comfortable area for talking. Have the equipment prepared and ready to operate, wear a watch, and dress according to cultural norms. Give a short, friendly introduction that tells the interviewee, again, who you are and the purpose of the interview, in case he or she may have forgotten or was afraid to ask you the first time. Verbally explain any permission sheet that you expect the interviewee to sign, confidentiality issues, and confirm details of any compensation. Always ask the interviewee if there are any questions or concerns that you can answer before the interview begins. Advise that he or she can terminate the interview at any point and not be penalized in any way. Tell how long you think it will last and ask whether this is all right.

When questioning, be aware of cultural norms and power issues that could arise between yourself, or the questioner, and the interviewee. Ask for follow-ups and clarification, and at the end, ask interviewees how they felt about being interviewed and whether they would be willing to be talked to again (Gupta 1999). You may want to foster a relationship with the interviewee prior to the interview or (for his or her morale) allow family members to sit in on the interview. If you are conducting an interview in an interviewee's home, family members may insist or be asked by the interviewee, to sit in on the interview. This is not uncommon, especially if the interviewer is a stranger. Group interviews may be more comfortable for new immigrant interviewees, because they can assist one another in translating and clear up confusing questions, without having to lose face by directly asking the questioner to clarify or repeat. The interviewer, on the other hand, will have to adjust to hearing many different voices and ideas. In this case, be sure to follow up on questions that might not have been fully answered, or use additional comments to elaborate on a new, important issue that arose in the interview.

A structured interview can be turned into an unstructured interview. These can be like "focused conversations" where the interviewer and interviewees discuss issues together, as they arise in the dialogue. Write down the names of all of the people whom you interview. If you decide to send someone else out to conduct the interview (perhaps someone who knows the language or community better), make sure that that person understands the purpose of the interview and follows the protocols that you have developed.

After the Interview

After finishing the questioning and leaving the interview scene, jot down a few notes about the context (who was there, where it took place, what people were wearing) and the highlights (surprising comments). This is a part of your analysis. Take time to analyze the data to look for common themes, stories, and significant anecdotes. These notes can be used to develop profiles of individuals and to conduct case studies (which can then be part of a community profile). Notes can also tell important stories about social change in a community, convey cultural information that is related to needs, and impart knowledge about the source of a problem.

Queens Borough Public Library's Adult Learning Center hired a consultant to ask questions of participating students about their experiences in the programs; because of the sensitive subject matter, it was decided that interviewing students would be the most productive approach. After the interviews, the researcher analyzed her results. She discovered information about the students, such as the importance of their self-esteem and personal motivation to learn. The tutors in the program should understand the emotional issues that students experience as they learn. These were developed into case studies, and additional interviews by the director of the program and another consultant (who conducted focus groups) confirmed these findings.

You can turn interviews into case studies and write them as stories. Anecdotes, in particular, can be advantageous for promotional presentations, for grant-funding reports, as well as in outreach campaigns (to be discussed in later chapters). Interviews, due to their in-depth nature, often bring up complex issues that can point the way for further research on a particular matter.

FOCUS GROUPS

Using focus groups can be effective for amassing many different perspectives and opinions on a matter and as follow-ups to interviews

(to confirm or explore more information) as well as precursors to interviews (to learn what questions are good to ask). Some interviews, however, can spontaneously turn into a type of focus group. Yet focus groups
are different in that they are intentional, focus on a particular subject,
and consist of people who do not necessarily know one another. Focus
groups also require a trained or knowledgeable facilitator who is non-
judgmental, is respectful, communicates effectively, and knows how to
work with difficult group dynamics (Gupta 1999).

A focus group requires a clear purpose and agenda, distinct param-
eters of communication, a target audience, explicit goals and objectives,
and clear questions (Alire and Archibeque 1998). Consider how a focus
group could illuminate a particular matter for which you or your library
needs more information. For example, a focus group could help library
staff explore attitudes of users toward computer usage. Questions may
revolve around how anxious or eager new immigrants are to use computers or how much experience they have in using them. Perhaps
certain knowledge gaps about a particular issue became evident from
other instruments (such as mentioned by interviewees, suggested in
community meetings, seen in observations, or discovered in windshield
surveys). The desire to fill in these gaps results in the decision to conduct
a focus group on this subject.

Preparing for the Focus Group

In preparing for your focus group meeting, target community members
who can help with understanding a range of perspectives on an issue,
ones who are willing to volunteer their time for an hour or so and do not
mind being documented (with note taking, video, or audio equipment).
They may be previously interviewed community members: random ones
selected from a telephone book or library database; or neighborhood
residents. Whom you choose to ask depends on your subject. Ideally,
focus groups consist of six to twelve individuals who share a similar
demographic characteristic (for example, one new immigrant group) but
live in different areas or represent different organizations. Address gender, race, and class if you desire many perspectives. Much criticism has
been targeted at one focus group study, the Benton Report, especially for
its cultural biases (McCook 1997; Zweizig 1997).

If the plan is to interview people about an issue regarding library use,
such as hours of service, perhaps select random walk-ins to the library
to be in the focus group. On the other hand, if the object is to check
the level of awareness of the library in the community, making random

phone calls to people in the area or surveying particular communities would be a better approach than focus groups—because you would need to get the views of nonusers of the library.

Consider logistics, such as scheduling, facilities, and compensation. The location of your meetings should be close to new immigrant communities' homes or easy for them to get to. It should also be somewhat familiar, so that participants feel comfortable. A quiet room with comfortable and adequate seating that can be arranged in a circle works well. Schedule your meetings at times conducive to the participants' work schedules and family lives. If this is not possible, paying a small fee can help offset costs and labor, as well as provide an additional incentive to participate. Having a bilingual facilitator is best when working with non-English speakers, but if this is not an option, bringing in a translator would work.

After selecting focus group members, send them a written invitation to the meeting. Follow up with a phone call. During this conversation, explain all of the logistical details, and encourage them to ask questions or express concerns. Assure them that the conversation will be in a language they understand and that it will probably be fun and interesting.

Create a list of clear questions to ask focus group members about the subject matter. Write these down; you may even want to prepare cards to hand out, so that people can see and reflect on the questions. Define the meeting structure and length, establish ground rules for communication, and decide how to troubleshoot problems should they arise. In setting the date with participants, be sure to communicate these particulars to them. Purchase light refreshments for the group; fruit juices, mineral water, coffee, and tea are good choices, depending on the group and the time of day. If it is around dinnertime, they will probably be hungry!

Focus Group Delivery

As participants arrive, greet them, offer them drinks and snacks, and seat them in a circle. Prep the focus group members for the focus group and encourage them to actively participate according to defined norms of communication. Explain these norms clearly and explicitly to new immigrants who may never have participated in a focus group before.

After you finish questioning of the group, encourage the focus group members to evaluate their experiences; use this data and the information recorded from the group to summarize key points in your report. Once a matter is better illuminated, focus group findings can lead to large- or small-scale surveys.

THE SURVEY APPROACH

Community surveys help to get a broad understanding of the issues that any specific group has. Libraries traditionally use surveys and are most likely familiar with this inquiry method. The challenge when working with immigrant populations is to make the surveys culturally competent in terms of their format, content, and delivery.

> **Basic Checklist for Your Survey**
> - Cultural competence (language, cultural norms)
> - Formats (visually appealing, understandable)
> - Delivery (clear, easy-to-do)
> - Several models of forms may be helpful (Alire and Archibeque 1998).

Designing Questionnaires

Create questionnaires that are bilingual or in a non-English language (with the help of a professional translator). Either way, frame all survey questions and their delivery in a culturally sensitive way. For example, in asking how many languages are spoken in the home and whether your respondents are from many different countries on the same continent (Latin America), make sure to include different languages (in tick-mark boxes), rather than having an "other" category. In the case of written, rather than oral questionnaires, offer participants assistance in filling them out, through translators/interpreters, especially for people with lower levels of literacy (in either their native language or in English). In this case, carefully consider the qualifications of the translator, as well as his or her social proximity to the participant. Avoid jargon, as well as overly simplistic questions, such as "Where do you live?" Open-ended questions must be understandable and not require excessively long answers; consider the relative merits of these and closed-ended questions (with multiple choice, yes/no responses, or interval scales), as well as their sequencing.

In formatting the questionnaire, take care to make it readable with plain typefaces and simple design; choose appealing color and graphics. Another factor to consider is whether the questionnaire will be mailed to people's home addresses; if so, who will be reading them? If the participants are undocumented immigrants, they may not want to give basic contact information, for fear of being deported. If this is the case, accept what they say, and move on to the next question. Do not try to force people to give responses. In composing the questionnaire itself, the more condensed it is, the higher the response rate will be.

Questionnaires may also be given orally, with respondents' answers being noted on the questionnaire. This is very similar to a highly structured interview (with fixed questions). The person who asks the questions must have a good rapport and understand the language or local dialect of the person he or she is speaking to. Decisions must be made about when and where the questionnaire will be given: over the telephone or in person; at a home, or in the library; during the day or in the evening.

A Word About Large-Scale Surveys

Your library may decide to do a large-scale survey (for example, on library use) across many different libraries and communities. This survey will use the questionnaires that were just discussed, but they may be slightly different because of the scale (fewer questions may be asked). Other issues come into play, such as cost. Doing large-scale surveys can increase understanding of a complex issue in the community from many different perspectives. For example, in surveying about perceptional barriers of the library and its services (community members' awareness about them), query both users and nonusers. To help you in conducting a large-scale survey, possibly hire consultants or university researchers. Other options are to invest in training, or to read books on surveys for their recommendations on design, sampling procedures, delivery, and analysis. A knowledgeable team of surveyors will design, implement, and analyze the data. One person will not be able to do it alone.

Before conducting the survey, the team will define the different types of targeted respondents, so that team members can tailor the questionnaire to these different groups. For this, look at previous research reports, and get information about the characteristics of library users and nonusers in your community as well as in other communities. Base your questions around these characteristics. Also consider a wide range of responses that respondents will give or not give. To encourage participation, perhaps provide incentives for new immigrant respondents, children's books or videos, for example. Pilot test the questions on a small group prior to the formal survey delivery. Once the questionnaires are returned, make sure that your team can analyze the results for qualitative information, as well as for quantitative data. For example, it is necessary to have anecdotes as well as descriptive statistics. Use a database to record and code data for ease in searching and retrieving the data. A database can allow easy storage of anecdotes as well as numbers, depending on how you design it. When it comes time to present the data, you will find it easier to extract and organize them.

Glenwood Branch library in Greensboro, North Carolina, took the survey approach with over a hundred Hispanic library users who were participating in its literacy program. They reflected the city's growing Hispanic community. The library's goal was to see what they wanted in terms of books, services, and programs. It hired a Spanish-speaking staff member to conduct the survey (written in Spanish, which was delivered both by phone and in person), to analyze the findings, and to make a report. The library's database helped with this effort. The staff member made these recommendations: the library should help these users with their English skills, reduce transportation barriers, provide assistance with child care, offer workshops in Spanish to help learners find and take advantage of helping organizations, increase cultural communication between Hispanic residents and organizations, provide orientations to Hispanic learners about library services, and provide a Spanish brochure and a library kit from the Greensboro Public Library.[2]

Again, be selective about the methods you choose, aware of each one's advantages and disadvantages. Base your decision about how to choose a method on whether it will best answer the questions and help in understanding a problem better. Ideally, it is best to use a number of methods to really understand a phenomenon in a comprehensive way. As you have already learned, interviews that are conducted well can provide in-depth information about an issue. Focus groups are helpful for learning about many different perspectives on an issue, as are surveys (large and small).

Community needs assessments are invaluable for planning how to improve the library's capacity to meet the needs of new immigrant groups. Needs assessment requires time and resources; it warrants careful planning. Decide which approach will work best for your library. When the assessment is complete, you should have a good idea of who your community is and what they need. Then create a strategic plan, as discussed in Chapter One. A good plan depends on your ability and willingness to learn about new immigrants' needs and their barriers to the library, using tried and true methods.

Chapter Three builds on the ideas of community needs assessments of new immigrant communities. It covers important conditions for outreach to new immigrant communities (such as funding) that need to be established before communicating (Chapter Four), policies and services (Chapters Five and Six), and collection development (Chapter Seven) are developed.

ADDITIONAL RESOURCES

ALA's literacy website: http://www.buildliteracy.org/toolkit/lri/lri.html

Beaulieu, Lionel J. *Mapping the Assets of Your Community*. Southern Rural Development Center, 2002. http://srdc.msstate.edu/publications/227/227_asset_mapping.pdf

Burroughs, C. M. 2000. http://nnlm.gov/gmr/3sources/0006.html#assess

Community Toolbox website: http://skyways.lib.ks.us/pathway/profile.html

Kretzmann, J., and McKnight. *Building Communities from the Inside Out*. Chicago: ACTA Publications, 1993.

National Network of Libraries of Medicine: http://nnlm.gov/libinfo/community/planning.php

Newsletter of the NN/LM, GMR. 18, no. 3 (June 2000: 1, 7. This brief article outlines key consideration for conducting a community assessment).

ENDNOTES

1. See the following activist library websites for more information: Progressive Librarians Guild; LibrarianActivist.org; Street Librarian; Information Professionals for Social Justice; Librarians For Peace; Librarians Against Bush; and Radical Reference. The websites might change but go to http://www.librarianactivist.org/activists.html for a full, timely list.

2. Research from the author's study of persistence, see all four of the reports at http://www.mdrc.org; and John T. Comings and Sondra Cuban, *So I Made Up My Mind: Introducing a Study of Adult Learner Persistence in Library Literacy Programs* (New York: DeWitt Wallace Readers Digest Fund, August 2000).

CHAPTER 3
Gathering Resources for Serving New Immigrant Communities

You have done your community needs assessment and gleaned some priorities from it that are part of your library's vision. Now, how should you implement this vision? Important steps to take—funding, partnerships and advocacy, overcoming language barriers, and developing good public relations/marketing—lay the foundations for developing positive relationships and ensuring that new immigrants' needs are met. Begin this process by reaching out to new immigrant communities. What does it mean to "reach out"?

Talking About Outreach

Outreach is not a simple concept, because it can mean many different things. In its broadest sense, it is services "outside of library walls" (Meadows 2004: 1). In more particular terms, it is "a program of library services designed to identify, contact, and serve persons who are educationally disadvantaged; members of ethnic or minority groups in need of special library services; unemployed and in need of job placement assistance; living in areas underserved by a library; blind, physically handicapped, aged or confined in institutions" (Orange and Osborne 2004). Although the broad-based definition is inclusive, it is ambiguous whereas the detailed one does not specify new immigrant groups. These problems of definition affect the status of outreach in the library and its capacity to make change (Orange and Osborne 2004). The first step is to assess whether the library understands outreach. Making a checklist can help.

Outreach Checklist (to review with all library staff)
- Does all library staff know about outreach? If not, what are the gaps in knowledge?
- How can you and your library learn more about outreach?
- Is outreach a core service, or an added feature, on the margins of your library's services?
- Does your library have an outreach coordinator or an outreach committee?
- What kind of outreach activities would be most beneficial for your library and community?
- What essential conditions need to be in place in your library for outreach to begin and to flourish?
- What barriers exist in or outside of your library for implementing outreach activities, and what strategies can you use to overcome them?

One way to make a case for outreach is to embed it in the original mission of the library—free and equal service to all. Then make it emblematic of all library services. This was difficult, although not impossible, for librarians in the past. With its heyday in the 1960s and 1970s, the burgeoning outreach movement began as an official recognition that unserved and underserved members of communities needed to be brought into the library fold. The movement emphasized the importance of both information and literacy for marginalized groups in communities (Weibel 1982). Yet the view of outreach activities more as special services of the library—rather than as core functions such as reference, cataloging, and circulation—has been difficult to overcome. As a result, not only do many outreach programs disintegrate when their funds dry up, but outreach ideas are not diffused throughout the library.

Consequently, new immigrant groups may never come to the library, and social exclusion perpetuates. The resources—let alone the consciousness—to turn outreach and its "extracurricular status" into an integrated library service have been a continual struggle, to the point of its often being perceived as irrelevant for "regular users" (Dodge 2005; Lawson 2004; Nauratil 1985; Orange and Osborne 2004: xiii; Owens 1987; Weibel 1982).

Think about it: When the library considers outreach as expendable, it sends a message to new immigrants that they are expendable, too. So the question becomes: "How does one create a welcoming environment to those [sic] who have long been considered themselves to be the uninvited guest?" (Wolmuth and McCook 2004). Creating opportunities for new immigrants to become not only users but also library stake-holders is critical for sustaining long-term mutually beneficial relationships. Only then can libraries measure up to the role of what one new immigrant referred to as "a truly community-minded institution." One library director advises, "Reach out to your community with good library services. Believe me, they will reach back to you" (O'Brien 2004: 97).

How can these ideas take hold? The *how* of outreach to new immigrant communities is important to explore. Let's examine some important conditions, starting with funding.

Results of Positive Outreach Activity, from the Perspective of a New Immigrant

I can listen to stories, learn English and learn computers—all free to the public. [The] Friends have established a scholarship fund for need[y] students . . . The Chinatown library is a truly community-minded institution.

FUNDING AND SUPPORT

In an era in which drastic reductions in library budgets are common, it is necessary to present a clear rationale for outreach expenditures, especially because of the perception of outreach as a luxury item. This is not always easy, because, as librarian Fay Zipkowitz points out, "Developing outreach services is an expensive process; demonstration grant funding is scarce or nonexistent; documenting need is time-consuming and takes away from other equally important services. . . . At a time of shrinking budgets, [librarians] are being asked, and want to, do more" (Zipkowitz 1996: 1–2).

Clearly, ongoing funding and resources are critical to creating and sustaining programs and services for new immigrants, as well as for conveying the unmistakable message of outreach programs as key library functions. Restructuring internal and external finances allows you to make library resources available permanently, especially when other services (health, welfare) for new immigrant communities begin to disappear (Larsen, Jacobs, and Vlimmeren 2004).

Adopt a new viewpoint on funding outreach services. Think about outreach in terms of new and old models (Larsen, Jacobs, and Vlimmeren 2004). The old model featured soft monies, a single location and library collection, a limited range of programs, and temporary staff. The new model includes permanent funding structures (stated in the vision), dedicated staff who represent the community as permanent employees (well-funded outreach coordinators), collections determined by community needs (through assessments), and an extensive range of programs and courses for new immigrants and other marginalized groups.

The idea is to institutionalize outreach, so that the community considers it a normal part of library operations. In this regard, some promising trends have been developing. For example, in a major survey by the Urban Libraries Council, more than half of all the libraries reported that they distribute funding for multicultural communities from their general operating budget, as well as from external grants. However, more often than not, the old money is omnipresent. Currently, libraries use project grant monies to start programs for new immigrants (Jacobs, Larsen, and Vlimmeren 2003). Since new immigrants are taxpayers, your financial plans should involve the use of a general fund and other resources to address both immediate and long-term needs of important constituents.

Financial Planning

Planning for financial support can and should be part of your strategic process of outreach to new immigrant groups in your community. Financial planning cannot be done in a vacuum, so the first step is to develop a savvy team of decision makers in and outside your library for guidance through the process. Include top-level administrators, as well as librarians and community leaders, in your committee. The committee should review current financial reports in addition to historical budgetary decisions to determine priorities for the reallocation of funds before mapping these onto the service plan. The committee's role also includes questioning priorities for targeting specific groups' funds—priorities that range from personnel to services, programs, and materials—and attaching outcomes to these priorities.

Next, create a list of new funding priorities with your committee. For this list, think of the big picture—considering all of the library's services.[1] Then, to each service, attach outcomes (specifically for new immigrant groups). Consider, for example, how improving personnel services might benefit new immigrant communities. Advisory boards that include community members can then work with these priorities, turning them into wish lists, delineating current budgets, adding in low- and high-cost items, and (based on current and future needs) reallocating percentages of funds for some services to other areas.

Let's look into some of the ways to obtain funding and possible sources for funds. Funding sources may come from within the library, as in restructuring the budget, or from outside sources, through grant seeking, fund-raising, partnerships, and collaboration. Whatever the sources for funding, good planning is key to succeeding.

Once the committee has identified priorities and how to fund them, establish a time line for implementing these services, based on the designated financial support; and determine whether the support will be continuous or one time only. Include all of the steps you plan to take within a given amount of time, say, one year, to develop and implement them. You can establish this time line in the form of a simple table with activities aligned with specific dates. Remember, ongoing community assessments, as well as full library staff participation, must guide your decision-making process about service priorities. It should be inextricably connected to your vision (Chapter One).

Checklist for Financial Planning
- Form a committee to review current and historical budgetary decisions.
- Make a checklist of priorities attached to outcomes.
- Return to the service plan and community assessments for your research.
- With this information, reassign priorities with outcomes.
- Create a time line for development and implementation of outreach services.
- Consider a variety of funding strategies for outreach to new immigrants.
- Apply for external grants, acquiring extensive grant knowledge and savvy as needed.
- Consider your contexts and limitations.
- Consider the perceived value of your services to new immigrant communities.

Use Multiple Funding Strategies

Using a variety of funding strategies, rather than just one, to make investments for new immigrant services can provide flexibility and strength to the program. In addition to federal funding, consider foundations, individual donors, corporations, library discretionary funds, and endowments (from the local Friends of the Library and philanthropists). These sources are especially useful for trying out innovative programming, as the Americans for Libraries Council's Libraries for the Future initiative suggests (see Additional Resources). Create a database of all of these funding sources, and designate one of your committee members to oversee it. In this database, also track time lines for services as they relate to grant deadlines.

Possible Fields for a Grant Database

Name	Grant Deadline	Time Line
Emily Robinson Foundation	month/year	Consultation—month
		Rough draft due—month
		Feedback on draft—month
		Second draft—month

Another possibility to consider is creating your own foundation. For more information about how to go about doing that, consult your state library's website. Most state libraries offer guidelines for creating foundations. If yours does not, check out other state library websites. The Seattle Public Library created a special foundation[2] that allowed staff members to visit model libraries to study best practices. It also hired a staff member to develop culturally relevant programs. Local businesses often delight in donating to foundations that support service to immigrants, because they see their employees' need for the library's help in developing their cultural awareness of American society, learning English, and using information on how to start a business. In many cities, such as Queens, almost 80 percent of all new businesses are, in fact, immigrant owned and operated (Larsen, Jacobs, and Vlimmeren 2003). So do not neglect this important funding source.

Applying for External Grants

Once your committee identifies priorities and outcomes and sets an appropriate time line for meeting the relevant goals and objectives, your library may decide to go after external grants for additional funding, either short term (twelve months, for example) or long term (over a number of years). Doing this, of course, requires grant-writing knowledge, general savvy, and resources. More specifically, the committee must know what terminology to use in the reports, have an evaluation component to study impacts (for example, whether new services have attracted more new immigrants), and line up support letters (from community leaders). Be sure the objectives are clear (what you will actually do), and be willing to go after all kinds of grants, including smaller (although potentially easier to get) seed money grants, for new services.

Does your library have grant writers or a grant department? If so, the time and commitment to apply for grants is already in the budget, so success may be greater (Alire and Archibeque 1998). If your library does not have grant resources, collaborative grant writing within library systems can help redistribute grants among libraries in communities. Other approaches to consider include training library staff in proposal writing, finding new agencies and associations to become involved in the application process, and using the support systems that some state and local libraries have. Working with consultants and contractors can be an effective approach, as can collaborating with volunteers, nonprofits, state workers, local colleges, universities, Friends, other agencies including PLA and ALA, and local associations. Do not spend energy and resources on applying for an inappropriate or unavailable grant. If a grant contact person is listed on the application form, write that person to ask whether your library's project is appropriate for the grant before spending resources on the application process.

Questions to Consider Before Outreach Grant Seeking
- Do you have a strong external grant strategy for outreach to new immigrants?
- Do you have local and national lists, or a database of grant sources that you can draw on, specifically for new immigrants?
- Have you read up on grant seeking, and do you know about the general process?
- Do you have access to grant and grant-writing sources, or can you collaborate with another library in grant seeking for outreach?
- Have you read the fine print of the grant and fully understood the criteria, and can you comply with the conditions and terms?
- Do you have a grant writer or consultant to assist you in the process?
- Is the time and energy required to apply for the grant worth it, and will the money you receive in return be worthwhile over a period of time?
- What is the time line for applying and how will you make the case? Is it feasible and viable? Be reflective about it, rather than grabbing at whatever comes your way!
- Do you have a variety of support letters lined up, or do you know where you might get them?
- Do you have assessment and evaluation systems in place, or can you create them quickly?

Federal funding has long been available for outreach services—through the Library Services and Construction Act (LSCA), for example, and through what is now the Library Services and Technology Act (LSTA).

Such funding has traditionally covered community language grants for underserved sectors of society; and these grants can assist your library in developing programs and collections for new immigrant communities (Quezada 2005). However, this is changing and less secure than ever before.

Drawing on federal monies can be especially important during a period of state and local budget crises; yet federal requirements constantly change, as evidenced in RFP guidelines. Keep apprised of these changes through reading grant news on federal websites, being on library listservs that advertise grants, and talking to colleagues who have grant-writing know-how. For example, most new federal guidelines contain strict requirements about accountability and partnering; so be sure to have rigorous quantitative and qualitative data, and partner with other agencies for federal grants. Also, the "one-stop system" of public services has become popular in recent years, so capitalize on collaborative ventures to capture federal dollars. Keep in mind that in addition to an increased emphasis on both performance accountability and outcomes-based results, the process of gaining federal funding has become more competitive.

What type of grants can your library pursue to support immigrant services? Consider these examples of grants for new immigrant services.

- The Newark Public Library, serving a 90 percent nonwhite population that is mostly Latino, received a planning grant to conduct a community analysis. The process consisted of interviews done by focus groups with translators, with results compiled into a list of recommendations.
- The Chicago Public Library has achieved renown for using federal funds for Spanish-language training to teach classes in the community (Alire and Archibeque 1998).
- The library system in Greensboro, North Carolina, responded to the needs of the growing Hispanic community there by writing a grant for outreach through book collections programs and services, many of which were developed from responses from local experts and associations.

Carefully consider contexts and limits of your grant sources. In many cases, for example, funds for outreach coordinators or outreach librarians come from soft monies, or development funds, for only a limited period of time. Although technology has allowed for easier and more expedient network collaborations—for example, with cataloging, acquisition, and interlibrary loans (Jacobs, Larsen, and Vlimmeren 2004)—it may also open up a Pandora's box of problems with data. For some libraries, privacy issues limit the ability to save and extract data on their populations for grant purposes; in others, databases on populations are nonexistent. One study of library literacy programs (Porter, Cuban, and Comings 2005) found that, in smaller libraries, databases proved to be complex enterprises to navigate. These databases required a great deal of technical support (a database manager), as well as cooperation among staff, to extract the data and fill out requisite forms, and they needed maintenance on a regular basis. Collecting data on new immigrants in an era of FBI requests for records (per the new Patriot Act) poses additional problems.

When you plan to solicit funding and support, take into account the value of outreach services. Return to your community assessment, and factor in your research on new immigrant populations whose funding the public and grant sources perceive as crucial. Then combine target groups to serve more than one group simultaneously. For example, the Seattle Public Library has targeted two immigrant groups—Vietnamese and Hispanic. Knowing that there are clear majorities of these groups, the library can more easily obtain funding slated for programs in their languages. The Queens Public Library secured funding in the form of a family literacy grant; thereafter, the library piloted a program in the Flushing branch for a mainly Asian population to acquire further funding for its branch libraries serving different ethnic groups.

Checklist of Possible Funding Agencies
- Federal level (e.g., LSTA grants)
- State level (e.g., State Literacy Resource Center)
- Local level (city council will have lists)
- Private (phone companies, local businesses, charities, computer companies)
- Other (become a member of different listservs, library and literacy, that advertise grants)

PARTNERSHIPS AND ADVOCACY

By collaborating with a network of agencies and individuals in communities to address new immigrant communities' complex needs and interests, the library can, at the same time, strengthen its role directly or indirectly in immigrants' lives.[3] Partnerships in all sectors are commonplace these days, and many libraries are already involved in various collaborations.

Partnerships are alliances that can serve multiple purposes, filling needs that the library alone cannot fulfill or finance. So, when they work well, partnerships are powerful. Let's take a closer look at how they can benefit new immigrant services.

Partnerships can exist for different reasons and on different levels to address changing community needs. They are sometimes formed for

- Exchanging information (e.g., calling a local adult education agency to see whether students on its waiting list could come to library-based literacy/ESOL programs)
- Making referrals (e.g., helping new immigrants locate local mental health services)
- Sharing resources and technology (e.g., giving out library cards to community college ESOL students)
- Developing joint planning and advisory boards (committee representation; for example, the sheriff's office, a welfare agency, and the library can plan the transition of inmates back into the community)

All of these functions can be conducted over a wide array of community agencies.

Partners with Purposes

Consider the following agencies for their potential contributions to your endeavors:[4]

- Local hospitals for dispensing health information about the library and for family literacy activities
- Ethnic and cultural associations for information on current issues of new immigrant communities
- Social services agencies for information about support services available to immigrants
- Police/fire for information on neighborhood crime and health and safety, emergency evacuations
- Museums/art centers for information on cultural activities, exhibits, performances
- Adult education agencies for information on literacy, learning, and language education
- YMCA/YWCA for information on recreational activities and social programs
- Universities and community colleges for vocational, certification, and continuing education

- Women's organizations for information related to family planning, sex education, domestic violence
- Government offices for information on documents, statistics, and changes in the law
- Private and public schools for information on children's educational options/requirements
- Political and legal advocacy organizations for immigrants

Such collaborations may be complex, especially in communities where agencies compete for funding and in cases of sharing costs in time and energy over and beyond set expectations, roles, and abilities. Consider these factors when setting up collaborations, so they can be more effective. Read about, talk to others, and involve your outreach coordinators in partnership efforts. Find information for developing relationships and best practices with community partners such as schools, health care facilities, businesses, and colleges at the website of the Urban Libraries Council, called Partnership for Successful Cities, which hosts conferences each year (http://www.urbanlibraries.org/december22005better neighborhoods.html.)

Other resources on developing partnerships exist (see Additional Resources at the end of the chapter), but talking to knowledgeable librarians may be your best resource of all. They can offer realistic perspectives of the process. Outreach coordinators can assist in assessment of which partnerships are potentially most appropriate, setting them up, and communicating between contact persons in the organizations involved. Especially helpful in developing rapport with your targeted population would be an outreach coordinator who is recognized as part of the community.

When seeking to better serve immigrant communities, one of the first collaborations to consider is with your local schools. Schools are central in communities and can provide convenient satellite sites for library activities. They also offer extension types of activities, to which libraries can contribute. For example, one library offered English lessons to Spanish-speaking parents who were school lunch-duty aides (Redwood City Public Library's Project READ). Santa Ana library hosts teacher open houses, PTAs, and university programs (Alire and Archibeque 1998). The New York Public Library's "Connecting Libraries And Schools Program" (CLASP) earned national recognition for its broad-based approach. This comprehensive program focused on parents and teacher workshops, family literacy, library cards, and class visits. A newer program, sponsored by the Wallace Foundation (http://www.

nypl.org/press/2003/wallacegrant.cfm), focuses on enhancing children's learning, studying, and homework. Remember that schools come in many different sizes and forms. There are private, public, alternative, and charter schools, as well as ancillary school-based organizations, especially after-school programs, and community-based schools. Most importantly, school librarians play an integral role in integrating the two institutions, so include them in any school–library collaborations and rely on them for important information about school needs and issues.

Social/human service organizations in your community (employment agencies, welfare departments, homeless shelters, community health clinics, domestic violence centers, lesbian/gay organizations, daycare centers, and senior centers) can also be important connections, especially for their knowledge of barriers in their clients' lives, and their experience of methods to reduce those obstacles directly. Some library literacy programs, for example, those in New York City, have partnered with one-stop job centers. These partnerships help students gain literacy skills necessary to advance in their jobs or to get a new one.

> The Fordham branch of the New York Public Library's Centers for Reading and Writing (a literacy program) did outreach to a substance abuse and prevention organization in the Fordham area of the Bronx. It let clients know that after their release they would have a welcoming place to go to. The literacy program director, as a part of the community, knew its landscape well. First she conducted an orientation to inform the recoverers about the library and its resources; then she answered questions and gave advice. Finally, she distributed literacy paraphernalia, which the recoverers eagerly grabbed up.

Other potential partners in your community can be found in the following: faith-based organizations (churches, mosques, Buddhist temples, and synagogues); sports associations; unions; jails and prisons; museums and other cultural agencies (performing arts and visual arts centers/galleries); police and fire departments; local businesses (both chain stores and local stores); social charities (e.g., Jewish Family Services, Goodwill, and Salvation Army); community service clubs (e.g., Rotary, Kiwanis, Lions, Jaycees, Girl Scouts, Boy Scouts, Junior League); local ethnic associations; women's organizations (NOW chapters); political and legal advocates for immigrants, and professional (especially law) associations, as well as government agencies and consulates. For example, in San Antonio, Texas, the public library works with the Mexican consulate to find out about Mexican nationals living and working in the area. Consulate documents can be used as valid identification for obtaining library cards.[5]

Keep in mind that grassroots organizations may not have conventional forms of leadership or organizational administration, but they have a strong base in some immigrant communities. They may even resist typical organizational structures, instead having loosely formed governance, which makes it difficult to collaborate using standard measures. But do not ignore them. Working with them will force the library to think outside the box! Build on their strengths, gain good contacts, and be inclusive in all interactions. Of special importance is this last point because a defined leader may not exist, or the decision-making process may differ from the standard. Examples of grassroots groups include twelve-step anonymous groups; activist groups that focus on social justice issues such as homelessness and hunger, gay and lesbian rights, anti-racism; and domestic violence groups. These groups can lend their expertise to work with outreach coordinators and train library staff on current issues in a community; they can also offer their communities timely information about library services and can even promote the library within the community. These types of collaborations increase library visibility as well as the level of services such as information and referral. They can also widen the distribution of books and materials that foster literacy, and develop programs. And, perhaps most importantly, such partnerships foster trusting relations with people who are not familiar with the library.

Adult educational agencies can also be suitable collaborators with libraries; their populations are similar, and they channel students into the local adult education system of which the library is a part. Community college ESOL programs with long waiting lists may refer ESOL students to the library for materials and services, for out-of-class learning, and for all types of media, for both themselves and their families. Moreover, libraries whose waiting lists are too long for their volunteer-based tutoring programs may recommend that people to go to another, undersubscribed program in their community.

Finally, consider partnering with cultural organizations outside of the country, in areas where new immigrants come from. This may help the library build connections with countries, and even visit them, learn from them, and assist new immigrants to come over and get settled. Many sources can initiate liaisons: community leaders, who know about local organizations in their villages or cities; international organizations such as Habitat for Humanity, Oxfam, or UNESCO; as well as fellow librarians or educators whom you meet at conferences. Even consider going to the International Federation of Library Associations (IFLA) conference to connect with these librarians and learn about global issues with migration. Reading up, attending conferences, contacting organizational members, using technology, exchanging materials, and visits can help develop long-lasting ties with new immigrant communities, because of the broad-based effort.

Potential Partners at a Glance
- Schools
- Human/social service agencies
- Faith-based organizations
- Political and legal advocacy organizations for immigrant rights
- Arts organizations
- Police and fire departments
- Community service clubs
- Jails and prisons
- Businesses
- Professional organizations
- Ethnic associations
- Adult education agencies and colleges
- Unions
- Women's organizations
- Sports organizations/associations
- Grassroots activist groups/organizations
- Organizations in other countries and international organizations

Keep in mind that personal contacts, rather than formal channels, often instigate collaborative relationships, especially in smaller communities. Sometimes personal contacts form the relationship initially, and then a written contract can assist in growing the project through a formalized, committed process of negotiations.[6] Be attentive to the culture of the organization you are dealing with in order to be able to communicate well with its members on all levels. For example, if you know that the negotiators speak different languages than you do, ensure that you have translators and representatives proficient in that language. The outreach coordinator can be a key liaison. The process of planning a partnership with individuals, with another agency, or with a set of organizations involves a series of steps. If you do not have much familiarity with the agency, follow these steps closely. If you already have contacts there, it may be necessary only to want to develop discussions, negotiations, and a contract.

- First, reflect on why and how a partnership is advantageous to the library and to new immigrant communities. List all of the outcomes to new immigrant communities that potential partnerships could achieve. Consider service areas in which the library is currently weak and how a partnership can make a service stronger.
- Second, with the outreach coordinator, develop a well-researched list or database of potential matches for a partnership. Include a number of partners and for specific purposes. Track interested, diverse venues for seeking out partners (from business development groups to arts and ethnic groups, community fairs, personal contacts, media, and the community press). List the informants too (including name, email, and contact phone number) for future reference.
- Research the agency on the web to learn basic information, noting in particular its mission, vision, and/or goals. Check out its past projects to see whether it has already worked with another library, and if it seems familiar with collaborations in general. Conduct informational interviews with colleagues or informants who have worked with the agency to see what they are like. Your outreach coordinator or community liaison should play a big role in this stage.
- Having gone through the list and identified particular partners for specific purposes, email or call the director, or the correct contact person; introduce yourself; and briefly tell about the library's interest in a partnership and what the library can offer the agency. Ask whether the agency would be interested in exploring the possibility of a partnership with your library and whether the person has any questions or concerns. Make clear that you will follow up with more information soon.
- Invite the partner with a formal, but friendly letter that follows up on the phone call and informs of future contact soon with logistics. Make sure that all of the information about the library is visible (name, address, website, etc.).
- Agree to meet with the agency to discuss guidelines, clear goals and objectives, and all other areas of interest to guarantee that the relationships and expectations are reciprocal, and the scope and time lines are made clear. Getting these details down on paper develops good rapport and a commitment to work together.
- Finally, create working contracts with a brief synopsis of aims of the partnership, goals, objectives, guidelines, and time lines. This contract will formalize the relationship and cement the commitment, as well as to make clear the worth of the partnership during trouble spots too. But if the contract is not legally binding, and both parties agree that things are not going well, the contract can be dropped.

The Queens New Americans Program[7] has established protocols and guidelines for developing and sustaining collaborative partnerships; the program's approach includes a systematic process of finding community partners through various sources and assessing their collections' development capacity, issues for certain groups, cultural adjustment issues, and cultural arts programs that "would encourage new immigrant groups to interact with established community."

Partnering Checklist
- Use all available resources (outreach coordinator, community gatekeeper, readings) to identify partnering sources and agencies in your community.
- Consider the advantages of partnering with those you have identified.
- Create a list/database of potential partners, making sure to consider schools, social and human service organizations, ethnic associations, and professional organizations, as well as community leaders.
- Consider ways to advertise for partners as well.
- Do research on partners to see who they are, their mission/vision, as well as their goals and past projects. See whether they have the capacity to collaborate.
- Contact potential partners to gauge their interest in partnering with the library, and determine whether a collaboration could develop working relations, contractual arrangements, and common goals.
- Return to the community assessment to see what needs and interests these partnerships can meet; and then go through this with your partners and community leaders.

Refer back to your community assessment to review the types of services that new immigrant communities want and need. Consider all types of needs and interests. These can range from practical needs for cultural adjustment (coping skills); survival information in their native languages on topics such as citizenship, employment, parenting; and resources, including cultural ones (book displays, celebrations, local artists).

As a result of a comprehensive partnering program, ethnic groups' awareness of library services increases, new immigrants may use the library more, and the library will more likely be viewed as a community center facilitating greater acculturation—which in turn leads to a greater degree of community action. These partnerships can enhance community renewal and turn into popular citywide initiatives.

> **A Successful Partnership That Became an Initiative**
> In 1997, with a matching grant from the library and a consortium of other agencies, the city of Seattle funded a two-year $500,000 New Citizenship Initiative, designed for 500–800 immigrants to obtain their citizenship through materials and information packets (in ten languages) located in twenty-two branches and distributed to other community-wide agencies. The initiative included a multilingual phone line of prerecorded information, an ESOL service directory, and web listings of all social service organizations providing ESOL and citizenship assistance in the Seattle area. It provided training for naturalization service providers and bilingual teachers (Kristi 1997: 23). The library reached out to its communities with well-sponsored needed services.

Community Liaisons Are Vital Friends

Because immigrants, and refugees often get initial information from their most familiar sources (often called "gatekeepers"), it is important to connect with these key individuals first, especially if you cannot afford to hire an outreach coordinator. These leaders, who are often bilingual or multilingual and, most importantly, bicultural, know cultural needs and can translate them. For this reason, they are like the glue that bonds new immigrants with the library. Involving gatekeepers in policy decisions is crucial in developing initial and close relationships with new immigrant communities. These vital friends can give you feedback about what new immigrants cannot say to your face.[8]

Known community workers (from police officers to social workers), as well as designated outreach coordinators, are critical liaisons for establishing these relationships. By focusing only on official community leaders, however, you may miss out on important information, so it is important to find the unofficial community leaders too. Although these informants may not have formal status or well-known positions in the community or even extensive formal education, they know what is happening on the street and are respected community members to whom people turn for advice. They may not come across as being officious, and although they may be much younger or older than a formal leader, they have strong ties to the community (Hall 2005).

Who are these people? A hairdresser or barber can be a community leader, and so can a local restaurant manager or waitress. Who is the neighborhood club or bar owner who sees residents nightly? Do you know the popular nail salon manager or worker who gives daily advice?

Or, what about the neighborhood psychic that community members go to when they need to make important decisions? Who are influential YMCA or YWCA staff members of whom people ask information? What about the matron on the block who knows the history of the neighborhood, or the gang member who knows what is happening on the street?

Find out where people in your community go for information—the places where potential outreach candidates hang out: local cafés and restaurants, recreation centers, bowling alleys, police stations, hospital emergency rooms, community clinics, the Ys, corners in neighborhoods, shopping malls, or a local park. Because it is sometimes difficult for librarians to begin collaboration with agencies or people with whom they are not familiar; use creative thought and initiative in establishing and nurturing these ties. Without community liaisons/leaders, it is even more difficult for you to really know how to meet new immigrants' needs and interests. Relying on a number of community leaders together as resources works best.

Community Leader/Liaison List
- Revisit your community assessments. Who or what is missing? Fill in the gaps by consulting with community leaders and your outreach coordinator.
- Make sure there are at least five community leaders/liaisons at any one time that you can consult with about the history of the neighborhood and changes in the community. These leaders may be found through your outreach coordinator (if there is one) or other venues.
- Ensure that these community leaders/liaisons are helpful and will help you and the outreach coordinator with additional contacts of many other people.
- Develop culturally competent communication (see Chapter Four) with community leaders/liaisons, so that this becomes a model for working with specific communities.
- Use the community leaders/liaisons to enter into creative partnerships with other agencies and groups.

Creative Partnerships

Numerous examples exist of creative partnerships between libraries and other organizations—both for-profit and nonprofit—that started out with individual contacts and grew into educational and informational types of collaborations. It is important that "librarians persistently seek new ways to serve their communities' needs and thereby make their libraries central to their communities rather than peripheral" (Constantino 1998: 69). The Queens Public Library has a model integrated type of program. There, staff actively create information about services set up by ethnic groups and put it online together with the names of agencies and a description of services such as community ESOL programs.[9]

> In the Redwood City Public Library's literacy program, Project READ, library staff collaborated with the local sheriff's office, the Junior League, and the community college to assist in training volunteers and peer tutors to work with inmates of a local jail in order to improve their literacy and GED. A fathers' reading program also proved valuable to the inmates.

Partnerships can also focus intensively on certain subgroups of new immigrant communities, such as the elderly or youth. In a Florida library outreach project for the elderly, a van holds a comprehensive print collection, as well as multimedia. Funded by LSTA monies, it offers courses to connect seniors to computers. Teens and college students assisted the seniors in learning technology literacy and even digital photography. Through a Wallace Funds grant, another project at the Enoch Pratt Free Library in Baltimore developed the Community Youth Corps program, a collaboration between the schools and the library. Participants gained high-quality work experiences and training opportunities, as well as access to library resources and service learning credit from their schools. Through focus groups, the teens planned peer-based activities, gained training in development and leadership, and worked in the library. After the grant expired, the collaboration created new after-school initiatives. At the Free Library of Philadelphia Public Library, another program for teens (LEAP) provides technology training, homework help, and social activities for youth, which neighborhood teens developed (Karp 2004; Milam 2003: 9; D. Taylor 2004).

Cultural and Social Events

Cultural and social events provide an avenue for introducing new immigrants to the library and for encouraging them to view the library as their meeting space. Community-wide events such as health fairs, spelling bees, and barbeques can be held at the library or sponsored by the library as well as through interagency efforts. These special events can particularly benefit immigrant communities, especially people who cannot come during library hours, who live far away from libraries, who are unfamiliar with library services, or who simply are too tired from working all day to come regularly to evening library programs. The events are also key marketing strategies, as we shall see.

Consider some examples. One community—Redwood City, California— holds a Trivia Bee that is sponsored by the library literacy program and allows learners in its programs, volunteer workers, librarians, community owners, and sponsors to come together once a year for fund-raising and intellectually engaging fun. In Seattle, the public library hosts exhibit booths at the Hispanic Sea Fair Festival each year, making available books and videos on Hispanic themes and in Spanish. People can apply for library cards, check items out, and get information about library services—including brochures on computer classes, ESOL, and young adult programs and books. The library also devotes another booth specifically to entertainment, which attracts many people interested in activities besides reading. These library booths are situated next to those of many other community agencies and businesses. Because such events are loose and informal, they attract groups of people not necessarily drawn to formality—youth, for example—both in and out of school.

A creative library–community partnership can be highly beneficial, especially when budgets are tight. Consider the full gamut of resources in your vicinity and make the most of them: volunteers, library staff, and patrons who live in the area, in addition to neighboring businesses, agencies, and organizations. The Seattle Public Library's student assistance program provides after-school jobs for youth at neighborhood libraries, and the students contribute their cultural resources to the library. And of course do not forget the Friends of the Library, library board members, and city council members, who can help in finding additional resources.

Become a Community Information Activist

Be creative and pro-active about your own role in the community and become an information activist. Information activists are librarians who go beyond their neutral roles to becoming key players in building education and information networks, and engaging in issues that concern new immigrant communities. Key players, as Joey Rodgers argues, do not think: "Library, library, library, but instead show up and talk about children, jobs, community safety, health or whatever issues the gathering is addressing" (O'Connor 2004: 93).

Information activists build effective collaborations between libraries and their communities. Therefore, you and the outreach coordinator need to become more knowledgeable about the new immigrant groups you are advocating for. Learn about the ethnic histories of immigration experiences and about local and national organizations that sponsor immigrants. Find out how immigrant communities have brokered information and continue to do so. And build knowledge about immigration law and reforms, as well as skills for conducting community needs assessments.

For this role, you or the outreach coordinator must also develop skills in public speaking and become visible as a public figure, especially by those who may not come forward with information. Some immigrants who are socially isolated and hidden (in the case of undocumented migrant workers) experience language barriers. In the capacity of outreach coordinator, facilitate discussions with bilingual community members to reach a common understanding, establish relationships, and solve problems. In collaboration with other agencies, schedule ongoing public engagements featuring dynamic speakers in or out of the library. Use the media, such as radio broadcasts in Spanish—for example, Seattle's "Ask a Librarian"—and community newspapers or newsletters that present important information and often include articles written by their ethnic-minority readers (Larsen, Jacobs, and Vlimmeren 2004).

Sponsorship of New Immigrant Public Speakers

In Seattle, for instance, a collaboration between the library (that provides space and the necessary technology), a literacy consortium that consists of community college directors, and a grant for Americorps staff has met with success. The consortium sponsors a group of ESOL students to advocate in the community. Members of the "Speakers Bureau," as it is called, are trained to give presentations in English and learn to overcome their language barriers. They get assistance in public speaking and come to know library resources. They discuss the meaning of their education, their goals in life, and what it was like to leave their countries and come to the United States. In all of these activities, they also attract other immigrants to the library.

Professionals who are immigrants can assist you in brokering community information. Together, with your team of community leaders, some of whom may also be professionals, you can develop lists of important information sources, define priorities, and create networks that continue to publicize important issues about and for new immigrant communities. For example, the Queens Public Library organized a meeting of Korean social workers who consulted on program issues and cultural sensitivity issues. The group recommended that a child abuse preven-tion program, in order to attract—rather than repel—interested people, be called "Overcoming Our Worries About Our Children" (Tandler 2004). In Hartford, Connecticut, an interagency collaboration program entitled "The American Place" (TAP) focuses on building awareness of community resources on many different issues, including education and cultural exchange, with the goal "to help you adjust to life in America while preserving elements of your native culture."[10]

Use Many Strategies to Become Informed

Critical for successfully publicizing library resources are computer technology and the digitization of important community information. The New York Public Library's Centers for Reading and Writing feature a computer management system that functions interactively, allowing community members to read learners' stories and write back to them with comments and questions. The centers attract tutors as well as patrons who want to learn to read. This reciprocal system allows people to communicate, exchange ideas, and build relationships online. It also generates timely information.

Through online and other types of information sources, find out about new laws that affect immigrants on national and international levels (the U.S. Patriot Act, California's Proposition 187, the terms of guest worker programs, human rights laws). Once you know about this information, you will gain status as an insider information advocate to immigrant communities—providing them with up-to-date information, access, legal references, and a strong community-based information and referral service that allows people to make direct contacts and ask criti-cal, complex questions.

Information activist projects can be formed through a creative col-laboration to deal with specific issues. One example of such a project is the "People's Law School" at the County Law Library in San Ysidro, California. The American Bar Association and the Western Law School joined together for this endeavor, using volunteer lawyers who are part of a Spanish pro bono program (Alire and Archibeque 1998). Consider training from law and immigration agencies on timely issues as well. In such cases be sure to sponsor an array of agencies with information that new immigrant communities need.

Another example of a successful collaboration is the Chicago Public Library's "port of entry" program, funded through an LSCA grant. In this endeavor, librarians participated in a training program conducted by six bilingual professionals to become sensitized to new immigrants' experiences and perspectives, to learn about immigrants' home countries and styles of communication, to avoid prejudice against certain ethnic groups, and to refrain from treating them as homogeneous entities (especially Latinos and Arabs, who in fact come from many different areas). A professional trainer reminded workshop attendees, "They will hesitate to ask you for your time. They may be afraid that you, a high official in their estimation, will treat them like ignorant peasants" (Trejo and Kaye 1988: 891).

Once again, return to your community needs assessment to review the findings, and disseminate this information. You or the outreach coordinator (or even the community brokers) may choose to set up a listserv to pass on reliable and valid information for review. Positive communication can counter rumors or myths that are spread throughout the community, and sharing information on an ongoing basis is critical for dealing with policies and issues.

If electronic networks for information exchange are not available, the exchange can be in the flesh. For example, INFOBUS (Virgilio 2004) travels the Memphis area to disseminate and gather information, and the librarians thus learn about all types of barriers and issues within the area. They have discovered that primary information needs are language development, employment information, and information on how to access health care and education. The biggest barriers to meeting those needs are lack of awareness and lack of multilingual resources. The librarians share information from one local community to the next and use more information to create surveys and services that will improve the library's role. They offer services and programs that are bilingual and in the native language of any given community.

Consider also working with established immigrant rights groups in your community. By working with both local and national immigrant advocacy groups, such as the American Civil Liberties Union (ACLU), the National Network for Immigrant and Refugee Rights (NNIRR), INS, and replacement INS services, you can assist immigrants in making informed decisions. Sponsor workshops (either online, or in the library) or regular listserv question-and-answer programs to assist new immigrant communities in accessing timely, crucial information. Be sure also to connect to national library listservs that post national legislative information. Access information from the Progressive Librarian Forum and the Progressive Librarians Guild, Social Responsibilities Roundtable, Street Librarian, and LibrarianActivist.org (with alternative perspectives on current issues).

Consider using local and national political organizations, which may have strong bases in communities, to learn more about political issues that affect immigrant groups in your area. Most political organizations have mailing lists, timely information about events, as well as knowledge about new laws that could be useful. On receiving political information, check out "facts" before disseminating it, and cite sources. Also, be inclusive; do not leave out smaller, lesser known parties or even less established, local student organizations.

A Word About Anti-Immigrant Groups

Do not worry about anti-immigrant groups approaching you to advocate for immigrant rights! However, be prepared for anti-immigrant groups to approach the library for information. Get a sense of who they are (perhaps make a reference list to share with library staff in other libraries). For this reason, it would be worthwhile to put together a plan of action and policies, as well as a committee to deal with these groups. If anti-immigrant groups approach the library, give them as much information as possible about what the library does with new immigrant communities, as well as all of the other communities the library serves, and answer as many questions as you can. Perhaps offer to present a talk to this group in the future, or send another member of the library staff to converse with them at a community event. Although it is unproductive to engage in arguments, encourage healthy debate. Make sure to tell them about the mission of the library, the policies of the library, as well as ALA's policies on equal access. If they need a space in the library to meet, let them sign up for a room. If they use library facilities, be sure they know the library's policies, especially on the harassment of employees and patrons, and hate language.

Beyond basic survival information, nurturing ethnic communities' historical and cultural information is also important. Immigrants need to be able to tell their "stories" (of their immigration experiences and motivations) so that you can understand the chronology of these needs (Lee and Sheared 2003; Sonenberg 2005). This process can additionally foster an exchange between new immigrants and native-born individuals who can share stories in the same language and—as in the case of a conversation club—find common ground.

Through listservs, community brokers, guest speakers, conversation clubs, speak outs, and other professional engagements, you can start to map out information networks in the community that identify important information areas and yield key informants. Mapping these informal networks and presenting them online or on library websites is beneficial, especially as they change frequently. These can be presented visually for easy access as well as through other preferred modes of communication.[11]

Are You a Community Information Activist?

1. Have you built effective collaborative partnerships with other important new immigrant agencies?
2. Do you have an outreach coordinator and community liaisons to assist you?
3. Have you or your staff participated in public speaking engagements in the community?
4. Have you used the assistance of professional immigrants in the community?
5. Did you use all types of strategies for gathering and disseminating information (online, training)?

If you have been following the steps outlined in this and previous chapters, you are now well on the road to better serving new immigrant communities. You have assessed your library's current services; surveyed needs of immigrant communities and barriers to service; found new ways to fund your endeavors through restructuring the library budget, grants, fund-raising, partnerships and collaborations; and become an information advocate. Chapter Four will show how to use your information advocacy to communicate effectively with new immigrant communities.

ADDITIONAL RESOURCES

Crowther, J. L., and Trout, B. *Partnering with Purpose: A Guide to Strategic Partnership Development for Libraries and Other Organizations.* Westport, CT: Libraries Unlimited, 2004.

Humes, B. *Public Libraries and Community-Based Education: Making the Connection for Lifelong Learning.* Washington, D.C.: Office of Education, 1996.

Kerka, S. *Developing Collaborative Partnerships.* Practice Application Briefs. ACVE, 1997. http://www.calpro-online.org/eric/docgen.asp?tbl=pab&ID=71

Kretzmann, J., and Rans, S. *The Engaged Library.* Evanston, IL: Urban Libraries Council, 2005.

Libraries for the Future Initiative. *Natural Partners, Foundations and Libraries,* 2005. http://www.lff.org/documents/Portrait_Partners.pdf

ENDNOTES

1. For more general information on financial planning, see Nelson 2001. For an excellent resource on serving Latino communities, see Alire and Archibeque 1998.

2. See Larsen, Jacobs, and Vlimmeren 2003; see Larsen, Jacobs, and Vlimmeren 2004 for ideas about developing immigrant programming.

3. See the ALA OLOS website (http://www.ala.org/ala/olos/literacyoutreach. htm) for partnering ideas, programs, and tips. In particular, as discussed in Chapter Eight and the Final Thoughts section, various types of literacy program recommendations exist.

4. For more ideas on community development and renewal, see Kretzmann and Rans 2005 and http://www.urbanlibraries.org/theconnectedlibrary.html.

5. The report, Milam 2003, has one of the first, recent national looks at library immigrant issues. See also Alire and Archibeque 1998 for more information on partnering with Latino organizations.

6. Archibeque and Alire 1998 have focused extensively on Latino collections. Do not bypass this source!

7. Fred J. Gitner, "The Queens Borough Public Library New Americans Program: Forging Partnerships for Diversity," American Library Association Diversity Fair, 1998, p. 1, at http://www.infolink.org/diversity/fredIFLA.pdf. Fred Gitner has researched and written extensively about their studies and program development. See also the following resources: Gitner and Chan 2001; Fred J. Gitner, "The New Americans Program: Forging Partnerships for Diversity," in *Bridging Cultures: Ethnic Services in the Libraries of New York State,* edited by Irina A. Kuharets, B. A. Cahalan, and F. J. Gitner, 166–169 (Albany, NY: New York Library Association Ethnic Services Roundtable, 2001).

8. See an excellent piece, Cuesta 2004; also Cuesta 2005. See also Vang n.d.

9. See more from Alire and Archibeque 1998.

10. See Hartford Public Library's, "The American Place" at http://ww2.hplct. org/tap/TAP.htm.

11. See librarian.org and streetlibrarian.org for additional ideas.

CHAPTER 4
Communicating Competently with New Immigrant Communities

This chapter covers communication—how to reach out to new immigrant communities in meaningful ways. Communicating competently involves overcoming language barriers, assessing library texts, and changing your modus operandi of interacting. Doing this requires all of your resources—community liaisons, bilingual staff, online sources—as well as taking advantage of training opportunities (in new immigrants' cultures). Most importantly, you must focus your efforts on learning, and not on marketing recruitment tricks. In doing so you can develop authentic communication and genuine relationships with new immigrant communities. You will begin to walk the talk.

THE LANGUAGE BARRIER AND HOW TO OVERCOME IT

Checklist for Overcoming Language Barriers
- Review oral and written forms of communication of the library that immigrant populations will potentially use, and change them if they do not communicate the message effectively.
- Make concerted attempts to improve communications with new immigrant groups in both written and oral forms.
- Use library volunteers (particularly those who are bilingual) in a variety of capacities to help break through the language barrier and connect to new immigrant community members, for example, as greeters.

- Consider the resources of your local community college and universities. International and work study students can be helpful.
- Use online resources to become more informed and disseminate information.
- Make sure the library staff contains as many bilingual/multilingual and bicultural staff members as possible.
- Ensure some training of library staff in new immigrants' cultures and languages.

What about talk? You might or might not be an English-only speaking person. If you or your library staff is monolingual, then overcoming language barriers presents even more of a challenge. Even though this may be one of the main problems for most libraries in dealing with new immigrant communities (Jacobs 2004; Quezada 2005), it is also essential for establishing positive working relationships with these communities. The language, content, and format of library communications must match with the language, culture, and information needs of new immigrant groups with whom you will want to interact. Strive to blend with the community in a seamless and community-sensitive way. This process starts with ongoing needs assessments (see Chapter One) and ends with services and policies (see Chapters Five and Six).

Keep in mind that you and your library staff function as bridges between the library and immigrant communities, and that many venues exist for communicating. Written forms are one method. It can be informants' and professional translators' work to translate electronic and print sources into the community's native languages. In the case of new immigrants, consider all types of languages, accents, and vernacular forms (such as Creole), including slang and dialects from a country of origin. Your needs assessment can reveal all these elements, especially through observations and talking with local people. In Hawai'i, for example, librarians and library staff commonly communicate in a form of talk story and in Hawai'i Creole English (which many new immigrants speak), to accommodate the local culture.

Your needs assessment should help you and your library staff to break down myths about new immigrants and to ensure cultural sensitivity about the differences between countries, between ethnic groups, and between language groups. Immigrant groups can also develop stereotypes and prejudices against other groups and native-born Americans. In such cases, fair representation is important. Advisory committees and task force committees, along with your community leader groups, can discuss and evaluate ongoing accommodation of different languages and ethnicities. Some library literacy programs, such as that of the Glenwood Branch library in Greensboro, North Carolina, have established focus groups among predominant immigrant groups in order to learn about designing effective programs.[1]

Examine Written Texts to See Whether They Are Culturally Sound

In written communication, be sure to use correct terminology and avoid Anglicization of the text. For example, use the "okina" (diacritical) in the word "Hawai'i." Signage in and around the library, library dress, electronic sources (such as websites), brochures, and other materials for outreach programs all feature written communication. Parts of these can be in English, parts in other languages. Materials targeted to specific populations may be in that particular ethnic group's language only, but other forms may use a variety of languages representing the cultural mix of the community. Remember that many new immigrant groups may be street savvy and competent in oral skills but less so in reading and writing skills; so they may need assistance with literacy in English as well. If your library has a literacy program, this factor alone may attract immigrants into the library for help with reading and writing. For individuals in groups that do not have advanced native language literacy, use pictograms and graphics for communication purposes (Vang n.d.).

Native language texts that are appropriate for the intended audience and without mistakes in grammar and meaning compose key components to your success with immigrant populations. Even in English, translating policies into plain language in a way that different patrons understand can often be difficult (Nelson 2001). Nonetheless, you should try. If your library has a literacy program, that staff can help in producing readable texts, possibly with students also assisting in the translations. Two libraries (Glenwood and Redwood City, California) hired multilingual Americorps volunteers to assist with their orientation sessions, to teach classes on different subjects, as well as to create curriculum. These personnel were especially valuable because of the cultural resources they brought into libraries. In addition, their labor was affordable (Sumerford 2005). Many had just finished college and spoke or were learning languages that were specific to a particular ethnic group—for example, Spanish or Montagnard (from the central highlands of Vietnam).

How Is the Oral Communication Between the Library and New Immigrants?

Oral communication is also crucial with new immigrant populations. This ranges from patron contact with bilingual reference, information desk, and circulation staff, to community-wide presentations, bookmobile services, and speaking events in the library. Some libraries (for example, the Toronto Public Library) have established "language lines" to assist library patrons with interpretation (Larsen, Jacobs, and Vlimmeren 2004). Other libraries have created phrase books and directories for assisting English-only speaking librarians to communicate. Consider all of your resources.

Community Language Liaisons

Native language speakers who work as greeters, pages or shelvers, consultants, students, or are even regular patrons can be critical players—permanently and temporarily—in accommodating a new immigrant community. Their ability to communicate in new immigrants' native languages and then translate to English makes them language liaisons for the library.

What if your library cannot recruit people who speak the native language and know about the culture? Or what if a budget crunch has led to hiring freezes and no money to hire an outreach coordinator? Consider volunteers. Train native language speakers, whether on a stipend or volunteer scale, to deal with library patrons. Greeters are volunteers who welcome people and direct them to their destination in the library. Wearing a name tag with a welcome message in another language creates a friendly and open atmosphere for new immigrants (McMurrer and Terrill 2001). These volunteers may also be translators who give tours—"library links" (just as the Minneapolis Public Library's program for New Americans is called). This important service helps immigrants who are not accustomed to using libraries in their home countries or who have little time to browse for materials.

Ethnic minority trustees can also assist you in important ways, by sponsoring language initiatives and recruiting more bilingual staff. They inform library staff on issues such as library use in the home country. They are often in the best position to recruit staff who are bilingual and culturally sensitive. Many immigrants may perceive libraries as government institutions to be distrusted (Alire and Archibeque 1998; Osborne 2005), and bilingual frontline staff who speak their native language can help dispel this suspicion.

Large libraries often hire security guards to protect, direct, and discipline patrons; but they can also be trained to greet patrons. They may be from the community themselves and know the people entering the library. Seniors can be greeters, and so can students from the local university or high school (perhaps in a service-learning position or else as recipients of library-sponsored scholarships that support them through high school and attract them to the library profession).

Professional consultants work in such fields as translation, linguistics, foreign languages, and education. A library with a particular language need that is near a university or a community college could consider student internships or professional consultations with language teachers and faculty in linguistics and ESOL. The library might recruit patrons to assist with translations as well; other consultants, community leaders, or a pilot audience could double-check these for reliability.

Ideas for recruiting volunteers may come from current staff members, religious organizations, community organizations, community leaders, an outreach coordinator, recreational centers, senior citizen centers, the judicial system, and the local ethnic media, as well as from community colleges. Queens Borough Public Library has both volunteers and paid staff who are bilingual and work with New Americans Programs, as well as in many areas of the library (Shriver 2002).

Using University and Community College Students as Intern Intermediaries

The Hilo Public Library computer-assisted learning program in Hawai'i employed work-study students, many of whom were Hawaiian, from the local university and other organizations, to assist with technical duties in the library. In return, the students received homework help from volunteers; they felt as though they were "giving back" to the library through this exchange.[2] Other libraries coordinate with universities for students to tutor adult learners.

Do not overlook the resources of international students. Working in the library offers them an opportunity to practice English communication, connects them to their own ethnic group as well as to native-born Americans, and helps them feel less isolated. International students can also assist with other library work such as cataloging. The Brooklyn Public Library used international high school and college students to assist in cataloging items from other countries, a project that addresses a common problem for libraries. Somali youth in Seattle helped librarians connect with immigrant Somali families and were able to share important adjustment information. A library in San Diego recruits young teens for an hour or two per week, working with them until they are old enough to become part-time employees. This supports the teens with their homework and contributes to a multicultural youth environment. Similarly, the New York Public Library has a youth club called the "Junior Lions," that delivers ESOL instruction and holds discussion groups for ESOL students.[3]

Online Sources

New immigrants can also use online sources, including websites and listservs, effectively to communicate in their first languages. Some Massachusetts libraries, such as Framingham (with its large Portuguese community) and Springfield (with its large Spanish-speaking community), actually have native language websites, as do other library systems (Quezada 2005). Attracting minorities through technology access is important since currently a digital gap often leaves immigrants out of the loop.

Other technological needs for immigrant communities include computer training and online tutoring, especially for populations with low levels of formal education. In Charlotte, North Carolina, and in Phoenix, Arizona, classes cover computer skills, ways of using the Internet, emailing, and word processing (Milam 2003). Webjunction sponsors Spanish Language Outreach Programs in most states in the country and in different geographic areas;[4] in conjunction with state librarians, librarians learn techniques and identify ways in which technology can benefit Spanish-speaking communities, thus encouraging the Spanish-speaking public's use of computers.

Bilingual/Bicultural Staff

Finding staff members who not only speak the language but also represent the ethnic community is crucial to your success in working with immigrant communities. This has been a key area of promotion for the American Library Association in recent years.

Professional staff who are bicultural and bilingual are vital to creating language matches and anticipating and diagnosing needs; and they can also become permanent members of, or stakeholders in, the library community. More specifically, having grown up with minority cultures' customs and mores, these staff members can be visibly identified as insiders to members of that culture. They know and speak a local vernacular; they may live in the community themselves and know informants; and they bring a sense of purpose and commitment to serving their communities in a long-lasting way through bilingual programs. Furthermore, they can operate as positive role models for young adults, as well as contact persons and outreach specialists (Alire and Archibeque 1998; Shriver 2002). Employing multi-ethnic staff increases the library's cultural competence as an institution that is attuned to diversity and offers equal access to all of its community members. Consult with your advisory board members before you try to recruit bilingual or multilingual staff members for the types of needs and services they may fulfill.

Library schools and libraries have attempted to attract ethnic and linguistic minorities to the profession: According to a 2003 Urban Libraries Council report, 48 percent actively recruit immigrants and refugee residents, and libraries overwhelmingly recognize the need for bilingual staff (Alire and Archibeque 1998; Cuesta 2005; Hall 2005; Larsen, Jacobs, and Vlimmeren 2004: 18; Milam 2003; Quezada 2005).

Yet in spite of their good intentions and efforts, libraries have generally failed to attract minorities into the profession. Although 93 percent of reporting libraries have customer service staff who speak multiple languages, and 80 percent said they have a few staff who are from immigrant/refugee populations in the community; immigrants are rarely trained library professionals and thus would be considered "unqualified" for most staff positions in the library.

Recruitment is tricky, because most LIS graduates are of Anglo-European descent. However, with new scholarship programs such as the three-year Spectrum initiative, mentoring programs such as REFORMA, and residency programs for academic librarians (Cogell and Gruwell 2001), the number of minorities in the field may increase in the future.

When trying to recruit immigrants or bilingual staff, your job announcements should be specific about the skills, knowledge, and types of programs being sought. Your ad might adopt the language of social service agencies to focus on helping activities. Involve committee members who are committed to outreach in interviews, including nonlibrarians from the community (Roberts 2004). Advertising through word of mouth may yield qualified applicants from different fields who would not have heard about the job otherwise. These individuals may have life experience and—if they had previous experience in social services positions—skills in listening and counseling. Ask professional organizations such as REFORMA, which have their own recruitment strategies. Multilingual paraprofessionals can also be good candidates for hiring, because of their familiarity with the culture of the library and the language and culture of particular constituents. The Denver

Public Library "grows its own" through paying employees to go through library school, and the Colorado State Library Advisory board provides scholarships.[5]

Training on New Immigrants' Cultures

Providing basic training in other languages and cultures also builds staff effectiveness with immigrant communities. In addition to ongoing in-house training, certain programs and workshops outside of the library focus on cultural competencies in new immigrants' cultures. Training can even concentrate on specific issues pertinent to immigrant communities. For example, staff at the Queens Borough Public Library received training from health care professionals on public health issues. Librarians elsewhere have benefited from training about job service (Kao 2004; Milam 2003).

It is not uncommon for literacy volunteers and staff to receive training on relevant issues through the Literacy Assistance Center, as in the case of the New York Public Library, Centers for Reading and Writing, as well as the Queens Adult Learning Center. The staff members receive training on a variety of topics related to literacy instruction, on adult learning, and from staff who attended literacy conferences and want to share their brand-new knowledge. Training of library staff members may be conducted on an in-house basis or at an off-site location. Most importantly, librarians need skills for outreach. In many ways, as Yolanda Cuesta states, outreach needs to be included in everyone's job description and should be a performance measure. Staff must have outreach competence and be knowledgeable in techniques for drawing in new immigrant communities (Cuesta 2004; Osborne 2005; Webjunction 2004). This includes certain abilities such as the following:

- Linguistic competence (being able to communicate effectively with new immigrants in their language by yourself or through a library liaison)
- Cultural knowledge (understanding the worldviews, values, beliefs, and social practices of a new immigrant group)
- Sharp analytic and empathic abilities to see the library from the viewpoint of the community (being able to evaluate the library's position in the eyes of its users through community needs assessments)

A Chicago library immediately introduces new staff members to outreach services as well as to other agencies in the area; and they hear accounts of librarians who are immersed in the community. The norm that the "library is the cultural backbone of the community" is established early on. After that, they practice outreach activities by attending community meetings and visiting other nearby institutions so they will feel comfortable being in the community (Greene 2004: 124).

Outreach training institutes can be helpful as well. In Seattle, for instance, a group of library trainers gathered for Webjunction's Spanish Language Outreach Program, an eighteen-month pilot program sponsored by the Bill and Melinda Gates Foundation. Well-respected in the field for her diversity expertise, trainer Yolanda Cuesta taught participants about the importance both of using terms and their context when reaching out to the Spanish-speaking community and of participating with other local organizations. A stimulating panel discussion among community organizers reinforced these points, and the conference participants appreciated the tools and models demonstrated.

PUBLIC RELATIONS STRATEGIES TO ATTRACT NEW IMMIGRANTS

Reaching out to immigrant communities starts with getting people to come to the library, but promotional strategies to achieve this do not suffice. Your public relations initiative must be comprehensive, integrated, culturally sensitive, creative, and far-reaching to sustain the relationship over time. Promotional strategies to new immigrant groups may currently operate at a minimum level in your library. Now is the time to take another look and to maximize them.

The New York Public Library can serve as a role model in making the maximum effort to promote library services to new immigrant communities. Because of its numerous and diverse populations, this library provides a fully comprehensive outreach service that is coterminous with its promotional strategies. Community specialists, for example, conduct fieldwork on various issues in boroughs and collaborate with external outreach advisory committees (of up to forty people) that communicate community needs.

Another example, the Seattle Public Library's "Libraries for All" campaign, attracted voters and increased financial support for more libraries and renovations. Seven libraries were slated for major expansion; five libraries were built in areas of need; two libraries were relocated; and two others were renovated. With an additional campaign, "Books, Bytes, and Believers," it directed another $5 million toward changing the book collections—and Microsoft added a further $2.5 million to this effort. This started because 69 percent of all voters approved a detailed plan by casting a "yes" vote at the election; afterward, the Bill and Melinda Gates Foundation gave $20 million, of which $15 million went to the branch libraries. Melinda Gates said, "Libraries help level the playing field by giving to everyone—no matter what their economic situation—access to the same tools and information" (Marshall 2004: 157). These resources assist the many low-income, new immigrant, and refugee groups in Seattle to access resources that might otherwise not have been available to them. One undocumented Mexican woman, who cleaned houses in Seattle, dropped out of her English language program because of her hectic schedule. Since then, she has gone to her local library with her children. The library bridged a gap in her education.[6]

If your library cannot afford such strategies, choose less expensive promotional activities. Pick and choose issues that are priorities and focus on these. Or, seek out local grants, instead of large ones, and use the assistance of city council members in securing them.

If your library has few resources for promotional activities overall, focus on a specific population and promote library services around its needs.[7] Your plan should identify the target population, the most effective ways of promoting the library to it (by distributing flyers, for example), and the best places in which to do that. Advertising may be in the form of print flyers, brochures, newsletters, and mailings; but also consider some other creative ways to promote your library services.

Oral presentations, graphic displays, and physical demonstrations/performances can be effective and inexpensive ways to attract new immigrant communities, although they do take some time. In addition, using word of mouth is an important and economical strategy, particularly with immigrant communities.

Word of Mouth

Word-of-mouth recruitment strategies, through immigrant networking, are particularly effective PR strategies with new immigrant populations—beginning with library patrons who share the news about libraries and/or with nonpatrons in community-based agencies, local stores, or neighborhood centers. These low-profile techniques can attract the newest generations of immigrants, who may not read or be familiar with institutional information channels but would trust a familiar face.

Make sure that your word-of-mouth strategies emphasize that the library is free and safe; that it welcomes new immigrants, and that language will not be a barrier to obtaining important information. This critical message must be sent because new immigrants can view libraries as intimidating institutions and as places that produce fear (rather than interest). One Somali woman said, "When I first came to the library, I was very shy, and couldn't express my feeling very much. I don't know how many times I cried on the way home" (Larsen, Jacobs, and Vlimmeren 2004: 44). This, of course, underlines the need to audit facilities to see whether institutional barriers for new immigrants exist. The audit is integral to targeting possible areas of confusion and problems for people who are not used to navigating the library. One library's literacy coordinator voiced the difficulty in attracting patrons who are intimidated by the public library image and facilities (Wong 2005). Even if the facilities are not inviting, frontline staff should reflect a sense of safety and openness that is clear to all new immigrants.

To communicate the library's message appropriately and successfully, your library must have access to translators. An outreach specialist can aid in this process, creating distribution lists on an ongoing basis, attending community events to keep updating the lists, and spreading the word to new immigrant communities. Use organizations' distribution lists and databases as well as key contact persons when starting a word-of-mouth campaign, especially to track basic information and projections of likely donations for marketing purposes.

What are some of the ways beyond the standard library publications to reach out to immigrant populations? Let's take a closer look at some traditional and nontraditional venues.

Public Service Announcements

Public service announcements (PSAs) about library events and services offer you an affordable way to reach immigrant communities. These short (30–60-second) "ads," which can run on different TV and radio stations, especially in other languages, also can be coordinated with the foreign language press in immigrant communities. For example, many people in Hmong communities work hard to support their children. Although they may not know about library programs or services, they would readily listen to a PSA (Vang n.d.). If foreign language cable or radio stations exist in your community, work with them on a regular basis, sending PSAs and then even advertising, if you get a response.

Ask for discount rates, if they are not free; barter and exchange advertising if appropriate; and use smaller, shorter ads.

PSA Guidelines

- Before creating a PSA, check the website of the media agency you want to submit it to, for its preferences. Most of them will have a criteria list for PSAs. If they do not, call and ask how to do it.
- Write the PSA on library stationery, and include all of the library's basic information, including address, email, website, phone numbers.
- Write a short descriptive paragraph on what it is you want new immigrants to know about the library (that services are free, you can get information from your home country, etc.).
- Know the time frame to air the announcement, amount of times for it to air, and word length or time length limits.
- Your PSA should be in the languages of the new immigrant groups you want to attract (be prepared to use volunteer translators if the stations do not have a foreign language announcer or writer).
- Highlight any special library events for new immigrant communities.
- Make sure to submit the PSA to the station at least two weeks in advance of the airing; but learn its deadlines.
- Make sure your PSA includes your contact number and email.

Exhibitions In and Around the Library

Exhibitions of artwork and crafts by immigrant artists or about local immigrant communities may liven up otherwise blank library walls while sending a message that the library is very interested in the cultures of the people in the surrounding community. Collaborate with local museums or galleries for shows; with schools, cafés, bookstores, and photographers from the area; or with library patrons who have photographed another country or a new immigrant community in the neighborhood. If the library sponsors the exhibit, make sure that library signage and pamphlets are visible and translated, if possible.

Staff members who recognize talented patrons might encourage them by giving them space to exhibit their work. Or put a key community liaison in charge of this task—with an available wall every month. This may well draw in new talent and audiences. These artists can also conduct workshops on their art in the library, thus attracting even more users, as well as building general community interest and understanding. Do not forget performance events—such as new or traditional dances or plays—that can be held in a theater space or auditorium.

Video documentaries of new immigrant communities may also help bring in both native-born and new immigrant artists, in addition to providing an educational and entertaining forum for ideas and issues. Your library might lend out equipment, if it has it, for these purposes. Certain stores or other businesses in your area may want to help out as well, seeing exhibits as opportunities to advertise and make connections with the community.

Remember that advertising and exhibits can easily fall into the cultural tourism trap (Quezada 1992) of turning new immigrant groups' work into novelties or pretty display cases to prove the library is "multicultural." This does not qualify as multicultural education, and it contributes to misunderstandings and stereotypes. These artists should have a say in how they want their work to be advertised, exhibited, and performed, and the library should allow them to convey their own messages to their audiences. Make sure the artists have plenty of opportunities to talk and write about their work, and give audiences space and time to respond (after performances, do a question-and-answer period or have written evaluations). Finally, ensure that these artists are on library committees and have decision-making power, apart from exhibiting or performing their work. Their contributions can be invaluable.

Book and Film Clubs

The traditional library programs of book clubs and film clubs can attract formally educated immigrant communities. These programs cost relatively little and can be easily promoted through word of mouth.

A more intensive and costly, but worthwhile, book club that can turn into a citywide program is exemplified by Seattle's "If All of Seattle Read One Book" campaign, spurred by the Lila Wallace Foundation grants. This book club idea took hold and soon spread across the country (Sonenberg 2005). Since then, several programs have developed around the country, including those of libraries in Citrus County, Florida, in Indianapolis, and in Alaska. The community of Greensboro, North Carolina, called its campaign for reading "One City One Book" and found that it attracted many new people to engage in discussions of literature, reflecting issues within their community. Your one city–one book endeavor might focus on a title with appeal to new immigrants. For example, one city chose a title that reflects the new immigrant experience: *The Middle of Everywhere: Helping Refugees Enter the American Community*, by Mary Pipher. A description of the cultural clashes in Lincoln, Nebraska, when refugees from more than 52 countries were settled there, this book has sparked discussions in Greensboro precisely because that area has experienced a similar influx and is now home to more than 20,000 Latinos, 8,500 Southeast Asians, 12,000 Africans, and members of thousands of other nationalities. A diverse community-wide committee led by Steve Sumerford, an experienced community library organizer, selected the book after a sensitive media campaign for the books over time.

Another library, in Charlotte, North Carolina, launched a book club for women, "Sisterfriends@your library," which operates at the library and the jail (McLean 2004). In 2001, when library users said they wanted to read and discuss women's issues, the library responded. The library program provides a calming climate (with aromatherapy candles) for women to relax and focus on self-care, as they discuss various books. When conducted at the jail, relaxing music and sound creates a similar environment. The library and jail groups read the same books and reviewed them. Women inmates published their writing in an anthology, called *Hungry for Home.*

A media campaign became indispensable for support to jail inmates; the club was cross-promoted through radio spots, brochures, articles, conferences, the library newsletter, and by word of mouth. The organizers issued a press release, mined data for current information, partnered with businesses (such as bookstores, for free books), and contacted publishers (for book signings by authors).

An example of an immigrant-friendly film club is the one at the Queens Public Library's Flushing branch. The staff held a film festival; it showed silent Charlie Chaplin movies, among others, which proved to be a lighthearted way of attracting students to its ESOL programs despite the differences in cultures. In the days after 9/11, this provided comic relief and a bonding opportunity for the many new immigrants who were traumatized by the event. Because language did not present a barrier to enjoying the movies (as they were silent), many new immigrants understood and appreciated the humor. Be sure to consider the interests and needs of your audience when showing a film. Libraries usually check out films rather than show them, but perhaps some of your video or DVD collection can be used for programs or even expanded for new immigrant audiences.

Guidelines for Film Clubs
- Make a draft list of possible videos or DVDs to show, and pilot it on various new immigrant patrons who would be most likely and least likely to attend a film event.

- Conduct a quick-and-dirty survey on opinions about what films new immigrants want to see and why. Simply stand outside the library and as new immigrants go past, ask: "What movies would you like to come to see at the library?" Write down these titles.
- Check out video club and box office hit selections to see which movies are most popular. Discuss your list with a staff film expert (there may be a number of closeted ones in your library).
- Get a sign-up list of library patrons who want to be on a film committee.
- Make sure that your films represent diverse countries and ethnic groups and that new immigrant communities consider them classic and/or popular.
- Advertise film clubs on the web, and seek out ideas through a library listserv about developing them further.
- Look at utube.com for ideas about making or showing videos.

If your library does not have the staff to host a program, consider sponsoring clubs that new immigrant community members start and help sustain them by offering space, screen, and chairs. If your library owns multiple copies of the book or film, people can use these or bring their own. Remember, you can collaborate with the local bookstore on book clubs too—advertising one another at the same time.

Print and Electronic Ads

You can use anything from flyers, brochures, and leaflets to electronic media/listservs and newsletters to communicate with new immigrant communities about library events as well as general and specific library issues. Distribute print promotions throughout your community and at special events and through other organizations, using volunteers or your outreach coordinator, if necessary.

Be creative, but think within your budget and your own abilities. Use graphics, color, different fonts, and paper to capture people's attention, and highlight certain topics, always keeping your audience in mind. Consult with local graphics designers, or local arts center staff, or maybe there are library patrons who will help you for free or give you a considerable discount. Sometimes, marketing or advertising agencies offer discounted services for not-for-profit and government organizations—or they might have staff willing to volunteer their services. Media-based nonprofit agencies also can help. In addition, creative members of your staff may be skilled in desktop publishing and can design something on the computer. If there is no one, take a class at your local community college or at your local arts council!

Who will see your ad? Seniors' interests are different from youth's, and they may prefer flyers over emails. Create flyers in the language of your audience; ensure (through a liaison) their proper translation. They should be in a variety of languages so your audience will both see and read them, and include graphics for those who may not be able to read in the native language, as well as for visual interest. List all partners and collaborators for sponsoring events, and give full credit to all contributors (not only the library), including logos if appropriate. Include important details, but not so many that they clutter the flyers. Certain types of information, such as hours, can be given in tables; graphs, auto shapes, computer clip art and templates also help in creating attractive flyers. At the circulation desk, give out monthly newsletters created by librarians with information about events or new books. Local retail businesses (such as grocery stores and coffee shops) and organizations (such as social services agencies) can also distribute them to attract people who ordinarily might not come to the library.

Ideas for Event Flyers
- Ask an artist or performing group who will be exhibiting at the library if it would like to make the flyer or contribute a description. If the group says no, make one and get its feedback.
- Use a designated staff member with experience in graphic design in conjunction with the event artists and a language consultant. There is always someone on staff who has an artistic flair and wants to showcase his or her work (make sure to give credit on the flyer).
- Consider using and modifying a flyer template on your word processing system, retrieve one from the web, or use a desktop publishing program to create one.
- Include basic information about the library with the library icon, schedule of the event, and contact information.
- Use appropriate pictures, icons, and graphics. Check out flickr.com for innovative photograph topics.
- Pilot test it on new immigrant patrons to get their feedback.
- Use appropriate bilingual language.
- Visual issues: Catch people's attention with eye-stopping titles, bulleted sentences, and not too many words. Use appropriately placed bolded fonts and sizes, colors, and paper that complements the design. Remember your flyer needs to be visually appealing and

readable, so it does not have to be complex. The goal is to motivate people to attend the event!

Like PSAs, press releases must be well written and checked for accuracy and appropriateness before they are read or distributed (see previous PSA guidelines). One library created a press release advertising an Isabel Allende event that was bilingual—written in Spanish on one side and English on the other. It included all of the relevant basic information (who, what, when, where, and how), as well as a photo and an attractive border around it to call attention to the event. The release also listed some of the extras such as food, live music, and "much, much, more!" (Alire and Archibeque 1998). Directions on how to get to the event may also be helpful. Create releases with your outreach coordinator and make sure you pilot test them on patrons before they go to press.

Now that you have attracted new immigrants to the library, started communicating with them, and reviewed some ideas for services and programs, let's take a closer look at the most effective ways to serve new immigrants. Chapter Five focuses on outreach policies. These ensure that the important issues about communication that were just discussed are in place and have a long-lasting impact on library relationships with new immigrant communities.

Economical Promotional Strategy Checklist
- Make a plan to focus on specific issues within new immigrant communities.
- Use a word-of-mouth campaign as the primary strategy.
- Locate free PSAs and target low-cost advertising venues.
- Contact your local arts council for advice.
- Sponsor art and performance exhibits that will not incur too many extra costs.
- Sponsor book and film clubs by providing space, advertising, and furniture. Read reviews and have patrons write them.
- Get as much feedback as you can from new immigrant groups—but without wasting their time.
- Use discounted print and electronic ads.

ADDITIONAL RESOURCES

Alire, Camila, and Orlando Archibeque. *Serving Latino Communities*. New York: Neal-Schuman Publishers, 1998.

Cuesta, Yolanda, and Gail McGovern. "Getting Ready to Market the Library to Culturally Diverse Communities." *Washington Library Association Journal* (March 1, 2002).

Elba-Pavon, Ava. *25 Latino Crafts*. Chicago: American Library Association, 2003.

Livo, Norma J., and Dia Chia. *Folktales of the Hmong: Peoples of Laos, Thailand, and Vietnam*. Englewood, CO: Libraries Unlimited, 1991.

Moller, Sharon Chickering. *Library Service to Spanish-Speaking Patrons: A Practical Guide*. Englewood, CO: Libraries Unlimited, 2001.

Venture into Cultures: A Resource Book of Multicultural Materials and Programs. Chicago: American Library Association, 2001.

Vigil, Angel. *Una Linda Raza: Cultural and Artistic Traditions of the Hispanic Southwest*. Foreword by Rudolf Anaya. Golden, CO: Fulcrum Publishing, 1998.

ENDNOTES

1. See Larsen, Jacobs, and Vlimmeren 2004 report on a Sno-Isle library that had focus groups for Russian- and Spanish-speaking groups. Redwood City's Project READ and the Glenwood Branch library of the Greensboro Public Library system, asked that learners in their learning programs form advisory groups.

2. From the author's study in Hawai'i. See her dissertation: Cuban1999; see also Cuban 2003.

3. These examples are all drawn from the following resources: Quezada 2005 (about involving immigrants in cataloging and other new immigrant topics); Alire and Archibeque 1998 for New York; Milam 2003 for a national perspective; and Larsen, Jacobs, and Vlimmeren 2004 for Seattle and Washington State.

4. See the Webjunction website for more information on its Spanish Outreach Program: http://www.webjunction.org/do/DisplayContent?id=13118; and Webjunction 2004.

5. These ideas on hiring draw from Alire and Archibeque 1998.

6. From an exploratory study of the author's on domestic workers and education in Seattle.

7. There are numerous library marketing resources. Alire and Archibeque's book (1998) on Latino populations draws from *Walters Manual for Marketing and How to Do It*.

CHAPTER 5
Changing Library Policies to Meet New Immigrant Needs

Working together, libraries can create institutions that provide and protect equal access, that help build communities, that integrate civic activities and that activate change.

(McCook 1997: 4)

In Chapters Three and Four you learned about strengthening your outreach capacity—through the distribution of resources, diverse partnerships, effective advocacy, and communication. Yet to sustain outreach and integrate it into your library's raison d'être, you need policies that will hold these inputs in place and allow them to penetrate throughout the library. This requires a strong commitment, even though it might incur struggle and resistance from different social sectors and cause turbulence of the kind that "rocks in a whirlpool" do (McCook, 2002). You may struggle to "stay the course," to support "downstream" issues such as outreach, even as they are caught by pressures to compete "upstream" and promote dominant practices such as outsourcing and profit seeking (Dodge 2005; McCook 2002).

Asserting outreach principles may also contradict you or your colleagues' ideals of neutrality, but, as popular historian Howard Zinn suggests, it is impossible to be "neutral on a moving train" (Zinn 1994). Your policy making is a practical strategy for advocating for new immigrant groups that need major accommodations in a discriminatory society.

This chapter will look at the philosophy and history behind equity and access, and why they are critical to new immigrant communities.

Then, it examines how to restructure policies (such as hours, community meetings and involvement, facilities, rules and regulations for behavior, technology policies, registration and borrowing criteria, fines and fees, and support services policies) in the interests of equity for new immigrant communities.

Principles of Equity and Access

Equity of access, traditionally embraced as a core value of public librarianship, originated over a century ago. "Equity of access" means "serving people of every age, income level, location, ethnicity, or physical ability, and providing the full range of information resources needed to live, learn, govern, and work" (Wolmuth and McCook 2004). Equity of access is one of five key ALA action principles making the library the "great democratic bargain" (American Library Association 1999; Barlow, Hering, and Mitchell 2001).

Landmark federal legislation, especially the Library Services Act (1956), the Library Services and Construction Act (1964), and the Library Services and Technology Act (1996), has financially supported libraries in offering equal access to marginalized communities such as new immigrants, who may find it hard to obtain information. Librarians have also advocated for equal access for the poor and homeless (1990), the illiterate (1970), women (1976), and African Americans (during the 1960s). Disability policies paid most attention to the importance of physical access, bolstering the equal access doctrine (Wolmuth and McCook 2004: 1).

Further, ALA's advocacy for equal access has resulted in a number of organizations and meetings, taking measures to embed antidiscrimination policies in their missions and activities for the constituents they represent.[1] The Public Library Association (of ALA) and the International Federation of Library Associations (IFLA) have also committed to many of these ideals. Yet to date, an immigrant and refugee advocacy task force, committee, or office is nonexistent. Never before has there been a time as good as the present for a focus such as this to protect new immigrants' rights.

Why? In the past, the FBI conducted surveillance of public and university libraries, under programs such as the Library Awareness Program, to restrict information to foreign nationals and to recruit librarians to report on them (Foerstel 1999; Rice n.d.).[2] This practice has intensified under the Patriot Act, which currently challenges immigrants' rights of information access and intellectual freedom. This threatens not only library principles but also new immigrants' civil liberties and their First Amendment rights to obtain information like everyone else (Jones 2004; Wolmuth and McCook 2004).

The Patriot Act, passed after 9/11 and renewed in 2005 after the July 7 London bombings,[3] authorizes unprecedented electronic and other surveillance of records and materials, as well as property searches. Most—if not all—of the people who are monitored and searched are immigrants, especially during and after 9/11. Men who look Middle-Eastern, simply sitting at computers, may raise suspicions.[4] As an information activist, you will need to be aware of these issues, in particular for Arab populations targeted as possible terrorists.

Victoria Toesing, former Justice Department attorney, defended the Patriot Act: "If I'm a terrorist and I need to use a computer system to email my buddies, guess where I'm going to go. I'm going right to the library that has refused any kind of records of who is using the computers" (Spencer 2003). The ALA has opposed the Patriot Act because it reduces librarians' autonomy and good sense about library users, it poses a threat to free-form information-seeking (no library user, immigrant or not, will feel comfortable using the library under surveillance), and it violates basic privacy rights. Some libraries in California (the Santa Cruz Public Library, for example) have reacted to federal legislation by shredding daily user records and lists of online users. Although ALA provides leadership around reactionary legislation, such as the Patriot Act, new immigrants rights must be protected. What would you do if an FBI agent came into your library and asked for records that contained "foreign-sounding" names? Consider the author's last name!

Another example of regressive legislation is the Real I.D. Act, which ALA, REFORMA, and the ACLU have tried to counter by proposing resolutions in support of immigrants' rights to free public library access. The Real I.D. Act requires that in order to get a library card all persons should present a standardized, state-issued, machine-readable national identity card that links personal information—a driver's license, for example. This requirement results in many immigrants being denied free access to libraries because they do not possess such identification. According to REFORMA, this law violates the Human Rights Declaration, the International Bill of Rights, and the International Covenant on Economic, Social, and Cultural Rights.

Knowing About Anti-Immigrant Acts

In 2004, the National Intelligence Reform Act and the 9/11 Recommendations (HR-10) Act gave rise to an anti-immigrant security bill, whose provisions of strict identification rules and increased border controls have had the effect of creating obstacles for asylum seekers and weakening processes of due rights: "The 9/11 Commission law moves the U.S. towards a dangerous new form of segregation where those without the right pigmentation or documentation will be further subjected to arrest and deportation," said Catherine Tactaquin, executive director of the National Network for Immigrant and Refugee Rights. "This will shamelessly undermine much-needed immigration reforms and further link immigration enforcement and services to repressive national security provisions, thereby endangering community safety and violating fundamental human rights." Moreover, the Department of Homeland Security now has jurisdiction over immigration enforcement as part of a multi-agency collaborative approach that pressures all stakeholders to apply tougher restrictions. Many view this move as posing a greater threat to immigrants' human rights (http://www.nnirr.org/news/press_releases/2003_09_05.html).

In view of such developments, do not underestimate or downplay the depth of anti-immigrant sentiments in the United States, or you will not be able to counterrespond effectively, especially when prejudice against immigrants directly affects libraries and new immigrant communities. The Denver Public Library, for example, experienced a growth in its Hispanic populations and therefore focused on revamping itself in order to accommodate better the Spanish-speaking members of its community. In response, the Coalition for a Closer Look organized resistance in summer 2005, protesting the library's collection of fotonovellas as (they claimed were) pornographic, illegal, and replacing English-language books. In addition to saying that their money should not be spent on these materials, the protesters demanded a number of changes—including the resignation of the head librarian. In its defense, a *Denver Post* editorial by Michael Gorman stated: "Arguing that certain books shouldn't be in the library is like arguing that certain words shouldn't be in the dictionary" ("Travelin' Librarian" 2005).

This case indicates how easy it is to stir up racist attitudes and English-only biases by focusing on marginalized groups and restructuring policies and services to accommodate them. Although the nativist group may claim unequal treatment, the library can argue that these reforms provide restitution for a group that has suffered discrimination.

Latinos in Denver, and in other cities with this problem, may have felt that their language and culture were under attack, and they may well stay away from the library because they no longer consider it a safe haven. Although a series of forums and meetings was held about the issues described, and various members of the community expressed their views, allegations about "clandestine changes" in the library continued to be made by the Colorado Alliance for Immigration Reform (CAIR).

Banning materials for certain groups infringes on the principles of equity and access at the core of the library's mission for the common good that reflect its democratic ideology. ALA provides directions for strong principles of equity. For example, an ALA proposition in 2000, "Twelve Ways That Libraries Are Good for the Country," instructed libraries to "keep democracy healthy." Yet principles alone are not enough. Policies need to be in place to ensure that these tenets are lived out to their fullest and sustained by the institution, not by one leader who may leave or is socially/politically vulnerable (Larsen, Jacobs, and Vlimmeren 2004). Policies should also focus on certain groups that have the greatest needs, who are part of the library's "social responsibility" (Coleman 1983; Nauratil 1985). How might these principles be actualized for new immigrants in a high-quality way and within an institutional context?

Organizations for New Immigrant Rights and Laws
Immigrant Solidarity Network: http://www.immigrantsolidarity.org/
National Network for Immigration and Refugee Rights: http://www.nnirr.org/
United Farm Workers of America: http://www.ufw.org/
American Civil Liberties Union: http://www.aclu.org/
American Immigration Lawyers Association: http://www.aila.org/
American Friends Service Committee: http://www.afsc.org/
Coalition to Abolish Slavery and Trafficking: http://www.castla.org/
Migrants Rights International: http://www.migrantwatch.org/
Sweatshop Watch: http://www.sweatshopwatch.org/
National Immigration Forum: http://www.immigrationforum.org/
National Council of La Raza: http://www.nclr.org/
National Immigration Law Center: http://www.nilc.org/
National Clearinghouse on Agricultural Guest Worker Issues: http://www.crlaf.org/gworkers.htm
Mexican-American Legal Defense and Education Fund: http://www.maldef.org/
Amnesty International: http://www.amnesty.org/[5]

RESTRUCTURING LIBRARY POLICIES
FOR EQUITY AND ACCESS

Policies are at the heart of an institution's culture, organization, and management. In a broader sense, unlike rules and regulations dictated from the top down, think of policies as agreements reached through consensus that represent the types of norms and behaviors of the library's community. The process for inclusion and access begins with mapping a progressive library vision and conducting community needs assessments, as discussed in Chapter One. This leads directly into developing and implementing outreach as a central project, with all of its conditions in place (Chapter Three). Thereafter, equitable policies should make outreach an integral part of the library's organizational infrastructure and culture (Chapter Four). Is anything missing from this picture?

To expand outreach in the library, with conditions that ease implementation, your library may formulate a vision and a strategic plan, conduct community needs assessments, and come up with findings. But this sequence will fail and innovative projects will wither on the vine unless accompanied by outreach policies that highlight new immigrants' needs. Like the hidden agendas of particular institutions, library policies can make or break outreach.

In practice, library policies repeatedly fail to reflect the needs of new immigrants and their communities; in fact, library infrastructure and cultural norms implicit in library policies may inadvertently set up barriers (Corona Research 2005). For example, the library's open hours may suit the needs of library personnel but not the needs of shift workers. Fines and penalties may be too high or so complex and unintelligible that they scare people away from borrowing materials. Rules for facility use may be unpleasant—for example, having to speak in hushed voices, during a literacy learning or computer training session.

Directors and their community task forces need to exercise leadership, which is essential in restructuring and sustaining equitable policies. Administrators must create and enact policies with energy and enthusiasm, and help to diffuse them throughout the whole body of library operations (Larsen, Jacobs, and Vlimmeren 2004; Orange and Osborne 2004). In essence, these policies create new norms and a new culture within the library that invite new immigrants to participate in a learning community; they also bolster community development. As the enactment of the mission of your library and community, policies model positive types of relationships and interactions.

Flexible, Integrative, Culturally Competent Policies

Design your library policies for "flexibility and integration" so they sustain the objectives of cultural diversity as well as the primacy of outreach (Milam 2003: 11). Make sure your policies address any issues that could discourage use of the library. According to your resources and capabilities, maintain standards for these policies, monitor their usage, and consider their different aspects (Nelson 2001). Policies must be lived out in the relationships that library users form with library staff, and library staff should uphold the cultural mores of these communities.

Consider how policies relate to new immigrant needs. The following policies are particularly relevant to new immigrant communities, and they constitute the structural nature of librarianship (see Chapter Seven for collection development policies and issues).

Hours

The New York Public Library's Center for Reading and Writing director in the Bronx observed that its programs were losing or excluding women who were unable to come at certain times of the weekday. In an effort to attract younger mothers, at one point the library began to offer programming from 11:00 a.m. to 1:00 p.m., when their children would be in day care and the mothers could come and study. This proved to be an effective strategy for giving them opportunities to learn.[6]

For many new immigrants, library hours are the biggest determinant to access. For those who work long hours, are housebound, are going to school, or have young families, access is especially difficult when a library's hours are restricted or determined by budget rather than by need. When facing a reduced budget, many libraries first resort to cutting their hours, even though this can pose the most problems for new immigrants (Corona Research 2005).

Reflect on your open hour policies and whether they fit with the groups you are attempting to attract. Consider your morning, evening, and weekend windows: Do they seem to exclude certain groups? Consult other organizations and library focus groups (Chapter Two discusses community-based assessments) before developing policies on hours. The Denver Public Library, for example, found that other key organizations were serving new immigrants—its targeted group—in the mornings; it therefore reduced its morning hours so that it could retain its evening hours—critical for students' study periods and for parents alike (Corona Research 2005). If you must cut library hours, use community needs surveys and advisory boards to find out which time frames would incur the least damage for new immigrants.

The staff of the Glenwood Branch of the Greensboro Public Library noticed heavy usage of its small computer lab room at certain periods of the day and on certain days of the week. Staff members decided to open it on Sundays and at staggered times during the days and evenings in order to accommodate restaurant workers who worked long weekly hours, but had some spare time during the day for several days a week. They opened the lab on the weekends, but not long enough. This change, however helpful to some, could not help everyone. One African doctor who was studying for his TOEFL wished that the library's hours were expanded. On Sunday evenings, when his wife, who was also a student, could stay home and watch the children, he went to the local university library to study, because it was open very late. At the least, library staff can give information to new immigrants who do not know about other local academic libraries with longer weekend hours. The lesson here is to change your hours to accommodate a majority of the population, and the minority can be directed to other community resources.

New immigrant groups benefit from weekend hours. Sunday library hours can be especially useful for non-Christians, but can also benefit other groups. In places where few entertainment options exist, libraries might consider Saturday evening hours to accommodate immigrant teens.

With collaborative, off-site, or mobile library services, hours for users can be expanded. For example, satellite print and electronic collections can be held in more accessible institutions that have longer operating hours: hospitals, cafés, clinics, community centers, parks and recreation areas, bookstores, and shopping malls. Bookmobiles extend borrowing hours and provide convenience to patrons with limited transportation options. You can also extend borrowing privileges and programs through other off-site services, such as laptop-borrowing programs, 1-800 hotlines, home tutoring, and mail-a-book services. The Queens Public Library's New Americans Program, for example, sends lists of books in various languages to its participants.

Consider all of your community associations and organizations, and see whether you can incorporate the library collections, services, or programming into them, even if only temporarily, before changing library hours. Consider offering access of information through Internet cafés in neighborhoods, as well as through phone and cable companies, to help new immigrants obtain technology connections, hardware, software, and information. These efforts expand the library and its hours well beyond its normal walls and open time.

Collaborative reference services can answer queries through libraries in different time zones (Barlow, Hering, and Mitchell 2001). Technology provides library users with a powerful key to getting information needs met. The valuable WORLDLINQ website at Queens Borough Public Library serves as a gateway to other websites (Brown 2002). Such convenient services especially benefit caregivers, people with disabilities, housebound individuals, and people without transportation; they also help prison inmates with little access to a diverse array of books.

ALC's "Libraries for the Future" initiative (promoting greater citizen involvement with public libraries) focuses on building better relationships between citizens, libraries, and their new immigrant communities (Barlow, Hering, and Mitchell 2001). In New York City, the library joined community health-based and social service organizations to sponsor health fairs, along with health literacy and information, throughout the community. In Minnesota, community organizers and a neighborhood council joined together to increase awareness of the library and intergenerational learning among new immigrant families. The innovative program focuses on program participants creating "culture bags" with information that teens gather for interviews with their older relatives about their lives.

Technology helps extend the library's reach, but keeping the physical library open is also vital. If contract terms prohibit staff from working some of the hours, consider using noncontractual community members to staff sections of the library during these times; this also creates more of a community-ownership model.[7] In addition, some library branches or services might be given higher priority for being open longer and for special purposes.

Find out which services new immigrant community members use most often and design your hours, staffing, and outreach activities accordingly. Revisit library hours, and consult with task forces and advisory boards before framing your policies. Attention to these policies results in more effective service, increased diversity of access points for the library, and it can even save the library, as well as taxpayers, a little money.

Community Meetings and Involvement

Community members often view the physical space of the library as an enormous asset, because few free, "safe," public places exist for people to meet in towns or cities. When libraries host community meetings, they essentially become involved in shaping community development. Be sure your policies for room usage are consistent with your community values, particularly in regards to groups who are eligible and for how long and when. Discuss these issues with all views represented. No groups should be discriminated against, unless of course, they are inciting violence, are using racist and sexist language, or are harassing people. If they do meet, make sure to advertise the event so that new immigrants can show up and hear their points of view. Community meetings can become forums for community organizing around problems or events, for hearing lectures about community issues, and for public readings.

Facilities

Welcoming, clean, and de-institutionalized facilities attract groups who may not be accustomed to using the library (Larson, Jacobs, and Vlimmeren 2004: 25). They exist in many different forms and are often based on cultural preferences. One obvious example, the San Antonio library, has a building known as the Red Enchilada—an allusion to the large Hispanic population in the surrounding area (Larsen, Jacobs, and Vlimmermen 2004: 54). The Glenwood Branch of the Greensboro Public Library was designed to feel (both literally and figuratively) like a second home for its many new refugee and immigrant populations. Large windows capture the sunlight, and a central open space, murals, and a large room for exhibitions and events contribute to the atmosphere. Modern and clean, it extends a welcome to all, particularly new immigrant populations, who enjoy the open, colorful spaces, multicultural collections, multilingual staff, and ESOL programming.

In Hilo, Hawai'i, the library incorporates vestiges of missionary culture along with elements of Hawaiian and local culture—Hawaiian motifs and representations. Sacred stones stand outside its entrance, and a library courtyard contains a garden with indigenous plants. The San Francisco Public Library marked diversity by inviting different groups—such as gay/lesbian, Filipino, and Hispanic groups—to decorate different rooms or areas with symbols of their different cultural heritages. These few examples show the importance of attracting people by physically reflecting the cultures of the community.

The internal *feng shui* of the building is important too. Library patrons should feel comfortable to move, read, and learn in comfortable spaces. Be sure the spaces in your library sufficiently accommodate growing communities; cramped and crowded libraries discourage users (Corona Research 2005). Where necessary, encourage facility expansion through library policies. This is especially important when you add programs that attract more people.

It is never easy to find the right answer. The Rochdale Adult Learning Centers in Queens participated in a two-year study to increase student persistence by offering more and diverse programming. However, as more students came, the program, housed in the back of the library, became more crowded and students spilled into other areas of the library. The popularity of the Saturday GED program in particular heightened the need for more space. Because the library was small, library and literacy staff had to carefully negotiate their needs. If little funding exists to build new rooms in your library, having constructive dialogues about sharing the space is critical.

Here are a couple of other questions to ask about your facilities:

- Does your library have room for strollers?
- Does it have so many regulations that parents are not able to enjoy their time there?

One participant in a focus group asked, "Can you bring a stroller, can you nurse, keep your eyes on the kids at all times AND still have a good experience with the kids?" (Corona Research 2005: 60). You will need to consider the cultural needs of your clientele and their individual as well as family needs. Are your policies suitable for both? Library policies for facilities design should be innovative and accommodating, for the interior as well as the exterior. Murals, gardens, furniture, and other open spaces without too many rules and regulations (to encourage creativity and free expression) benefit users and staff.

Rules and Regulations for Behavior

A planning committee should decide rules for library behavior and demonstrate cultural competence. In other words, sensitize your library staff to cultural norms that may differ from typical, mainstream, middle-class norms; and then adjust to them within reasonable limits. For example, take into account the need for some women to nurse and to feel that their children are safe. The latter includes factors such as noise levels, eating, playing, bathroom use, hall use, the number of people per square foot, and both verbal and nonverbal interactions with staff and with other library users. Remember the culture of "being a professional" means that members of the public may not appreciate the language of the helping professions (Edelman 1974). Examples would be using library lingo to communicate and maintaining a reserved air while speaking with patrons. On the other hand, try not to dichotomize librarians and the public, because within each category, some groups and individuals may have different preferences.

One older man in the Flushing community of Queens, New York, liked to use the library because it was one of the few quiet and peaceful places he could come to read and concentrate: "In the library," he said, "it is very quiet, yes, quiet. Nobody smoking. Nobody eating, no worries. You can pay more attention to learn something very well."[8] However, a teenager might come to the library to meet people and would be there regardless of noise levels. The planning committee also needs to make decisions about the criteria and enforcement of these policies—for example, on how many warnings are enough to give before someone is suspended because of behavior intolerable to other users. Of course, certain behaviors should not be tolerated at all, such as sexual harassment or racist language, and people who are dangerous. Ensure that the security guards, as well as library staff, are on the lookout for sexual predators, especially in the children and young adult sections, and that new immigrant families, as well as other library patrons, can expect that their children are safe when they come to the library.

Communicate policies about behavior clearly and educate users about them. This education can occur at the time of registration and at some sort of orientation, when the library might give its new users the opportunity to ask questions and get them answered. Many ways exist to fairly negotiate these policies, and compromises can be reached. For example, the library may ban users who are known to destroy library property from certain sections of the library, yet allow them to continue to use library resources, especially those that are online. Once staff members get to know users, they can try to form workable relationships and lines of communication, to reconcile different perceptions of what constitutes acceptable behavior. Librarians have had to deal with the issue of homeless users, in particular; and as homelessness increases among new immigrants, new matters to discuss will likely emerge.

Technology Policies

New immigrant patrons often show interest in both local and global issues. They want to know about concerns in their communities here *and* abroad. Therefore, be sure your library's technology policies support what is called "glocalization" (Barnett 2002). What is glocalization?

Usually people consider technological resources to be more global than local, but libraries have sought to make Internet resources serve local purposes. Enhance the visibility of local issues by providing various options for community-based links in the neighborhood—from online tutorials to book clubs to chat groups (Barnett 2005). At the same time you can provide broad-spectrum information—through an online reference assistance system that helps people search for information if search engines do not assist with queries or fail to interpret them accurately and supply adequate answers (Barlow, Hering, and Mitchell 2001).

In addition, check to see that the library balances the electronic and print collections, which are often considered to be at odds with one another. More importantly, be sure that community members participate in decisions on achieving such a balance to alleviate problems about whether computers "are taking over" (which was a major complaint at the new San Francisco Public Library, for example).

What are your policies on computer usage? Be sure your policies are sensitized to the following issues:

- Age groups regarding time frames for use (most likely seniors and teens will be using the library at different times of the day and week)
- Types of software (video games, word processing, and desktop publishing entail different costs, upgrade demands, instructional and technical assistance)
- Behavioral regulations for youth (contained within a separate area of a library, or are there rules on noise, how many are allowed at one computer, filters, etc.)

For example, video gaming can be limited to after-school hours; it can accommodate more than one user at a station, and it can be relegated to noisier areas, rather than intruding into quiet areas. Purchase popular types of video games that target different populations. In other words, include casual, entertainment-types of games as well as the more serious ones that focus on learning (Gee 2003; Hayes forthcoming; Squire and Steinkuehler 2005).

Seniors and even middle-aged people may use the library computers more in the mornings and afternoons before school gets out; and they may also require more assistance in starting to use them. Consider what one middle-aged immigrant woman said about her first experience with a computer, "I never, never go on that. I am so nervous, my skin trembling, my hands sweating. I tell him I never put my hands on a typewriter, nor such a computer."[9] Your library policies should support such instruction; otherwise computers will be available but unused by those "technologically low-literate" adults.

Policies for instructional assistance must address factors such as:

- Times (a basic instructional session can last for 15–30 minutes, depending on the patron's previous knowledge and need, whereas a more advanced session can last longer—these need to be posted and advertised)
- Assessment (before you begin teaching someone, assess what they know and what they want to learn, as well as see whether they understand what you have taught)
- Methods (ensure that patrons know there are diverse methods of teaching—workshops, classes, one to one. These methods should all be hands-on, contain ongoing assessments of learning, and allow for plenty of practice and experimentation)
- Level of support (patrons should know they can ask for more help and be directed to community college or library classes)

Do You Have Guidelines to Ensure Assessment of Basic Technology Skills and Knowledge Like These?

- Can you turn on the computer and manipulate the mouse? Do you know the keypad? (point to each part and explain these if the patron does not understand)
- What kinds of things would you like to do on the computer? Here are our software programs (show and demonstrate software programs that would be of interest to patron)
- Are you familiar with the Internet? If so, what would you like to learn more about? (show different Internet access points, including the library)
- Would you be interested in taking a class? (give information on classes in the library or in the community)
- Let's practice. Please demonstrate what I have taught you and tell me what you are confused about, or would like to know more about.

Use individual assistance (by teen tutors or senior mentors, for example) to determine and build basic computer skills in immigrant populations. Structure these individual sessions through a guide that has clear wording and pictures, or icons, of terms. Training sessions can be given to anyone—these sessions should focus on imparting basic knowledge of computers (hardware, software choices) and contain handouts of steps for usage with visuals. The facilitator should constantly ask learners whether they understand the lesson and what else they want to learn.

Classes are another option. For example, "Wired for Learning" at the Seattle Public Library gives participants valuable computer experience and skills. You can also structure classes as workshop seminars that are given on an ongoing or periodic basis. Whatever format you use, be sure the classes adjust to learners' previous knowledge and skills and do not use a lecture format. Instead, model the actions and then have learners try them out together in pairs. The facilitator should ask learners to learn together and encourage students to ask questions. A basic guide will enable students to practice at a later point.

The library can also offer more advanced classes and have an expert run them either in the library or in community colleges (for example, advanced searching, using the Internet to find a job, etc.). Yet another option is to work through public libraries' literacy programs, which are generally staffed by trained professionals and volunteers with knowledge about good teaching.

Seattle Public Library's "Wired for Learning" classes help new immigrants learn how to create email accounts, use the Internet, word process, and learn basic skills in reading, writing, and math. The room setup in clusters allows all the volunteers and staff to interact; and the classes encourage students to ask lots of questions about the computers and about their learning.[10]

In the Hilo Public Library, for example, a learning program helped highly educated library users with their technology skills. These students, in turn, have the potential to be volunteer tutors, because they understand computer learning from the viewpoint of a new student and remember well how they learned. Redwood City's Project READ program helped students with low levels of English language literacy gain technology skills. In this program, the literacy program volunteers assist ESOL adults in gaining basic technological literacy and the ability to navigate the Internet.

These examples illustrate that technology policies and programs can and should target different educational levels. For people at low (print) literacy levels, for example, policies should support the purchase of the newest English literacy language software (notably "Rosetta Stone"). Those who are highly print literate also need support and instruction in using computers to search for foreign language newspapers and to use other important links that can be highlighted and put onto the library's home web page.

Most importantly, make sure your policies concerning computers are flexible. Base your technology policies on assessments, conducted on an ongoing basis, of people's learning and their needs. In your needs assessments, address the following issues:

- What kinds of computer software do users desire and why?
- What kinds and levels of instruction do users need?
- What hardware components does particular software require (audio, headsets)?
- What issues interfere with usage?

Computer policies should also be culturally sensitive, as in a program at one library that set up a separate room for Muslim girls, because the library staff knew that without it, these girls would not be able to come to the library (Larsen, Jacobs, and Vlimmeren 2003).

Shortages of space, money, and time create problems for libraries in accommodating diverse users who need the computers for different purposes: to locate books and browse online, for email or research, or for entertainment. One major problem most libraries face is the need for more computers; so one-time-only "injections"—saturating a library with first-generation computers and no upgrades—offer only Band-Aid types of solutions to providing access (Barlow, Mitchell, and Hering 2005; McCook 2005).

In the central Queens Library, it is not uncommon to see lines of students waiting to get online after school. As a result of the high demand and low supply of library computers, time is limited and short, making it difficult for users to do research and to reflect on the information discovered and retrieved (McCook 2005). However, libraries can develop ways around this problem by cooperating with other agencies for sharing computer use in other facilities, such as schools, Ys, and community centers. They can also collaborate with local computer companies for hardware, software, and expertise.

For example, the purpose of the organization Npower, in Seattle, is to assist nonprofits with computers. The assistance this type of organization offers may involve library partnerships or may even provide technological assistance to library users in their homes. Likewise, the Seattle Community Technology Alliance assists many different agencies with computer access and use.[11] In addition, you can support new immigrant families through leasing out computers with good software programs and giving parents home-based instruction as well as technological assistance, which has been implemented at several libraries across the country, including San Jose, Redwood City, and San Francisco. These literacy programs may loan laptops to families and offer technical assistance and instruction so that they definitely use them. Immigrant parents often purchase computers for their children but use them in very limited ways for themselves, only for email, for example. Yet with keyboarding and other instruction, these adults can become much more computer literate.

Technology policies can encourage distance education opportunities too, as well as the use of high-end technology such as computers that function as phones, plus cell phones, iPods and iPodcasting, CDs, DVDs, and videos. Do not forget "low-end" technology, such as photocopy machines (necessary for paperwork), which is often just as necessary to new immigrant families. This is especially the case if your library is supplying government documents, such as citizenship information.

Registration and Borrowing Criteria

Registering more library users is an important goal for outreach programs, and one way to achieve this is through a collaborative process with other institutions. Simplifying the procedures of registration also assists in the process, which can mean using as proof of identification other types of cards that people already have—for example, ATM cards and utility bills, or other basic documents (Corona Research 2005). You may also want to use only a signature.

Conduct an orientation for new users to explain library policies and registration, and familiarize new library users with staff and available resources. Limit or soften any factors that might intimidate new patrons regarding the process of library use, and remove or reduce punishments for breaking rules.

Borrowing periods can range, depending on the types of material borrowed, and staff can communicate these in person when the material is checked out; materials should also have clear return dates, perhaps in the form of a calendar, attached to them. Charge circulation staff, who are the frontline, with communicating these policies verbally; and encourage them to accommodate as best they can the many different needs of new immigrant library users. Having circulation staff of the same ethnic group as the community you serve often ensures good rapport and understanding of information. Checking materials out can be made easier through supplying self-checkout machines, similar to

ATMs, which give privacy and efficiency to the process (Barlow, Hering, and Mitchell 2001). On the other hand, this technology may intimidate some immigrant communities, and so they will appreciate a friendly and helpful staff person. Again, check this matter against your needs assessment. Offering a choice may be the best way to accommodate differing needs and preferences.

Fines and Fees

Negotiate fines and fees within your committee, among users themselves, and through a process of continuous review. As Robin Osborne explains, "I can understand that librarians want to control their inventories, but libraries should be welcoming, accepting, compassionate, and forgiveness is a good thing" (Osborne 2005). Some libraries, for example, have instituted a "Random Acts of Kindness Day" forgiveness policy for fines. Remember that in addition to exhibiting such sentiments, you will need to communicate the policies effectively in plain language. You may need to explain, for example, what "free" means, and how this principle differs from requiring "fines" (Osborne 2005).

If materials have been lost or damaged and are not returned, consider allowing people to substitute other materials or else contribute to the library in some other way in recompense. It is important that they are able to compensate the library in some practical way, rather than feeling ashamed (for instance, if their child tears a book) and never using the library again.

Think about innovative ways to get materials back to the library. For example, you may want to design a system of mail-in arrangements and multiple drop-off locations to maximize the return of materials; some libraries may volunteer to collect materials from people's homes, call or email people when their books are due, and lengthen the borrowing periods if no one else needs the books.

Are your print materials well protected and fully accessible? Do what you can to better protect the library's books and other materials, so that they are less likely to be damaged. In addition, if possible and in cases in which it is legal, make electronic copies in order to avoid having to buy duplicates and replacements; or direct users to websites where materials are free and permanently storable on home computers. Library subscription websites with valuable materials can also assist people with obtaining information, as well as downloadable books. Having more printers in the library will enable and encourage people to use in-house services, too.

Support Services Policies

New immigrants may not use a library that is beyond walking distance from home because they lack private transportation, encounter parking problems, or cannot afford or find public transportation. Bookmobiles, satellite sites, and online resources counter such obstacles. Keep in mind, however, that many people enjoy being in the community space of a neighborhood library and prefer being able to browse shelves and ask questions directly, even though their complex living situations may make it difficult to come on a regular basis. Here are some examples of transportation difficulties that you may not have considered:

- One Mexican woman came to the library to use the computers, but when her brother, who got a new job, could no longer drive her each way, she stopped coming. How can your library help someone like her? Consider: mailing books, online reference services, carpool committees.
- Some users walk miles to get to a library rather than pay the cost of public transportation, but when they arrive they may feel exhausted and discouraged. One woman was too shy to ask her friends for the subway fare in New York City and walked across the Brooklyn Bridge to come to the Seward Park branch library's literacy program. The library staff there could not help its patrons with the cost of transportation because it was too difficult to judge users' eligibility.[12] What are some ways that your library could help a walker like this woman? Consider: carpooling, advocating library trustees to subsidize funding, advocating public transportation services, and creating traveling programs or satellite sites.

Consider ways to simplify the process of getting to the library. Try to enable new patrons coming to the library in person, rather than making it a complex endeavor for both parties.

The need for child care is another obstacle to use of the library, especially for women with infants. Some libraries provide child care, although it may be temporary and short term. The Glenwood Branch library provided babysitting services, run by staff on a short-term grant, to women who went to a women's literacy class. Because of its temporary nature, it was not considered to be a formal child-care service and did not require a license. The women learners really appreciated the service and came to the classes because of it.

Child-Care Services Checklist

- Can you collaborate with nearby professional services to offer low-cost child care near the library? Do you have a list of all child-care services in your city or area?
- Do you have a group of trained child-care/day-care professionals (retirees or current workers) who can provide low-cost or volunteer babysitting for children in a safe space in the library? Can you reserve space for child care near the children's section of the library?
- Can you offer family literacy programs through the children's librarian that assist parents and children to learn together?

For any type of child care that the library will provide, it is essential to communicate to parents about:

- The policies involved (these should be clearly worked out by the director of the library and all library staff should be aware of them; e.g., parents may not leave the library when their child is in child care)
- Liability issues (legal issues could arise, so get advice from the library's legal department, especially regarding health and safety; e.g., keeping the cleaning closet shut and locked)
- Cultural norms (ensure that the service is multicultural in that it should not purposely try to inculcate middle-class ideas about parenting. Nor should it attempt to discipline children through physical punishment; e.g., staff are not allowed to hit the children)
- Ratio of children to adult caretakers (you will need to have enough well-trained staff to ensure that each child gets quality care; e.g., when one staff member takes children to the bathroom, another must oversee the other children)

Some volunteers who babysit for children may be mothers themselves and can exchange babysitting services in the library or outside of it. For example, a group of young mothers may be involved in a literacy program, and they could take turns with helping out with child care. If your library is physically attached to a YMCA or YWCA (Sumerford 2005), it might be possible for parents to receive child-care services and to use the library.

Chapter Six will discuss how to enact these equitable policies through accommodating services and programs. These connections are important, because "equity of access cannot be achieved without equitable service delivery" (Orange and Osborne 2004: xii).

ENDNOTES

1. See also the Office for Literacy and Outreach Services (ALA OLOS); the Black Caucus; the Gay, Lesbian and Bisexual Task Force (GLBTF); the Feminist Task Force; the ALA Committee on the Status of Women in Librarianship; the Social Responsibilities Roundtable; the Intellectual Freedom Roundtable; the Special Committee on Freedom and Equality of Access to Information; the Ethnic and Multicultural Information Exchange Roundtable (EMIERT); and the Office of Diversity. In addition, are the American Indian Library Association, REFORMA, the Chinese American Librarians Association, and the Asian/Pacific American Librarians Association. See also Wolmuth and McCook 2004; American Library Association Diversity Brochure, ALA Action, No. 4 in a Series." http://www.ala.org/ala/ourassociation/governingdocs/keyactionareas/morediversity/diversitybrochure.htm.

2. See the article by Eric Lichtblau, "At FBI: Frustration over Limits on an Anti-Terror Law," *New York Times* (December 11, 2005), which cited an FBI email (of an agent who wanted to implement the Patriot Act). This agent was quoted as saying: "While radical militant librarians kick us around, true terrorists benefit from OIPR's failure to let us use the tools given to us." See http://www.nytimes.com/2005/12/11/national/nationalspecial3/11patriot.html.

3. As of December 16, 2005, the House of Representatives passed a tough new immigration bill that requires employers to check employee legal documentation and calls for fences along borders. See http://www.denverpost.com/nationworld/ci_3317304.

4. See recommendations and articles on ALA's website "FBI in Your Library" and a piece entitled "A Chill in the Library" (July 23, 2002). http://www.ala.org/ala/oif/ifissues/fbiyourlibrary.htm.

5. Many of these resources came from the National Organization for Immigrant and Refugee Rights.

6. From the author's study of persistence in library literacy programs; see Porter, Cuban, and Comings 2005.

7. When deciding to staff the library with community volunteers, make sure that they receive training, that they get criminal background checks, and that you sharply assess (through a casual or formal interview) their expertise so that they can directly apply it to the service they are overseeing.

8. Data from the author's study of persistence in library literacy programs, published and unpublished reports, and interview notes; see Porter, Cuban, and Comings 2005.

9. Data from the author's study of persistence in library literacy programs, including interview notes and unpublished reports; see Porter, Cuban, and Comings 2005. Presentations of the author's study include Sondra Cuban, "Literacy Education Brokers: The Unique Roles for Library Literacy Programs within the Adult Education and Literacy System," American Educational Research Association, Chicago, April 21–25, 2003; Sondra Cuban, "'I'm Looking for Another

Link': Building Persistence Pathways for Adult Learners in Programs and Communities," American Educational Research Association, Chicago, April 21–25, C 2003.

10. Unpublished paper by Kristin Morgan-May, a master's student at Seattle University, called "The Seattle Public Library: Information Learning for Patrons" (for Sondra Cuban, November 23, 2004).

11. For more information, see the Seattle Community Technology Alliance website: http://www.ci.seattle.wa.us/tech/overview/default.htm.

12. From the author's study of persistence; see Porter, Cuban, and Comings 2005.

CHAPTER 6
Accommodating New Immigrants with Library Services

You have learned about how policies can be changed to meet new immigrants' needs. Now let's talk about services. Of course, your policies should accommodate and clearly communicate the services that are available to new immigrant groups. Beyond that, library services should be targeted to and responsive to new immigrant communities. Design your services to accommodate new immigrants' daily lives and needs.

A PLAN FOR SERVICES

As the first step, work out a careful plan for services. Customize your plan to fit local needs, using your community-based assessments and fitting it to your library's organizational structure. Modify your general guidelines for service planning to new immigrant groups (Nelson 2001). These guidelines entail making decisions that evolve from clear rationales based directly on community needs in particular neighborhoods. In addition, consider your library's resources in regard to offering these services. Decision making can be done through a committee or through administrative channels. A review board can then pilot your initiatives to ensure the timeliness and high quality of the planned services.

Finally, reflect on library services as a whole. You will probably want to ask the committee questions about its realistic implementation of the plan—the pros and cons of how new services will create new opportunities and how they may become possible threats to other services and populations. For example, if you institute a computer skills class for new immigrants only, how does it make other community members (who are not new immigrants) feel? If this is the first time the library is offering these services, consider how staff members will react in terms of their attitudes, labor, skills, and possible need for training—and in regard to future benefits for themselves, the library, and the community. Engaging staff in preliminary planning discussions can help alleviate fears, share perspectives, modify ideas, and create an intracommunity response. For example, staff that would not be involved in computer instruction may feel excluded, unless you give them the opportunity to participate in the conversation.

Most importantly, link the service planning process to the library's vision and mission (discussed in Chapter One) and to its goals. These goals direct objectives, which then lead to activities around a particular issue. Although this may sound a bit mechanical, it has value in keeping you organized and thoughtful. Let's walk through these ideas.

Goals, Objectives, and Activities

Everyone talks about goals, but what are they, really? Robert Mager (1988) describes goals in terms of larger outcomes to be achieved and people's understanding and awareness. Goals have a place within the context of the library's vision and its mission statement.

Let's look at an example of connecting a service goal to the mission. A service response, such as community referral, may be under consideration. The committee and a review board may promote a community needs assessment and confirm it through a consensus staff discussion. They will then write goals in a clear way, thus leading to specific objectives and finally to activities that carry them out.

Take the example of community referrals. A goal for community referral might be:

The adults in [this] community will understand that the library is fully committed to providing diverse, numerous, and timely community referrals to meet their needs.

Goals are linked to objectives. Objectives, unlike goals, refer to actions. As observable performances, they refer to what people do under certain conditions or in particular circumstances. An objective for community referral might be:

The adults in [this] community will be able to access the full range of referrals through personable, culturally competent library staff, who will query, inform, and determine (through a collaborative, caring process), the wide array of agencies, recommending high-quality ones that could best serve their needs.

Follow up your goals and objectives with more specific activities. The activity that follows from this may be outlined as:

The library staff person will engage in relationship building and meaningful exchanges with users to learn about their information needs, through a series of reference inquiries and searches for timely, appropriate information; that staff person will also communicate in a culturally competent way to ensure that the user understands the information that was exchanged, has the ability to act on it or, if not, to make personal contacts to guarantee implementation of the process.

As these examples demonstrate, the library staff has to have a variety of competencies in order to carry out the activity, especially cultural competence in communicating with new immigrant communities. This glue activates your service plan and holds it together.

Becoming Cultural Competent

Cultural Competence Information
Attend diversity workshops and conferences
Receive training on cultural competence
Read books on it
Consult health organizations for information

You might become more knowledgeable about cultural competence by reading a book on the topic. But this, alone, will not make you more culturally competent in communicating with new immigrant communities. You will need to engage in a learning cycle of gaining knowledge, opportunities to practice, a reflection period, and occasions to experiment with new behaviors and get feedback. For this, consider training in cultural competence for yourself and your staff. Numerous institutes and consulting firms can be involved; some even offer free services.

What Could Happen at a Cultural Competence Course/Workshop/Seminar for Library Staff
- Get a chance to reflect on their own cultural backgrounds and write autobiographies that they share with their own families and others as feedback
- Through a local expert, learn about the myriad of cultures that exist in their communities and the library

- Critically assess past and potential cultural clashes that occur in their communities and develop strategies to work them out
- Watch videos or films about cultural topics in society that serve as springboards to discuss how these issues influence local ones
- Engage in group exercises that map cultural differences and raise cultural awareness
- Get chances to role play in dealing with cultural conflicts
- Gain knowledge and practice from trainers in developing skills associated with cultural sensitivity such as listening and empathy
- Learn about how to create and run dialogue circles (with ground rules for communication, a facilitator, promoting discussion, and sharing of thoughts and feelings)
- Learn about the meaning of cultural competence
- Gain knowledge about the customs and belief systems about various cultures and subcultures in the community in order to become less judgmental and not stereotype based on limited knowledge
- Consider complex case studies of cultural differences
  An example would be family behaviors and values: Consider the differences between the ways that families interact in different cultures. U.S. mainstream culture encourages autonomy and separation from the family. Immigrant adult children may run into conflict when they are expected to take care of their parents, and their friends or colleagues see this as unrewarding or oppressive. Individuation is unknown or rejected in some cultures. Think about how to sensitize your library to these issues, and help fill cultural gaps by providing services that accommodate these values.

In addition, consider creating cultural competence guidelines and standards, which you can adopt from other organizations (look at organizational websites on health in your community and attend conferences). For example, Terry Cross defines cultural competence as:

A set of congruent behaviors, attitudes, and policies that come together in a system, agency, or amongst professionals and enables that system, agency, or those professionals to work effectively in cross-cultural situations . . . the word "competence" is used because it implies having the capacity to function effectively.[1]

Cross outlines essential ingredients for cultural competence: the abilities to culturally self-assess, to be conscious of dynamics and how cultures interact, and to develop adaptations to diversity. Self-assessment refers to the ability to reflect on your actions and their effectiveness.

Being conscious of dynamics means being aware of communication styles and body language. And cultural knowledge entails being attuned to how different cultures deal with institutions and with one another in a variety of ways. These elements should function at every level and be put into practice within your library.

The community itself, however, can also decide the definition of cultural competence, because generic definitions may not be satisfactory. So, go back to your community leaders for their opinions. Engage in a process of learning about cultural competence, so that you take on a new identity, as someone who can communicate effectively, handle concerns, and relate well with new immigrant communities. That is a major part of cultural competence.

CULTURALLY COMPETENT SERVICES

With your new knowledge, you can turn your core areas of services into ones that are culturally competent. Then, you will want to add in new ones. Typically, consider a variety of service "streams," ranging from business and career information to information on current topics and titles, to be the core areas of the library (Nelson 2001). More alternative types of services range from translation assistance to conflict resolution services. This chapter covers both of these types of services with respect to new immigrant groups. Chapter Eight discusses outreach services such as basic literacy, lifelong learning, formal learning, and information literacy as part of programming.

Core Services

Fundamental library services consist of interlibrary loans and cataloging, as well as reference services—such as business and career information, consumer information, current issues and topics, and local history and genealogy. To make these services broad based, targeted, and tailored to new immigrant and individual needs, means conversing with people about their needs and building relationships in the process of helping them.

Business and Career Information

Because business and career information for new immigrants can vary from community to community, be sure to include local and national organizations for work contacts, and be attuned to the in-demand skills and occupations of certain groups. Collaborate with other local organizations and analyze labor market trends in your community. You can do this by reading the newspaper and discussing interesting articles with fellow staff. Some libraries, for example, may focus on helping patrons to invest, and offer investor education and information (http://www. investoreducation.org).

Your library may decide to respond to an economic crisis. One city in Michigan, for example, suffered from severe unemployment, and to counter this, the library became an employment assistance center giving monthly workshops. "We started asking not just 'What do you need from your library?' but 'What are the issues that concern you?' " Because of this service, the community passed a ballot initiative for increased library funding, raising the library's annual per capita funding (Barlow, Hering, and Mitchell 2001).

Libraries can collaborate with community-based organizations that offer training to new immigrants. For example, the Refugee Women's Alliance (REWA) in Seattle, Washington, offers English classes and training in certain areas for African women refugees. Casa Latina, another organization in the same city, serves Hispanic migrant day workers, many of whom are men. The library collaborates with these community organizations through referrals and educational programs that extend learning beyond the classroom and provide information and connections, especially to people who cannot get to a library.

Other new immigrants may have specific work experience and want to start their own businesses. You can connect these individuals to community organizations that will help them improve their networks and find appropriate loans; some of these organizations may even offer classes that help new immigrants understand how to get started in a specific type of business or career. Many community colleges and adult education programs run such classes, and libraries can sponsor them, offering meeting space or staff to assist in the programs. Some libraries collaborate with employment programs that facilitate referrals, with partnerships already in place. These can include job counseling together with career assessments. This type of service helps people who are starting careers in a new country and trying to figure out options and availability.

Consumer Information

Consumer information is vital to new immigrants, especially because of their language barriers and real concerns about being exploited in stores, at work, and in other private and public domains. New immigrants often need to be educated about legal issues such as taxes (when, how, and where to fill out forms; how the tax system works in the United States), the courts (for parking tickets, how to attend, how to provide one's defense), health costs (what is covered by insurance policies; why certain tests are more costly than others), driver's licenses and registration (taking tests verbally in another language than one's own; registration expirations), and housing (renting, buying, problems with landlords, coping with repairs, and identifying hospitable neighborhoods to move into). When students in a pilot health literacy project in a library literacy program were asked what their health concerns were, many of them expressed a need to learn more about insurance costs. Some of them also wanted to know more about doctors' costs in general.[2] This issue is particularly important because health care is viewed as a consumer item in the United States.

A critical approach in understanding consumerism or "consumption" is vital for combating media pressures to buy for social status. This can help those parents, for example, who may feel reluctant about purchasing products for their children, but simultaneously think that this is the American way. Because you have been trained as a librarian to be a critical thinker and reviewer, you can readily guide new immigrants through materials such as consumer reports and help them to become critical consumers, developing their own criteria and sustaining their own values.

Current Issues and Trends

Ongoing focus groups can help you keep abreast of "hot issues" and trends among new immigrants, and enable you to deal with these and with any rumors spreading through the community. New immigrants often want news, information, and education about the Immigration and Naturalization Service (INS) and laws regulating sponsorship, citizenship, applications, and requirements. They need to understand how laws could affect their livelihood in the United States and about traveling back to their countries of origin. They may also require information on how laws affect their access to various community services. A multimedia approach in providing information and educating new immigrants about these issues can cater to various styles of learning and information seeking. You can complement focus groups with films, guest speakers, and Internet sources about these issues.

Local History and Genealogy

Local history and genealogy can assist new immigrants with connecting to diverse groups within their own communities and to the history and culture of the place they are moving into. Such information aids their understanding of the attitudes of older generations of immigrants, of people transplanted within the United States, and of people born and raised in the community. Library collaborations with museums, local history associations, and other immigrant associations can support these efforts. For example, the Glenwood Branch library literacy program took a group of its students to visit a civil rights museum to understand the history of black/white relations in the South.

Interlibrary Loans and Cataloging

Interlibrary loans are often slower in public libraries than in academic libraries. Consortia of public libraries can focus on speeding up the process for users and provide the types of materials that new immigrants demand, such as native language materials. Also, consider making your library catalog more user-friendly; for example, by showing users where books are located in the library, so that people do not get lost in their search. For the same reason, the cataloging system (both Dewey and Library of Congress) can also be simplified to abbreviate call numbers and codes (Osborne 2005). Automated catalogs can have multilingual interfaces as well as subject heading searches. Moreover, books with subjects that are of interest to both adults and children can be interfiled, as can children's books and teen books for low-ability readers (Osborne 2005; see also Chapter Seven). Use native speakers to assist you in appropriately cataloging native language materials.

Other Services for New Immigrant Populations

Although core services accommodate basic needs of new immigrants, other alternative services can extend accommodation. These extended services include community networking and referrals, translation services, direct and indirect support services, conflict resolution and interethnic awareness, neighborhood sustainability, and entertainment and recreation.

Community Networking and Referrals

Reciprocal networking—library users, community-run businesses, and nonprofits meeting to discuss problems, seek solutions, and exchange ideas—benefits all community members. Librarians can serve as intermediaries in these community networks, linking people to assistance and support beyond the library's traditional information and education role. This help is especially important for people who are in transition and isolated from other agencies. For example, the Redwood City Public Library has links to a shelter for women and to food banks that help its users—some of whom are homeless or in poor housing conditions—acquire basic services through personal contact and information networks. Libraries can provide meeting places, facilitate the process of seeking assistance, and map out networks.

Whom Do I Network With?
- Partner list from Chapter Three
- Social services (homeless shelters, mental health agencies, community clinics)
- Ethnic associations
- Job centers
- Government agencies
- Chambers of Commerce
- Private charities
- Faith-based organizations
- Senior centers
- Day-care centers
- Public schools

Translation Services

Many organizations depend on clients' family members to translate for them. This can create an awkward situation and in some cases is illegal; for example, if a child is translating sensitive information for parents. Professional translators can make it easier to overcome language barriers and exchange information. This is a major part of institutional cultural competence. One user, unable to read a letter from her doctor, paid hundreds of dollars to a neighborhood translator, only to discover that the letter was not meant for her—it had been sent to the wrong address. She then decided to come to a literacy program at her library.[3]

How Do You Find a Professional Translator?
- Word of mouth: ask someone who uses translators.
- Contact your local university or community college linguistic or ESOL department.
- Contact a translation association or agency.[4]

Social Support Services

Although social support services such as counseling may not be provided directly in libraries, library collaborations with social service organizations can help users access external sources to get their needs met. Trained librarians can and do counsel; this service assists users in discovering paths to further support and services. Counseling can assume the form of a reference interview, guidance counseling, or a referral to psychological counseling. These library services can also compensate for the lack of social service counseling in the community, especially on certain issues—for example, where to receive family planning advice and services. In addition, social services can encourage community members to persist in their learning and assist them in finding appropriate education (Porter, Cuban, and Comings 2005).

Conflict Resolution and Interethnic Awareness

Consider collaborating with professional mediators to help people negotiate various problems with personal relationships or with external issues. Perhaps you can provide library space for this service, or you may get more involved as a trained mediator. Because libraries serve many different ethnic groups, they can also operate as a forum for resolving interethnic conflict and help build awareness of diversity issues in the community. For example, tensions can be exacerbated when librarians discuss "multicultural work" while focusing on only one immigrant community (viewed as the "new" one) and neglect to bring in historically disenfranchised native-born communities such as African Americans (Cuesta 2005; Sumerford 2005).

Consider bringing in public speakers, such as from local police and legal aid organizations, to present issues and exchange ideas on how different ethnic groups can work together to resolve problems and exchange cultural information for learning to take place. This type of endeavor might also entail people from different ethnic groups gathering together to talk about a certain community issue in the form of what the Highlander Research and Education Center calls a "learning circle." This circle encourages people to be sincere and straightforward, while observing ground rules for communication. A facilitator can assist in this process.

Groups That Support Conflict Mediation and Immigrants
- Highlander Research and Education Center: http://www.highlander center.org/

- Peacemakers Trust: http://www.peacemakers.ca/links.html#peace
- Ask neighborhood schools, counseling agencies, police, peace and justice organizations, as well as universities for local referrals

Biracial or multiracial individuals or families can present and discuss notions of ethnicity and identity, and share insights on how they negotiate different cultures and social perceptions. Such discussions may especially benefit new immigrants coming from more homogeneous cultures to this country of multiple cultures. Participants can ask questions and develop wider social relationships, so that they can confront and deal with cultural stereotyping. In addition, new immigrants and older generations of immigrants can compare their differing experiences with mainstream America, to make more solid their knowledge and understanding of cultural traditions and change.

Neighborhood Sustainability Development

Libraries can be important focal points for community organizations in collaborations to increase local and active participation of new immigrants. They also can be key players in designing future directions for new immigrant communities. Community assessments are a starting point. This agenda may include discussing the assessments, having community-wide dinners or retreats to focus on a specific problem, and possibly involving the library staff as facilitators. These events can also bring in experts and guest speakers to discuss broader national issues that affect community cohesion and development. Webjunction's rural sustainability program[5] is funded by the Bill and Melinda Gates Foundation. Roughly 700 staff in 15 states attend workshops that help them develop action plans for community renewal projects focusing on making community technology more accessible This is especially important in light of the recent demographic changes in these communities and new immigrants' need to access technology.

Entertainment and Recreation

The library's multipurpose nature allows it to be used in many ways. Many people use the library not only for finding information but also for recreational purposes (reading fiction, for example). Programs such as community dances, bingo games, video gaming, sports activities, comedy nights, poetry slams, festivals and dinners, and other activities can attract new immigrants and encourage them to feel that they belong and are contributing to the library environment. A library in Arlington,

Virginia, for example, had potluck dinners with local families, through its youth services program and the schools (McMurrer and Terrill 2001). These activities built the library's image as a community center.

Identify which activities are popular and in demand through your community needs assessment (discussed in Chapter One). Media assets also broaden the library's repertoire; television, iPods, videos, DVDs, and movies may be made available, and sometimes even musical instruments can be borrowed. If space permits, your library can have a music recording and listening room for community use.

Optional Service Delivery Models

You have probably decided to selectively adopt the mainstream and alternative services described in this chapter based on your resources, your local contexts, and less so on whether they are considered to be "best practices." You may also implement them slowly over time rather than all at once. Consider also offering a service delivery model that highlights several services for new immigrant communities. These models (Corona Research 2005) can be designed around specific community needs or interests:

- Cultural hub model (emphasizing author events, films, entertainment, and recreational types of services)
- Contemporary library model (a consumer focus through cafés, bookstores, research services, up-to-date collections offerings)
- Learning and language library model (English classes, native language classes, English software, and computer access)
- Classic library model (a focus on traditional collections and materials)
- Youth inspiration model (services specifically for youth)
- Online model (Internet access, a home/school/work website with information, distance education, and downloadable books and music)

With these various models, consider barriers that new immigrants might encounter and how they could compromise the models' implementation and success. An online model is difficult, if not impossible, to achieve in poor neighborhoods without reliable access to connections. A learning and language model might fit best with new immigrant populations who need support in cultural and social adjustment. Yet it would not be appropriate for older generations of immigrants, who might prefer either a cultural model with multicultural authors from this country or—because they are more established and might be in a better position to pay for services—a contemporary model (Corona Research 2005).

Your library system may also develop branches that focus on particular themes of the community. The community itself can decide these themes. One library (in Greensboro, North Carolina), located in a park, had an environmental theme as part of its collaboration with the parks and recreation departments (Sumerford 2005). The library collection and services focused on issues related to the environment; it offered workshops for kids, walks with a ranger in the park for seniors, and a program on solar homes. The library also hired an environmental librarian. In April, National Poetry Month, the city had a poetry festival and the librarian created programs around the theme of nature poetry. Another branch library in the Greensboro public library system, situated in a transitional neighborhood, concentrates on art and literacy for children and their parents. An art studio has been built as an addition to the library space, creating an experimental space that both reflects and balances out the neighborhood's transitional quality. Now that you have reviewed some of the ways you can expand or adapt services for new immigrant communities, let's consider how your collections can better serve new immigrant populations. Chapter Seven discusses multicultural collection development in detail.

ENDNOTES

1. Terry Cross et al., *Toward a Culturally Competent System of Care*, vol. 1 (Washington, D.C.: National Technical Assistance Center for Children's Mental Health, Georgetown University Child Development Center, 1989), pp. iv–v.

2. From unpublished reports of the author's study on persistence. See Porter, Cuban, and Comings 2005.

3. From the author's study on persistence, published and unpublished reports, and interview notes. See Porter, Cuban, and Comings 2005.

4. See the guide: *Translation and Interpreting: Languages in Action*, Office for European Communities, 2001. See http://ec.europa.eu/dgs/translation/bookshelf/traduc_int_en.pdf.

5. See this website for more information: http://www.webjunction.org/do/Navigation?category=498 as well as http://www.webjunction.org/do/DisplayContent?id=11132.

CHAPTER 7
Building Multicultural Collections for New Immigrant Communities

You have laid the foundations for structuring new immigrant services and policies. Now you will need to build culturally competent library collections. Your collections should:

- Support new immigrant communities' needs for information
- Foster literacy activities for civic, recreational, and educational purposes
- Nurture the desire to use the library and its resources
- Contribute to the formation of multicultural relationships

Are you there yet? Ask yourself these questions as you put your collection together:

1. How does your library meet the needs of new immigrants through your library collections? How do you use the collections to build literacy, diversity, and strong community relationships?
2. What is your library's philosophy of collection building, and is it aligned with a multicultural orientation?
3. What are your library's barriers to creating a multicultural collection? How can these be reduced to meet new immigrant communities' collection needs?

Let's consider an example from the author's study of persistence (Porter, Cuban, and Comings 2005):

I had come into the donut shop from the library. I had just walked back from the library with books. And Saya [a Cambodian donut shop owner] said,

"Are those books?" And I said, "Yes." And she said, "I wish I could read." I said, "You can't read?" She says, "No." I said, "I'll teach you." (Mary, a tutor, to Saya, a learner)

The story of Saya and Mary illustrates the power of a culturally competent library collection. Mary, an Anglo-European native of southern California and an elderly customer of a local Cambodian-operated donut shop, often said hello to Saya, the owner. Saya often picked up newspapers that her customers—including Mary—had left behind, but she could not read them. One day Mary and Saya discussed Saya's education. Mary discovered that Saya had barely gone to school as a child and as an adult was too busy with her young sons and the family business to go to a local adult school class to learn to read. She did not have any English language reading materials in the home because she could not read English. After Saya talked about her needs, she and Mary decided to work together to improve Saya's reading abilities. Mary did not know where to find books that would match Saya's reading level, so she decided to start with the public library.

Mary began with children's literature and later advanced to other genres and levels after attending the library's learning program, Project READ. There she learned about good adult materials and how to teach reading to adults. Eventually, Saya started to read newspaper articles from the donut shop and came to view the library as a useful place for her literacy development. Saya said, "She [Mary] always go to library, looking for the book for me, and she said, 'You better hurry up; we've got to bring the book back!'" Mary and Saya became friends and between sessions took walks together in the neighborhood where they lived two blocks away from each other. Without the library as a reference point, it would have been tough for the two women to break through barriers created by class and race/ethnicity and to sustain their work and friendship. This library supplied them with a culturally competent collection and much more.

A MULTICULTURAL EDUCATION PERSPECTIVE FOR YOUR LIBRARY

Collection building for new immigrant communities constitutes much more than getting books or computers for the library, and giving people access to them. Collections provide important means for knowledge sharing, literacy development, and community building around cultural diversity. Although most libraries have made efforts to provide multicultural resources for their communities, they have paid less attention to the rationales behind this effort, other than arguments for equity of access and the need for diversity.[1] Mary and Saya, for example, were not just reading together; they were exchanging cultural knowledge and forming important relationships.

Let's consider multicultural education in the library. This perspective provides a philosophical foundation for building collections that prove that diversity is the library's "greatest strength" (Quezada 1992). Multicultural education's underpinnings are rooted in a commitment to social justice and transformation. The National Association for Multicultural Education calls it a philosophy that focuses on "freedom, justice, equality, equity, and human dignity as acknowledged in various documents, such as the U.S. Declaration of Independence, constitutions of South Africa and the United States, and the Universal Declaration of Human Rights adopted by the United Nations" (http://www.nameorg.org/resolutions/definition.html). Although there are a number of interpretations of multicultural education, its originators, James Banks and Cherry Banks (2004) have focused heavily on how multicultural education—with its emphasis on developing culturally competent skills, knowledge, and attitudes—can help diverse groups to function in a democratic society and for the common good. Collections become resources for this practice.

Libraries need to incorporate the precepts of multicultural education into collection development to combat society's social, cultural, and institutionalized racism, which is systemic, insidious, and upholds exclusive norms. What is institutional racism? Institutional racism has been described as "a network of institutional structures, policies, and practices that creates advantages and benefits for whites, and discrimination, oppression, and disadvantages for people from targeted racial groups."[2] Examples of institutional racism in collection development may involve policies (limiting access to certain materials) and/or overemphasis of authors (representing only the classic canon—dead, white males). When collection development policies consciously strive to reflect all of the stories and perspectives that exist in communities, they challenge what Audrey Lorde calls "the mythical norm" of white, male, thin, young, heterosexual, and Christian (Baumgartner and Merriam 2000: 4).

When people from other cultural backgrounds do not see their experiences and lives reflected in the library collection, they often feel excluded, as though they are outsiders. Author Gloria Anzaldua (1987, 1990) called this position the "borderlands." Because her complex identities defied conventional societal categories, she essentially existed in an unnamed territory. She writes, "Borders are set up to define the places that are safe and unsafe, to distinguish us from them. . . . A borderland is a vague and undetermined place . . . the prohibited and the forbidden are its inhabitants" (Anzaldua 1987: 3).

Be aware of these borderlands, and do your best to eradicate them with your collection. Invite patrons to use multicultural literature, to create "a bridge between readers' real-life experiences and their learning, providing models of culturally competent authors" (Quezada 2003). Immigrants may be drawn to authors who address:

- Immigration and its effects (e.g., the complex emotions that occur when arriving in a new country)
- Biculturality (the sense of belonging to two cultures and negotiating norms)
- Return to a country (the complexities involved in returning to family after a long hiatus somewhere else)
- Negative portrayals of ethnic groups (how new immigrants deal with common stereotypes of themselves by native-born groups and by other immigrants)
- The meaning of "home" (how new immigrants identify their homes when they move frequently to new places)

PROCESSES OF CREATING A MULTICULTURAL COLLECTION FOR NEW IMMIGRANTS

Steps to Build a Multicultural Collection
- Do a preselection study.
- Take steps to reduce barriers to collection use.
- Develop multicultural collection policies.

A Preselection Study

Who will be using your collection? A preselection study is similar to conducting a community needs assessment (discussed in Chapter One; Larson, Jacobs, and Vlimmeren 2004). It can help you to determine what people need and want from library collections. Remember, you cannot assume that all new immigrants or refugees—of different age groups and from different countries—will want the same types of materials.

In the past, library researchers conducted reading surveys to determine selection and acquisition of materials, and they remain valuable today.

These studies typically focused on the general public's reading interests and purposes. Researchers classified these according to the following purposes (Berelson 1949; Gray and Munroe 1929; Karetsky 1982; Waples and Tyler 1931):

- Instrumental (reading a newspaper)
- Aesthetic (reading about art)
- Cultural (reading in order to learn about different cultures)
- Psychological (reading self-help books)
- Sociological (reading to learn about societal issues)

Although for various reasons most studies did not include immigrants, you can use the categories to start surveying new immigrants' reading needs and interests, and reflecting on how your library fulfills them. These categories really have not changed over a period of thirty years, except that electronic sources have produced more venues, interests, and options of subject matter.

Use the Reading Categories To
- Conduct polls of new immigrant users and their reading interests: "Do you like to read about art?"
- Survey library staff for their perceptions and knowledge about new immigrants cultures and reading interests: "What do you think (a particular ethnic group) likes to read, and why?"
- Check the collections to see whether all categories are sufficiently represented.

The largest known library reading survey that included immigrants and low-income groups (a mix of educational levels) was the *Library Materials Study* project, conducted by Helen Lyman (Lyman 1972, 1977a, 1977b). Focusing on cultural issues, she discovered a wide range of reading interests among the community members surveyed. Further, the community leaders in her survey reported that their communities' needs were less related to survival than to self-realization and a sense of their own identity. These informants also expressed the desire for diverse subjects within library collections, as well as a wide range of services in parallel. Lyman noted that these needs differed according to the ethnic groups and their experiences. From this, she deduced that because ethnically themed material encouraged highly affective responses among readers,[3] libraries should select and purchase it and then match it with the reading level and culture of patrons for programs and for services.

Lyman also recommended assessment of the personal qualifications of materials evaluators, because these people play a crucial role. They should include a broad spectrum of knowledge, sensitivity to and awareness of the underlying ideas and values of the material, and attunement to what is being communicated to the reader. Concern for reading levels alone is not enough. Lyman focused her study on reading-level assessments for those who have low levels of literacy, and she wrote about various formulas that librarians could use with this population.

In the process of conducting reading surveys, you may find that new immigrant communities are not using the library. In the 1980s, the Queens Borough Public Library conducted a public opinion survey and discovered that Spanish-speaking residents were not library users (Abboud 2002; Alire and Archibeque 1998). In response, in a number of branch libraries, the library increased its collections of books and other materials in Spanish and in other targeted languages. Books in seventy languages, videos, records, and CDs are now in these collections, and each year millions of them circulate—more than some major public libraries' circulations combined. Moreover, the director has traveled as far afield as Singapore, Thailand, and China to purchase library materials, in addition to buying from local distributors. In this context, the Queens Borough Public Library has set a precedent for other libraries, which over the last twenty years have experienced a heavy demand for foreign language collections (Abboud 2002; Greenlee 2005).

Take Steps to Reduce Barriers to Collection Use

There are ways to ensure that conducting the collection development process takes into account common barriers to new immigrants' usage of the library and of the collection. Here are some pointers:

- Start with basic information about local new immigrant communities (your community asset maps), adding to it information about what they like to read and for what purposes (from your preselection surveys).
- Involve new immigrant communities to advise on subjects and genres in selection decisions.
- Create bibliographies and reading clubs, and sponsor new immigrants who write books, articles, and reviews on materials.
- Check out the reading lists about immigration experiences on the ALA website: "Becoming American," "New Immigration Stories" at: http://publicprograms.ala.org/newimmigration/materials/

Also consider your course of action. These pointers can assist you with the *process* of building a culturally competent collection:

1. Work in stages and build the collections slowly over time (it may be most resourceful to focus first on one or two communities).
2. Become part of a library network (including academic libraries that can help process materials, provide web links, and offer inter-library loan assistance) in order to optimize access and ownership of multicultural resources as well as to advise about best practices (Alire and Archibeque 1998; Godin 1994; Larsen, Jacobs, and Vlimmeren 2003, 2004).
3. Take into account specific regions when you collect and acquire materials (geography and demography). Consider your neighborhood and its different ethnic groups, as well as your region of the country (for example, Somali communities in the Northeast).
4. Ensure your collection selection is locally designed (by and for new immigrant groups) through an advisory committee (that you set up with the help of community leaders).
5. Create a flexible implementation timetable. Be sure it is easily changeable and is accompanied by innovative policies to guide it.
6. Assess language barriers (yes, again). You or your library staff may not have sufficient skills to discern the quality, the vernacular language, or the political perspective of the materials. Bring in some community experts to help.
7. Assess literacy issues. New immigrant populations with less formal education might need easy reading materials in English for coping, or fotonovellas, rather than translations of *The Da Vinci Code* (Quezada 2005). Those new immigrants with higher levels of formal education might enjoy the latter more. You will even need to check out this preconception!
8. Review your budget. Costs and geographic factors can also pose barriers; for example, overseas shipping rates, nonavailability of materials, uncontrolled temperature in tropical climates, low publishing volume, poor paper quality, and bindery problems.

Strategies to Overcome Cost Barriers
- Purchase materials through foreign language networks (such as OCLC or the Multilingual Materials Acquisition Center) and major book jobbers that now order multicultural materials.[4]
- Use the web as a gateway for electronic resources and subscriptions, as well as for cataloging assistance.

- Get donations (conduct them discreetly, with assigned criteria, and on an individual basis).
- Collaborate with bookstores (independent and chains, used and new), publishers, and distributors (online and in person), and choose diverse ones, rather than only the largest.
- Purchase materials from international book fairs; if you cannot go, ask a friend!
- Tap into local educational resources such as volunteers and advisory committees to support and make decisions on selection and acquisitions. People on these committees can be community leaders or individuals who work in community-based organizations and are language experts. Advisory committee members can also attend conferences, informally train staff who are not familiar with new immigrant collection and diversity issues, and create classes in a particular language for librarians as well as opportunities for cross-cultural discussion and exchange.

To enhance your collection's diversity, purchase an array of multicultural multimedia in a variety of forms and genres. Library networks—including educational research and immigration centers—can assist with the process. Try not to depend on mainstream reviews for selection because small presses, which may be your best sources, are often underrepresented in this process. Check out all types of sources. The National Center for the Study of Adult Learning and Literacy (NCSALL), for example, has established a good guide to literacy materials based on surveys of library literacy programs, *What Every Library Should Have* (NCSALL 2004), which contains diverse materials. The goal is to see collections as part of easing the transition of new immigrants to both adjust to their new environments and keep connected to their native countries (Alire and Archibeque 1998; Larson, Jacobs, and Vlimmeren 2004; Shriver 2002).

Reference Guides in Languages Other Than English: How to Find Good Materials

Use all the resources at your disposal. Many reference and reader's advisory guides exist for Latino literature or Russian literature or multicultural authors and fiction. You can find updated sources by searching most academic (community college or university) or other public library web pages under "multicultural sources" or "multicultural materials," which usually includes a listing of standard references of general multicultural sources as well as particular ethnic groups. Many of these, however, are classics. Your best source of all is going on library listservs (for example, REFORMA's listserv) and asking your colleagues! They can suggest updated references that are tried and true.

Sample Multicultural References
- Marshall Cavendish Multicultural Reference Center (EBSCO)
- *Encyclopedia of Multicultural Education* (Mitchell and Salsbury, Greenwood, 1999)
- *American Immigrant Cultures* (Levinson and Ember, Macmillan, 1997)
- *Criticas* magazine (http://criticasmagazine.com)
- *Gale Encyclopedia of Multicultural America* (1995)
- Libraryjournal.com
- ALAs "Library Services to the Spanish-Speaking" (in RUSA)

You also will need to think about purchasing materials in other languages. Some of the standard library distributors, such as Baker and Taylor, Ingram, and Brodart, handle material in most other languages, but you will need to check out others (see list). How does an English-only collection development manager go about selecting titles in the major language groups that are represented in the United States, such as Spanish? For this, you will want to develop a few strategies.

Involve librarians who represent that language group. You can connect with them via a listserv or through their association website, such as the Asian/Pacific American Library Association; through a state association, such as the Hawai'i Library Association; or even through a major U.S. library that deals with many language groups, such as Queens Borough Public Library or New York Public Library. Look at their collections. If that does not work, search libraryjournal.com on your own or "book distributors" in the specific language, and you will find some good lists of distributors and books. Libraryjournal.com, for example, has a comprehensive book distributor list in world languages (it describes the kinds of languages, what types of resources they offer, the countries they specialize in [for example, Cuba], names, contact emails, and websites). With this information, you can compare prices. In addition, check out *United States Book Distributors Directory*.

After you peruse a distributor's online or print catalog, involve your outreach coordinator and your advisory committee who can help you to review and select the sources. Again, your best source for selecting books and book distributors is by asking your colleagues about their experiences in your local vicinity and in your state association. This would especially be the case for language groups that are not well represented nationally and in the book distributor and publishing agency (such as Albanian or Haitian-Creole). Still, certain book distributors service these too (see Multicultural Books and Videos in list). There is no better place to do this than at a major conference (for example, ALA); but if you cannot get there, numerous listservs on ALA and articles on libraryjournal.com can help you connect and learn! Go to the Reference and User Services Association (RUSA) website as well as ALA's Diversity Online lists for contact, print, and webliographic information on various ethnic groups and collections.

Spanish Book Distributors to Check Out
- Bilingual Publications
- Brodart
- Lecturum Publications
- Libros Latinos
- Sante Fe Books Corporation
- Spanish Audios
- Vietos Tropicales
- Mariuccia Iaconi Book Imports
- Multicultural Books and Videos

Here is a major urban library system's sampling of vendors that sell materials in languages other than Spanish that are used for immigrants:

- Midwest Tapes—all languages: http://www.midwesttapes.com
- Multicultural books and videos—Bengali, Urdu: http://www.multi culby.com
- China Books and Publication—Chinese
- Haitian Book Center—French, Haitian Creole: http://www.haitian bookcentre.com
- D.K. Agencies—Gujarati, Hindi, Punjabi: http://www.dkagencies.com
- Gefen Publishing House—Hebrew: http://www.israelbooks.com
- Opes, Inc.—Korean
- Raker Library Services—Portuguese
- Russian Publishing House
- Polish Bookstore and Publishing

Develop Multicultural Collection Policies

Develop policies with some baseline principles and logistical considerations. First and foremost, your guidelines should be accessible to different language groups and expressed in "plain language,"[5] an important component of cultural competence (Osborne 2005). The guidelines should also exemplify your library's ethos of the ideas of "service equality," meaning that you need to prioritize access issues (NBLC 1990: 39). At the same time, they should reflect the fact that a demand orientation could jeopardize the acquisition of materials that might not have high use but that are critically important for new immigrants. To some degree, align policies with national library policies and programs (http://www.ala.org/ala/rusa/rusaourassoc/rusasections/codes/codessection/codescomm/colldevpolicies/collectiondevelopment.htm), so that there is a sense of shared objective—diversity. Policy guidelines for collections can focus on[6]:

- Housing and site selection (whether permanent or in bookmobiles, medical clinics, and other community centers)
- Their maintenance (whether they are out of date, worn, weeded regularly; rebound, or replaced with duplicate copies); staffing (the staff should be multilingual or language experts and reflect language groups of a particular surrounding community; there should be enough staff to take on these responsibilities)
- The language of the materials (they should foster both English and native language literacy)
- The language of the automated systems (they should be not only in English but also in other languages; there should be card catalog systems as well, and non-English instructions on how to use the system)
- The size of collections (the collections for new immigrants should be in proportion to their representation in the community, and oftentimes larger, because there may be fewer resources for them in the community)
- Marketing (if information about the collections is sparse, there should be ways of ensuring that new immigrant communities will learn about them, such as through brochures and registration forms in multiple languages)
- Bibliographic access (which should be provided by distributors, with transliterations; multilingual subject searches should be available)
- Physical accessibility (whether they are in the back of the library and visible or hidden; whether they are available on interlibrary loan or for in-house use only, and how quickly they can be obtained)
- Cataloging barriers that the Dewey system may present due to its complexity and inherent Eurocentric prejudices

Guidelines cannot tackle every issue and many unexpected logistical barriers can arise. Ask yourself some practical questions as you develop your guidelines, and keep asking them on an ongoing basis: How will these guidelines be enforced? How will they be backed up with funding? Are staff members trained sufficiently to deal with decisions about collections of multilingual materials, and do they understand their various dimensions, compared with those involved in selecting other materials? Have they communicated among themselves about their criteria? Is collection development linked strongly to programs and services, or is it disconnected from them? All these points are critical to consider and yet are pretty pragmatic and material based.

"Blah, blah, blah," you might think. "I learned this in school." What you probably did not do in school is take a long hard look in the mirror and interrogate who *you* are in the collection development policies. Research has shown that it is *you*, the librarian, whose character and culture make a key difference in the process of selecting materials. If you have developed knowledge about your own identity and of multicultural education, you do not have to fall prey to a tradition of defaulting to other authorities and perpetuating the status quo when selecting materials. Becoming conscious of who you are and what you like is integral to the selection process. Your selection decisions will be based on these (often) unconscious issues. Ask yourself, for example, whether your current selection process may be inherently biased and tacitly censored.

This requires what Shelley Quezada (2003) calls a "soul-searching audit" of librarians' own cultures and the "ways in which other cultures look at the world" with the idea to "become more comfortable with being 'uncomfortable.'" White antidiscrimination educators, with whom you may already identify, focus on questioning their own conditioning and practices, without erasing how their race is implicated (Manglitz, Johnson-Bailey, and Cervero 2005: 1266).

For this reason, think about attending an antidiscrimination training. You may also want to join an organization or group in your community devoted to dealing with racism, sexism, or homophobia. This training is important for your library staff's growth and development in thinking through critical decision-making processes about collections. One of these might be to question the ingrown prejudices in your cataloging system (racism, sexism, anti-Semitism), and how many non-English materials are often lumped into "foreign language" sections of the library.

Learn to be a critical evaluator, rather than perceiving yourself as "neutral" or objective about collection development. The myth of the "neutral professional" (Buschman and Carbone 1991; Jensen 2004) is rooted in keeping the current status quo and power relations intact. An astute librarian acknowledges the types of power relations involved in collection development decisions, especially with the needs of marginalized groups, and then intervenes on this dynamic. For example, you might ask yourself whether you should collect two extreme views of a subject (such as a country's political history) or one neutral one, knowing there is not a perspective that is really "neutral."[7] The notion of "balance" is very deceptive.

No federal mandates or overseeing capacities monitor the degree to which libraries are culturally competent, and public relations efforts and marketing efforts are only partial solutions (Larson, Jacobs, and Vlimmeren 2004). Therefore, take a hard look at how your own identities (assuming you have more than one), values, and knowledge affect your collections decisions.

Check out policy handbooks for guidance. The Reference and User Services Association (RUSA) website of ALA has much information on multicultural collection building and includes *The Guidelines for Multilingual Materials Collection and Development and Library Services*, first published in 1990, then revised in 2002 by the RUSA-MOUSS Library Services to the Spanish-Speaking Committee in 2002 (www.ala.org/ala/rusa/rusaourassoc/rusasections/rss/rsssection/rsscomm/spanishspeaking/rev_guidelines.doc). This thorough policy guide focuses not only on collections standards, promotion, and maintenance but also on general services, such as outreach, programs, marketing, and staffing. The Canadian counterpart, *A World of Information: Creating Multicultural Collections and Programs*, also notable, includes a broad-based approach to collection development policies. The IFLA *Multicultural Communities: Guidelines for Library Service* from 1988 covers similar important issues from an international perspective, including staffing, definitions of targeted language minority groups, extension services, technical services, and cross-cultural issues regarding usage (http://www.ifla.org/VII/s32/pub/guide-e.htm).

The Multilingual Materials Acquisition Center (MultiMAC) at Newark Public Library serves as a statewide clearinghouse and resource center for library materials in world languages that meet its new immigrant needs. The LSTA and a grant administered by the state library fund the center. The languages of the materials include Arabic, Chinese, Tagalog, French, Gujarati, Haitian Creole, Hindi, Korean, Polish, Russian, Spanish, and Vietnamese. It contains educational, recreational, and informational materials, as well as ESOL materials, immigration aids, parenting information, and current event titles in all languages. All of the materials are listed in the catalog and OCLC's Worldcat, and bilingual subject headings in Spanish are provided. A bilingual Spanish cataloger does Spanish cataloging, and freelancers and professional translators are hired as needed (Betancourt and Rimpau 2004). The Ethnic Materials Information Exchange Roundtable in the ALA, as well as REFORMA, has also supported the development of these policies and is an important resource. These holistic policy guides can be adapted for local contexts and specified for new immigrant communities.

Remember that national and international political issues and laws—including copyright laws, the digital divide, and tax dollars—need to be dealt with in policies and guidelines too.

Policy Statements

Policy statements announce how your library handles decision making around formats, targeted new immigrant communities, subject matters and budgets. These should be connected to overall library goals, vision statements, and services, and be flexible, clear, and culturally competent (Alire and Archibeque 1998). Moreover, they should be purposeful and connected to your preselection study. Here is an example regarding language formats:

Our library is committed to collecting materials in the language for these communities [name ethnic communities in the area] so that they are able to access information, get their information and literacy needs fulfilled, and bond with the library. Our preselection study conducted on [cite date] indicated that these were important issues to these communities. More specifically, participants said [summarize your research in terms of the above reading interest categories and give anecdotal evidence for each one you mention].

As the example illustrates, policy statements should clearly delineate rationales for allocating funds for these collections. One study (Milam 2003) found that non-English collections were used heavily—half of all the books that the San Diego Library lends are in a language other than English. But across the nation, over 30 percent of all libraries in the survey reported collections in fewer than ten different languages. The absence of these languages in your collections, and the need to obtain them, becomes a rationale that you can state in your policies. Connect your policy statements to ongoing needs assessments (see Chapter One), and barrier assessments for using the collections (see earlier) (Neely and Lee-Smeltzer 2002).

MULTICULTURAL COLLECTION DEVELOPMENT ACTIVITIES

Collections can be divided into two basic purposes: recreational (designed for entertainment and leisure) and educational or instructional (designed for acquiring basic and more advanced skills and knowledge). Each of these types of collections can incorporate multimedia, be housed in a variety of places, be selected through a variety of ways, and exist in multiple languages. Moreover, these collections (both print and electronic) can be shared within a library network and generate smaller interrelated collections within certain areas of the library (for example, literacy collections). Many sources are available online and in print about collection building for new immigrant communities. Some of these are *Criticas*, RUSA, ALA's Diversity Online, Libraryjournal. com, and various library websites around the country that are known to collect immigrant materials.

Recreational Purposes

Offer recreational types of materials for new immigrant communities so they can see the library as having a multipurpose function rather than supplying only instrumental types of information (for enhancing survival and coping skills). Doing this sends the message that the collections are for many different family members and for fun and creativity as well as learning. Most importantly, your collections should signal the library's desire to serve and bond with all of its communities. Promoting recreational materials is a way to acknowledge that adults play multiple roles in their lives, including those of parents and consumers. Bookstores and other types of for-profit centers appeal to family literacy by offering traditional library recreation activities, such as story hours and cushioned chairs for reading, in order to sell their books. Libraries can build on these activities, modifying them according to their budgets, and tailor them to populations that otherwise would not likely be reached. Because libraries are not businesses and do not need to sell anything, they can offer entertainment types of activities that are different from bookstores. Moreover, bookstore staff has no training in the critical use of recreational materials.

Toys, Games, and Music

Adding toys to the library collection is often a wonderful way to reach out to new immigrant communities. Many new immigrant parents or caregivers may not have the money or time to shop for quality toys for their children or know where to find them. Moreover, they may feel pressured to purchase toys advertised on TV or in store windows; and they may not have the consumer knowledge to know where to obtain toys that are sustainable, that they wholeheartedly approve of, and that are safe. Parents and caregivers want to feel that their children have access to quality toys for learning, for fun, and for socializing. Many new immigrant parents or caregivers obtain toys from street vendors in their neighborhood, share them with extended family members, or get them through thrift stores. Libraries, too, can use these outlets in order to learn what toys are most popular. Unfortunately, many parents go to large stores and pay exorbitant prices for toys for their children.

Keep in mind that for new immigrant parents, toys can also be a source of conflict: they want their children to have what they themselves did not have, but their children have an endless demand for toys. In addition, support your collection with knowledgeable staff. Parents frequently work long hours, and often an older sibling or a grandparent is in charge of the children after school; this person will likely need assistance in selecting appropriate toys. As toys become more complex and more frequently electronic, caregivers may need help with selection decisions and with literacy for understanding operating and repair information.

Board games—from different parts of the world—come in handy on rainy days. Children's librarians can work with adult reference librarians to create informal caregiver groups; and they may even choose speakers to come in to share their knowledge about toys. For example, there may be discussion groups about guns, fireworks, the use of helmets, and gender-free toys. Consider giving children the opportunity to make toys at the library through programming. These toys may be kept in the library for future visits. Librarians, volunteers, and clubs of parents or caregivers can help teach children how to build toys and read instructions.

Librarians and caregivers can work together to create the kinds of toys used in the children's own cultures and present them to parents from other cultures, rather than just relying on a Cambodian Barbie as a way into the culture. For example, with Russia, these might be wooden nesting dolls. Another way to extend the library's role in recreation is to collaborate with local parks and recreational facilities, or local Ys, for swim tokens, fitness equipment, play opportunities in the community, and child-care facilities.

Video games. Video games are popular with people of all ages. Immigrant adults, as well as teens, play video games for entertainment and for learning (Gee 2003; Hayes forthcoming). Learn which games to choose and for whom, and how to support them in the library. Use surveys to make selection decisions—for example, through an advisory board of video gamers. Various web links, blog spots, and listservs, as well as gaming conferences, can also be used for selecting video games, and gaming experts can collaborate with librarians about selecting and using the games.

How Do I Choose Video Games? Start Here
- The Shifted Librarian: http://www.theshiftedlibrarian.com/
- SuperPatron Friends of the Library: http://vielmetti.typepad.com/superpatron/games/index.html
- Internet Librarian and Internet Librarian International
- Videogame symposiums and Sci-Tech fairs
- Video game developer websites
- Published online video game lists of various companies
- Magazines devoted to video games such as Playstation
- Websites specifically for gamers such as Gamespot.com
- Online reviews of video games
- Video games in education websites
- Gaming sites: http://www3.essdack.org/socialstudies/videogames.htm#Sites
- Local teens and middle-aged patrons in the library
- Local video game stores in your neighborhood or video game store lists online

The library's decisions about acquisitions should also consider issues such as unsuitable content (sex and/or violence), the library's use of filters, cultural factors, and parental decisions about suitable content, especially where new immigrant families are concerned. Parents may not be able to read or understand English-only descriptions of the video games available.

Encourage video game users to form teams, and promote a constructive culture of video gaming by supporting your collection with programs and knowledgeable staff. Remember that video games, largely considered to be recreational, are also educational. Learn more about digital literacy (the use, creation, knowledge, attitudes, and manipulation of different technologies); for example, see Gee, *What Video Games Have to Teach Us About Learning and Literacy* (2003). Popular games

(*Civilization III*, *Sim City*, *The Age of Empires*, *Rome: Total War*, *The Age of Mythology*, *The Sims*) can be used to host game nights for teens. The Santa Monica Public Library, California, for example, has sponsored a game night in which teens play *Counterstrike* (first-person shooter game). The event gives librarians insights into youth culture and allows teens to see the library in a new light (Squire and Steinkuehler 2005). Not surprisingly, this program has raised interest in the library and is establishing valuable new relationships across the two communities— teens and librarians.

Be sure the games that you select are gender sensitive, but without stereotyping girls and women (Hayes, forthcoming). Educator Elisabeth Hayes recommends against excluding girls and women from certain games based on "pink and blue" ideas, or assuming that all girls and women like the same games and use them similarly; she urges that educators orient and assist new women gamers, and provide a supportive social context (12–14). Although it may be impossible to avoid selecting video games with cultural stereotypes, educating about these would be important. Consider obtaining video games in other languages as well.

Downloadable books, music, and videos. It is now legal to download some music and books. In the future, more will be legitimately available. This will change library computer options—including printing conditions, download capacity, and instructions. The library may make iPods available for downloading music; librarians can instruct on the process and about various music sites. Consider subscribing to online music companies, and create your own recommended play sets for library users. Various companies offer Internet phones and calling options that you might be able to extend to patrons. In addition, make videos and DVDs available at the library. The library can loan video/DVD players to patrons, supply listening devices for use in the library, and offer appropriate computer instruction to new immigrants.

Materials Reviews

As you build your collection for new immigrants, formally and informally invite their feedback. Ask new immigrants to write short reviews of both print and electronic sources in their own languages for others to use. You can make these available in many ways: online, on library web pages, in the form of e-zines (magazines written for a specific community), or as blogs (writings that appear on a weblog site); through listserv discussions that are started online; through online vendors; and through librarians and advisory groups working together to improve usage of globally available materials of different subjects, genres, and formats. They can also deliver reviews verbally, presented in audio form on podcasts or videos, for example. Volunteers can sort, update, and archive the printed or recorded reviews. Consider inviting new immigrants to write reviews of favorite websites for display on the library's home page, as well.

Sharing Stories

When creating community, allow or encourage people to share their stories. Encourage new immigrants to write their own stories, share their parents' or grandparents' stories, and support others in telling their stories in the library and beyond. These stories can be orally based and dictated, web based and interactive, or captured on videos and web cams. In some literacy programs, students write their stories, which are then typed, bound, and archived. During learning celebrations these stories can be read to other learners, other library users, or the general public.

In the age of the Internet, also encourage library users to write blogs and online print journals to share their stories. These activities promote pride in cultural heritage, preservation of languages, cultural wisdom, and exchange. Elderly immigrants might work with the children of older generations of immigrants, for example, to engage the children in learning the language of their own culture through stories. This activity might be especially advantageous to adopted children or adults or to others who are interested in and are researching their roots. Personal stories often unearth a rich cultural heritage, displaying the complex identities of library users and bridging cultures. Pictures, performances, show-and-tell sessions, and their storytelling can supplement the initial sharing of stories. These can be coordinated through collaborations with local historical museums, community centers, and other agencies. Pictures and images are particularly effective because they are "more direct, more immediate than words, and closer to the unconscious" (Anzaldua 1988: 32).

News from Home: Television, Magazines, and Newspapers

Many new immigrants strive to stay connected with their countries of origin by reading widely about cultural trends and events, sports, business, entertainment, the weather, trivia, as well as politics. They seek a wide variety of opinions on these matters, ranging from each political extreme. Newspapers and magazines that cover this type of information can be made available both in the library and online through listservs, library web page blogs, and email. Offer new immigrants the opportunity to communicate with family members in their home countries on library computers. They can compare and contrast the news that they hear from that source with news that they get in this country from bilingual radio stations, television stations, small presses, or ethnic presses. The Hartford Public Library's cultural exchange website for new immigrant communities focuses on ethnic newspapers and provides a media directory; it has another site devoted to restaurants, recipes, and food markets. Consider sponsoring or partnering with a local radio or television station that provides information that new immigrants want to know—information that is culturally beneficial—from social to political events.

Popular Materials

Comics, fotonovellas (popular comic strip type of books with stories in Spanish), and other types of printed materials with strong visual appeal are essential for people who may have limited English literacy skills (Shriver 2002). Make pictures and graphs accessible to those who are low literate in English and/or in their native languages. You can find these materials through information available online through library networks (for example, go to REFORMANET, which can help). Audio materials are also important to new immigrant communities. Groups of library users can be formed to translate books on tape and to create their own stories for others to share. You may also choose to order such materials, based on local and national needs assessments and reviews. Popular materials cover a variety of topics and are available in diverse electronic formats. Book readings, author discussions, lectures, and reviews can boost the usage of popular materials by people who may be interested yet did not know that the library had these materials.

Subjects of interest to new immigrant communities vary widely, partly based on their past and present experiences. New immigrants generally want materials from authors of their home countries as well as from authors in the United States who speak to the experiences and perspectives of new immigrant groups—especially about family life and relationships, as well as spiritual well-being. Genres with appeal to these groups range from self-help to romances and mysteries to religion and quality literature, including the classics. Keep in mind that individual interests as well as educational levels come into play in reading and genre choices. Be sure to collaborate with literacy program educators and instructors, and with school librarians, to learn about readability levels and how to use formulas to assess reading materials.

Educational and Instructional Materials

Educational and instructional collections focus on the worker/professional, citizen, parent, and consumer roles that adults commonly have. As employees or job seekers, new immigrants may want to learn new skills and/or receive a more advanced education, in order to move out of occupational ghettos or advance their careers. New immigrants who are employers may want to know about business networks, codes of ethics, and human resources issues in the United States. In becoming U.S. citizens, new immigrants often look to libraries for support in preparing for the citizenship tests and learning about immigration laws and civic issues (including becoming a licensed driver). Libraries can support new immigrants as parents too by providing reading programs to children and serving as child advocates in the public school system.

Libraries can also help members of new immigrant communities become better educated about all types of consumer issues. These include where to find the best resources for medical attention and shopping, as well as how to get information about social service and human service agencies.

Beyond offering collections for people's personal recreational interests (for example, in gardening), libraries have educational collections that focus exclusively on literacy and language development. These include self-help manuals, as well as manuals for tutoring and teaching English as a second language (either for individualized or small-group instruction) and audio materials for learning English. Many popular ones are listed in New York Public Library's Centers for Reading and Writing and Queens Borough Public Library's Adult Learning Centers websites.

Library users may also want to seek out information about the educational system in the United States, tests required for entry into schools and colleges (including the TOEFL and GED), learning disabilities, and other types of disabilities that affect learning. These materials ease cultural adjustment; they can be in print or electronic (for example, online testing subscriptions, such as Learning Express, or web links such as Firstfind.info) and may be considered as adjuncts to the main collection.

Consumer Collections

New immigrants often use the library to read *Consumer Reports* and gather other information for purchasing, exchanging, and selling items.

They may need information on the U.S. economy, the labor market, banking, and the stock market. Because housing is a basic need, using manuals for information about purchasing and selling houses, renting, interest rates, and mortgage loans can greatly assist decision making.

Transportation is another basic need. New immigrants require information on where to find train, bus, or ferry tickets at affordable prices; the routes of public transportation; or where they can buy or sell their cars. Do not overlook this type of information in your collection; and if you can get it in other languages, all the better.

Finally, many new immigrants have questions about health care, especially about insurance. Such information should be made available online or in print. Library staff can assist new immigrants in navigating "eBay" types of sources as well as help them find agencies that offer free services and more detailed information. Some new immigrants may find it interesting to read about how large corporations advertise their products to their communities. Critiques of consumerism, including journals such as *Adbusters* can fill this need.

Citizenship

New immigrants—especially those wanting to become U.S. citizens—sorely need information and materials on laws about a range of subjects such as immigration, sponsoring family members, civil rights, human rights, marriage, divorce, labor laws, driving, and cultural adjustment (Shriver 2002). People can learn about these subjects from a number of websites and immigrant resources directories (available in some libraries). Remember that these resources need to be monitored and updated regularly. Bookmark website links such as "Life in the USA" (http:// www.lifeintheusa.com/services1/libraries.htm) for library users. Some libraries, such as Hartford Public Library, create their own local and national sources (http://ww2.hplct.org/tap/TAP.htm--hartford). Remember, for easy access, it is important that these materials be in languages other than English.

Extensive documentation, tests, and preparation are all important for new immigrants applying to become U.S. citizens. Libraries can provide assistance by making special (longer-term) borrowing arrangements for pertinent materials; by photocopying and highlighting useful information; and by having audio books that support learning in the library. Also having reserve copies of vital material on hand in the library provides prompt access by a number of users. To find these important resources, check out books by CASAS called *Bibliography of Citizenship Materials* (for free, http://www.casas.org/DirctDwnlds.cfm?mfile_id=1442&selected_id=808&wtarget=body) and *Becoming a Citizen: A Selective List of Resources to Prepare for the U.S. Citizenship Exam*. Or, look at the many government websites on citizenship, including the "Citizenship Project," and "how to become a U.S. citizen." New York Public Library has an excellent citizenship site: (http://www.nypl.org/branch/services/citizenship.html). Immigrant experts and volunteers can help users find citizenship information in the library, and they can answer questions and address concerns when immigrants' rights are violated.

Instructional Manuals and How-to Books

Like other library users, new immigrants need information on educational certificates and licensing, business English, study methods, repair or construction, cooking, gardening, and any number of daily tasks that require some level of expertise. To serve such needs and offer a complete range, match your collection. When it comes to serving new immigrant groups, the sources must often be multilingual. Contact local adult education agencies to find out what sources they may offer that will complement your collection.

Literacy and Language Learning Materials (ESOL)

Of course, one of the most obvious needs for new immigrants is for materials that support literacy and language learning. Libraries generally collect these materials, particularly in those libraries with direct instruction programs in literacy and English as a second language, where the collections may be more developed due to constant usage and monitoring of the collection. The New York Public Library, widely known for its comprehensive collections, also has in its branch libraries an impressive collection of lifelong-learning materials that supports technology instruction and ESOL programs (Milam 2003). Many of these collections house materials of different genres (arranged near signs that indicate easy reading), published by both larger (New Reader's Press, for example) and smaller (such as Peppercorn Books) presses. Librarians who have developed best practices in collecting learning materials for new immigrant populations often present on this topic at library conferences, where they may distribute bibliographies and webliographies.

Sample Publishers of ESOL
- Grassroots Press
- ALTA

- Teachers of English to Speakers of Other Languages (TESOL)
- Contemporary Books
- Cambridge University Press
- Linmore
- Oxford University Press
- Pro Lingua Associates
- University of Michigan Press

Look for resources that list high-interest but low-vocabulary works from publishers, such as picture books (the *Oxford Picture Dictionary*, a standard in most collections). Checking out New Readers Press and Literacy Volunteers of America ESOL materials will help. The Center for Literacy Studies (http://cls.coe.utk.edu/library/esolbib.html) has an excellent bibliography of these books as do the Center for Adult English Language Acquisition, CAELA (http://www.cal.org/caela/esl_resources/publishers.html), and the New England Literacy Resource Center (http://www.nelrc.org/). Literacy and ESOL program directors, some of whom may not be librarians, can and should update general library lists and communicate with librarians about new immigrants' needs. If your library does not already have a general in-house collection that literacy and ESOL students can both use on site and also borrow, establish one. Some literacy programs in libraries extend borrowing privileges to participants and even register students as library users.

Literacy and language learning software changes constantly; therefore, be sure knowledgeable personnel help with collection. Many software companies offer trials for literacy and language learning programs, computers, and software. Take advantage of those opportunities, and if you can, extend the trials to your immigrant patrons, inviting feedback. One literacy program (Redwood City's Project READ) set up review boards for student evaluations of software and had experts in the computer industry and at the university monitor them. Tutor training programs can help tutors select materials for students to use independently or with staff, or else they can enable students to select materials themselves, based on their interests. Webliographies (a list of websites about a subject, "Organizations for Research and Information on ESOL Populations," p. 169) offer the same options in selecting materials.

Some libraries offer individualized instruction to learn English. In the case of computers, for example, one library sponsors a site called Learn English on the Net (http://www.mvls.info/literacy). Public access channels on television and TV 4-1-1 can also help. These modes of access may be especially advantageous for homebound learners who cannot attend classes. Popular ESOL software includes audio programs and graphics programs such as Rosetta Stone. Literacy software may focus on both phonics and whole language approaches to learning, whereas the Internet may be used for more radical/critical approaches to learning and community development.

Many standard library collections include materials for family literacy, workplace education, life skills, learning disabilities, adult education theory, ESOL, and health. Moreover, GED and pre-GED (in math, writing) materials—as well as ESOL materials in all formats—are often in high demand by students and tutors alike (NCSALL 2003). Make sure these materials—especially GED, pre-GED, and driver education—are available in non-English languages, as well as online resources, by state. For example, check out GEDillinoisonline at http://www.gedillinoisonline.org/ or the more general GEDonline at http://www.gedonline.org/. Include English language grammar materials, poetry, fiction, biographies, and self-help materials in your collection, and be sure to update them regularly. Many materials purportedly teach "adult basic skills" and are thus categorized simply, so that adult learners can find and read them. But one single category may not be enough. Consult any of the committees you have created for categorizing, and query members about labels that reflect the needs and interests of new immigrants. Although you may consider this material separate from the main collection with respect to how it is cataloged and housed, duplicate copies may be interfiled into the general collection.

Supplementary materials, such as newspapers (for example, *News for You*), student writings, and picture dictionaries, are often popular with new immigrants. Many of these materials are available online as well as in print. Make these materials accessible to teachers, tutors, and adult learners who are enrolled in non-library-based adult literacy programs and need to be encouraged to come to libraries for the collection and for accessing diverse materials. All other people in the community (such as Saya, described earlier in this chapter)—whether they are in such programs or not—must also be able to use the collection for their personal benefit. Keep in mind, however, that many of these materials are most helpful when trained instructors help people use them. Patrons may need assistance both in selecting materials and using certain levels, series, or genres.

For this reason, you may want to give assessments for literacy and oral/aural levels before proceeding with collection development.

These may include standardized and nonstandardized literacy assessments, users' goals for reading, and their interests and needs. You can make these up yourself, using icons and tick boxes, and deliver them orally. Or, you can search for them on websites, consult experts, and ask about them on listserv discussion boards, such as the National Institute for Literacy (NIFL) website on assessment which offers much information on instruments (see list below).

What Kind of Assessment Should I Choose?
- Go to a website for ESOL and read up on assessments.
- Join a listserv on literacy assessment (through the National Institute for Literacy) and ask members about their favorites and why.
- Consult a local literacy agency for how it assesses and uses its resources.
- Consider criteria:

    1. What does it assess? (reading comprehension levels, writing levels, speaking, listening, long-term and short-term goals, social support needs)
    2. Do the questions intimidate the learner? Are they appropriate?
    3. How will the assessment be administered? (through the library staff, through a literacy agency)
    4. Is the assessment in another language?
    5. Is a lot of training required to administer the test?
    6. Is a formal assessment needed at all, and can you just use some literacy materials in the library to assess basic ability and understanding?

In the long run, using commercial assessments and materials may not be as effective as simply asking students to bring in real-life materials from their homes and communities in order to assess how much they understand and for literacy learning (as Mary eventually found, with Saya). These materials, even if ephemeral, can become a part of your literacy and language learning collection, too.

Literacy and library personnel can and should set up networks and site visits between each other, as well as attend conferences and share collections information across listservs. One example of a very beneficial listserv for librarians working with literacy issues is LIBRARY_LIT, where you will find discussions on literacy, literacy research and education centers, and clearinghouses and their resources (http://lp-web.ala.org:8000/guest/info/LIBRARY-LIT).

Organizations for Research and Information on ESOL Populations (remember these may change)

Texas Center for the Advancement of Literacy and Learning (TCALL): http://www-tcall.tamu.edu/

System for Adult Basic Education Support (SABES): http://www.sabes.org/

National Institute for Literacy (NIFL): http://www.nifl.gov

National Center for the Study of Adult Learning and Literacy (NCSALL): http://www.ncsall.net/

World Education: http://www.worlded.org/WEIInternet/

National Center on Adult Literacy (NCAL): http://www.literacy.org

Teachers To Speakers of Other Languages, Inc. (TESOL): http://www.tesol.org

U.S. Department of Office of Vocational and Adult Education (OVAE): http://www.ed.gov/about/offices/list/ovae/index.html

Center for Applied Linguistics (CAL): http://www.cal.org.

Center for Adult English Language Acquisition (CAELA): http://www.cal.org/caela/

Women Expanding Literacy Education Action Resource Network (WELEARN): http://www.litwomen.org/welearn.html.

New England Literacy Resource Center (see also other state literacy resource centers): http://www.nelrc.org/

Center for the Study of Adult Literacy (Georgia State): http://education.gsu.edu/csal/

Canadian Congress for Learning Opportunities for Women (CCLOW): http://www.nald.ca/cclow/

California Adult Literacy Professional Development Project (CALPRO): http://www.calpro-online.org/

American Library Association's Office for Literacy and Outreach Services (see "literacy readiness inventory!"): http://www.ala.org/ala/olos/outreachresource/servicesnewnonreaders.htm

A MODEL OF MULTICULTURAL LIBRARY COLLECTION DEVELOPMENT: THE GLENWOOD LIBRARY

The Glenwood Library, a branch library in Greensboro, North Carolina, focuses heavily on multicultural collections for literacy, information, and community building (Sumerford 2001: 97–105, 2004: 39–41). This library has:

- Nonprofit and multicultural collections to serve numerous immigrant and refugee communities—African and South American students studying in the local colleges, a growing community of Mexicans who work in local service and manufacturing industries, and Laotians, Cambodians, and Montegnards

- Multicultural fiction and nonfiction materials tailored to the diverse clientele as well as educational materials: new immigrant patrons use the library's ESOL collection, ESOL software (ELLIS, TOEFL prep, and Rosetta Stone are popular), videos, and manipulatives—including maps, learning objects, and arts and crafts
- A community-based approach to library services—one that has grown naturally according to needs and demands, and regards literacy as its central mission
- A community-wide reading initiative known as the "Community of Readers," to improve literacy through many types of services sponsored by collaborations with various organizations such as Amistad de Guilford, an important center for Hispanics in Greensboro, as well as the local universities for cultural and educational events
- Partnerships with ethnic/immigrant associations to improve community relations; with the local community college for teachers of classes offered on an in-house basis; with other educational agencies for tutors and service-learning volunteers
- Multilingual Americorps members who work at the library; and have working relationships with social service agencies for referrals and assistance
- Staff attendance at international book fairs, conferences, and professional development opportunities in ESOL and cultural issues
- Advisory groups that counsel on various aspects of the collections, library operations, and sponsored events
- Small-group English language instruction program, a class on women and literacy, a citizenship-preparation class, a conversation club (both in English and in Spanish), family literacy groups, a computer lab, short-term book clubs, and field trips to Raleigh to campaign for more library funding or to the civil rights museum
- An expert multicultural coordinator who facilitates courses, workshops, liaisons with community agencies, and presents training for tutors and the public

Strategies for Locating Publishers of New Immigrant Materials
- Consult local and national listservs about attractive publishers.
- Consult ESOL websites (named earlier).

- Go to book exhibits at conferences: TESOL, ALA, PLA, IFLA, and your local associations; visit alternative types of book fairs in your community.
- Consult your multicultural library committee on an ongoing basis about the types of materials the members want and need.
- Go to various used and new bookstores, as well as bookselling street vendors, and see what community members are buying.
- Make home visits if you can, and see what books people have in their homes and what computer software they use.

Now that you have reflected on your collection building strategies, making them usable to new immigrant communities, let's take a look at how to make them come alive. Integrating your collections into programming can help this process. Chapter Eight will focus on programming for new immigrant communities.

ENDNOTES

1. See ALA's diversity website (http://www.ala.org/ala/diversity/diversity. htm), which contains some excellent references on multicultural resources and materials.

2. These ideas are drawn from Marianne Adams, Anne B. Lee, and Pat Griffin, *Teaching for Diversity and Social Justice: A Sourcebook* (New York: Routledge, 1997); Feagin 2005: 7; Pamela Taylor in Sondra Cuban, Jeffrey Anderson, Pamela Taylor, Laurie Stevahn, and Kay Beisse, "Where's the Justice in Service Learning: Institutionalizing Service-Learning from a Social Justice Perspective," presentation at the American Education Research Association, April 11–15, 2005; and L. Derman-Sparks and C. B. Phillips, *Teaching/Learning Anti-Racism: A Developmental Approach* (New York: Teachers College Press, 1997).

3. See also Sherill's research (1972), which is included in Helen Lyman's larger study.

4. For more information, check out the following resources: Joanne Godin, *A World of Information: Creating Multicultural Collections and Programs in Canadian Public Libraries* (Ottawa: National Library of Canada, 1994); Alire and Archibeque 1998; Larsen, Jacobs, and Vlimmeren 2003, 2004.

5. "Plain language" (or, Plain English) means communicating so that your audience understands the meaning the first time they read or hear it. Your audience should find what they need; Understand what they find; and Use what they find to meet their needs. From http://www.plainlanguage.gov/whatisPL/index.cfm).

6. These ideas draw on these resources: NBLC 1990; Larson, Jacobs, and Vlimmeren 2004; American Library Association, *Guidelines for the Development*

of a Multilingual Materials Collection. [Revised in 2002 by the Library Services to the Spanish-Speaking Committee, Reference User Services Association, American Library Association]; Alire and Archibeque 1998; Quezada 2005; Osborne 2005.

   7. Many of these ideas are drawn from Wayne Wiegand's historical work; see Wiegand 1986, 1989, 1998. See also Buschman 2003; Buschman and Carbone 1991; James P. Danky and Elliott Shore, eds., *Alternative Materials in Libraries* (Metuchen, NJ: Scarecrow Press, 1982); Judith Serebnick, "Book Reviews and the Selection of Potentially Controversial Books in Public Libraries," *Library Quarterly* 51, no. 4 (1981): 390–409; Judith Serebnick and F. Quinn, "Measuring Diversity of Opinion in Public Library Collections," *Library Quarterly* 65 (1995): 1–38; and Barbara H. Smith, *Contingencies of Value: Alternative Perspectives for Critical Theory* (Cambridge, MA: Harvard University Press, 1988).

CHAPTER 8
Connecting New Immigrants to Learning Opportunities

A culturally competent library provides a welcoming environment that is a "place in the world" for new immigrant communities (McGinnis 2001). How do you build this treasured learning place? Drawing from the author's research on learners as well as literature in the field of adult education, this chapter discusses programs for new immigrants as well as community-wide collaborations.

Start with a vision, for example, to be "inclusive of different skills, cultural backgrounds, and cognitive abilities" (Osborne 2005). Hopefully, you have created this vision through assessing your library and community's resources, expertise, assets, desires, and needs (see Chapter One).

Second, become an active helper to new immigrants, identifying and interpreting their unmet and stated needs, while presenting them with new learning opportunities (Carr 1983; Knox 1983). This role requires special skills in both communicating with and relating to other people on their terms. It also means knowing about how adults like to learn. The following descriptions of learners, tutors, and literacy program directors in library literacy programs are drawn from the author's study of persistence (Cuban 1999; Porter, Cuban, and Comings 2005).

Sherlette Lee, the director of the literacy program at the Wakefield branch of the New York Public Library and herself an immigrant, demonstrated these qualifications when she counseled Jesse, an immigrant learner who attended her program. Jesse commented, "At first I was kind of scared, but Miss Lee made me feel very comfortable after sitting and talking with her. . . . She was telling me that I'm not the only one, and at least I'm making a step toward bettering myself. I remember her telling me that."

As learner advocate Archie Willard put it, "If you really want someone to understand you, you make real efforts to use language they'll understand."[1] Yet many librarians have exactly this problem, because they have not been trained to be culturally diverse communicators. Yolanda Cuesta, a library diversity trainer, states, "We could build the understanding that librarians need to work with the communities, identify community leaders and work with community experts and share the trust. You can't do it by sitting at a desk. You have to develop skills to integrate community information into services" (Cuesta 2005).

Knowing your community is especially important in light of the fact that many new immigrants may come to the library after being turned away from other agencies. Community colleges, for example, require admission tests that many immigrants with low skills cannot pass. They often do not have as many classes as there are people waiting for them. One agency director in the Northeast—a region that has experienced a surge in immigration over the last ten years—said, "there are many thousands of people who are in need of ESOL who are not able to find an open class appropriate for their needs . . . there is little money for the Dominican woman and her family members who want to be able to help the children with homework. The backlog begins here" (Lieschoff 2004; Sataline 2002).

As federal, state, and local education budgets are slashed as well as severely regulated under long-term conservative administrations, committees are calling on libraries to fill in for secondary and adult education, and to offer a broad array of learning opportunities for immigrant learners.

Third, realize that new immigrants have wide-ranging learning goals. Many immigrants report that finding work is a high priority, yet they may have a problem transferring their already developed skills and knowledge from their native country into an American context (Osborne 2005). As discussed in the Introduction, it is not uncommon for highly educated immigrant professionals to be engaged in low-skilled work, especially in the low-paying service industry. But there is more work to do, especially to help those new immigrants that have less education.

As we all know, literacy is an advantage for qualifying for jobs as well as for socializing and communicating on a daily basis. Being comfortable in casual interactions in stores, on the street, with doctors, and with neighbors are survival skills (Sticht 2005). New immigrants may want to enlarge their social networks beyond their immediate milieu—as one study (on second-language learners in a San Diego library literacy and ESOL program) showed (McDonald and Scollay 2002). The learners benefited from the program by experiencing greater happiness as they improved the quality of their lives. As multipurpose agencies, libraries are primed to be extensions of adult learners' social networks.

Fourth, realize that, regardless of their immediate goals, immigrant learners are often in transition when they come to the library. Be aware of the types of changes that learners seek, and focus on those, rather than trying to change learners' identities—to Americanize them, for instance. As learners enter into new programs, they may experience both excitement and apprehension as they try something new. The library can respond by accepting immigrants while they develop coping skills, deal with conflicting demands, and learn new skills and practices (Cuban 2003; Drago-Severson 2001; Fingeret and Drennon 1997). With time, a dynamic community of new immigrants forms within the library—immigrants who feel integrated and develop a sense of belonging.

This community-building role for libraries can help counteract the language and power issues between immigrants and native-born individuals in public areas such as the workplace (for example, in situations that require speaking only Standard English).

One woman in a library learning program said that she was not allowed to speak Spanish at work: "I just met a new girl; she's from Puerto Rico. She's good in Spanish, as long as we don't speak. They don't let us speak Spanish. The language. It's gotta be only English."[2]

Immigrants may also feel that their English is not acceptable because they have accents, use slang, or else speak or write in local vernacular or in other languages such as Ebonics (AAVE) or Hawai'i Creole English (HCE). They may put themselves down and say they speak "broken English"—self-denigration that is exacerbated by others scorning them for not using Standard English or official English. Another woman in the same program exclaimed, "I can't speak well. So kind of shame of myself, you know," echoing another student who had said, "I want before I die, I want to knows English. I was thinking now [it] is really broken English." These students may want to learn the rules for using English, but do not want to be ridiculed for not using them all the time; for example, a Hawaiian woman required to attend that program said she wanted to learn but she "didn't want to know the vowels."

Learners often internalize dominant views about themselves as parents and speak only their native language at home, but worry about not passing Standard English and "correct educational messages" on to their children (Luttrell 1996). For example, a Mexican-American woman (in the program cited previously) said she did not teach her Hawai'i-born children Spanish for exactly that reason. On the other hand, many immigrants consider language preservation important; grandparents may insist that their grandchildren be sent to language schools, because the children do not use or refuse to speak their ancestral language in public or at home.

Fifth, remember that new immigrants are not the only ones that need to learn. As a librarian, you must take on the responsibility for educating the public about critical issues facing immigrants and refugees today. Native-born Americans—in the workplace and elsewhere—need to learn about immigrants' rights, such as the right to use public schools (children of undocumented immigrants included), the right to practice their own religion, the right to legal representation, and the right to good wages and labor opportunities. Make native-born Americans aware of recent laws that reduce opportunities for immigrants to form communities, to assert their rights, and (in the case of guest worker programs) to prosper in the United States (Bacon 2005; *The Change Agent* 2000).

For all of this to happen, you must offer numerous types of programs and services tailored to immigrants' lives, both actual and aspirational, as the community needs assessments dictate. Ample resources, funding, technology, and collections are prerequisite (as discussed in Chapter Three). Through learning programs, you can create "pathways" for new immigrants to pursue their own learning goals, undertake lifelong learning, and both connect and feel integrated with their communities.

Before getting started, consider the many different types of program strategies, and link these to your collection and services (discussed in previous chapters). This chapter's focus is on literacy and ESOL programming, then on intergenerational mentoring programs, community organizing, cultural arts exploration, and technology.

Checklist for Getting Started on New Immigrant Programming
1. Create a vision of what is needed, based on new immigrants' needs and interests.
2. Become an effective helper and communicator to new immigrants.
3. Respond to new immigrants' far-reaching goals, and offer learning opportunities that counteract discrimination in other areas of their lives.
4. Educate the rest of the community on new immigrants' rights and interests.

PROGRAMS FOR LITERACY AND ESOL LEARNERS

Currently, most public libraries offer literacy services of some type—whether it is simply information and referrals, collections, technology, meeting space, or collaboration with community colleges and local literacy agencies. A smaller minority (about a third) offers tutor-based or computer-assisted instructional programs that are either in-house or collaborative (Estabrook and Lakner 2000). This chapter will focus on these last services, as they are important in libraries becoming active community-based educators.

Library literacy programs are unique in that the library shapes their physical space, their underlying principles, and their organizational features. These programs have different names: "learning" programs, "literacy" programs, "ESOL" programs, "reading and writing" programs, and "computer-assisted" programs. The well-resourced ones can have long and staggered hours, multiple technological learning resources, layered staffing with volunteers, and diversified multimedia materials in conjunction with few demands for patron documentation. These characteristics work together to make library literacy programs flexible, open ended, and sufficiently informal to address immigrants' various needs. Yet even in the best-designed programs, not all immigrants are aware of the services, and even when they are, they participate at different levels.

In a recent study of persistence among library literacy learners (1999–2003), learners persisted in ways that are different from those prescribed for them.[3] When the community acknowledges and understands these different pathways, literacy programs can better help learners persist over a lifetime of learning in their communities. According to the author's findings, learners follow five types of pathways:

- *Tryout*. Immigrant learners shop around for appropriate programs or come just once, uncertain about whether they can meet the program standards. They may realize they cannot attend all of the time and never return. It is safe to assume that all learners begin as tryouts. Make an effort to include them the first time they walk in the door. Stress the flexibility of the program, and encourage them to return and keep in touch. Before they leave the program, give them information about other community programs.
- *Short term*. These learners come because they need specific skills to achieve a goal (e.g., pass a driver's test) or to move on to another type of program (e.g., for the GED) or to advance in a job. They stay for a short time (perhaps a month or more), learn the skill, and leave.

Before they leave, find out what they achieved and where they are going. Encourage them to return when they need additional help with something or to become a tutor or mentor to other students.

- *Intermittent.* These learners may have responsibilities that prevent them from attending regularly. They may be able to come for only short spurts over a long time span. In these cases, give them activities to do while they are not in class, and provide ways to keep in touch.
- *Long term.* Some learners need a community within which to socialize. Encourage their full use of the library, treat these participants as mentors to other students, and give them plenty of learning opportunities, so they can keep busy and continue learning.
- *Mandatory.* These learners are required (by parole officers or caseworkers) to attend a program. Do not assume they are unmotivated. Help them find a learning interest, build on it, and sustain their learning as they transition from mandatory to another way of participating.

Most programs favor the long-term pathway, because those learners are consistent and easier to track. In reality, these learners are few and far between. Probably the most significant pathways to cultivate are the tryout and intermittent pathways, as many students start on these.

Keep in mind that these learners may encounter a variety of barriers that prevent their active and regular attendance in your program. You can accommodate for this through flexibility, collaborating with other organizations (social service) for support services, and offering diverse learning opportunities. As your library becomes better integrated into the system of community colleges, adult schools, public schools, and other nonprofit literacy agencies in your community, more immigrant learners will find out about your library's learning program. Of course, this happens only if you plan and implement your learning community well.

Planning a Learning Community

You Will Need to Consider
- Creating a collaborative climate
- Recruiting and keeping a cadre of good tutors
- Recruiting students
- Doing literacy and ESOL needs assessments
- Doing intake interviews
- Staffing issues

Creating a Collaborative Climate

Although a few planning guides exist for designing library literacy programs (Zweizig, Johnson, and Robbins 1989), they tend to emphasize technical, quantitative issues. But consider qualitative considerations, such as how to form a community of learners and maintain an ongoing relationship with them.

Be sure your learning community fosters peer collaboration and friendship. This goal fits neatly with the library principles of accommodation and personalized service (Wagner 2004). What does this look like in practice?

The following examples are from the author's study of persistence in library literacy programs (Porter, Cuban, and Comings 2005). A Trinidadian man working at a construction site noticed a co-worker having problems with reading and writing, so he invited him to a literacy program that he himself had attended ten years ago that was still operating. The two men were immediately accepted into the program, and together they regularly rode the subway twice a week to class, where they learned reading and writing together in a small, tutor-led group. They became friends with each other as well as with other men in their group.

Learners often have effective referral systems that your program can build on. One Chinese learner, a soccer coach, attended the Flushing library regularly for computer instruction. He also used a number of local community education agencies that he had learned about through his own investigation, with help from the library and through word of mouth. During the summer he attended a church-run ESOL program, he used the computers at another branch library when Flushing's computer time slots were already taken up, and he attended both a community college English class and a small learning group in another library literacy program.

Encourage many languages to flourish in your library. At one library, a learner who was not confident in his English language skills opted to teach Spanish to a small conversation group for native-born speakers of English. Not surprisingly, his conversational skills in English grew because he interacted with members of the group in a comfortable way.

Build on all of the skills and strengths that learners bring to literacy programs. People should not be ashamed about the skills they are perceived to lack. For example, when one learner saw that others needed assistance in math, she started (with the support of the staff) a small math-tutoring group.

Finally—and perhaps most importantly—offer learners in-house and external support services; and utilize as many local, state, and federal resources as are already available to immigrants. Immigrant learners often have child-care, health, transportation, and other types of obstacles or barriers preventing them from attending the programs. How can your program help them? Consider partnering with other agencies or offering in-house counseling. One learner who had an illness attended the Oakland Public Library's Second Start program; this provided counseling referral services, stress-reduction classes, and on-the-spot counseling done by a student representative, as well as transportation tokens and food donated by local restaurants. He appreciated the friendly environment created by his fellow students and the staff, and he felt that it counterbalanced his life outside of the program.

Recruiting and Keeping a Cadre of Good Tutors

Tutors can be a great source of support to students as advocates, even though their formal roles in literacy programs are limited to ESOL, reading, and writing instruction. Their professional expertise and networks, higher levels of education, and willingness to connect learners to many resources beyond literacy programs and to give advice while learning about the learners' different cultures as "co-learners" is important.

In the persistence study, we found many tutors who had stepped out of their roles to help learners. Consider the tutor, a college student, who helped a young man who had been arrested and detained in a jail in another state get legal assistance so that he would not be deported to Mexico. Still another tutor, a newcomer to a city, assisted a homebound and isolated woman in finding employment. Yet another tutor moved lessons to jail, after her pupil was incarcerated. These homegrown strategies can make all the difference to learners, but are rarely mentioned in tutor training sessions.

Recruit tutors who are available, committed, and of diverse nationalities, without being too rigid or inflexible about their tutoring responsibilities. Conduct recruiting through other volunteer agencies; through public speeches made in the community; through information (and application forms) made available online, flyers, college fairs, local referrals, professional networks; and through coordination with companies that expect their employees to volunteer. One program, Project READ, of the Redwood City Public Library, coordinated with a computer company for volunteers and conducted on-site recruitment and orientations.

Encourage tutors to feel that they are part of the community, that they are learners also, and that they can play multiple roles with learners. Although certain programs ask tutors to commit for nine to twelve months, some tutors may feel that is too long. These tutors can work as substitutes or as drop-ins when other tutors leave; at least one program has found that drop-in tutors were helpful after their training and sustained their commitment.

Foster communication among tutors. Tutors and students should be able to speak freely without censure, about their own lives, and even about problems they may have with one another. Too often, students or tutors disappear, without saying a word to anyone. If there are opportunities for tutors to communicate about problems and exit the program with a sense of closure, more tutors might persist than currently do.

How do you attract and maintain tutors? Consider the reasons for which tutors volunteer their time in the first place. Most tutors come to programs in order to help. They do not really want to keep logs of their hours, test students, and work solely on computers or in multilevel groups. If your program requires these aspects, you will need to train tutors. If the tutors resist doing these activities, try to work within their limitations and help them develop cultural competence.

Initial training (which may run from between two and twenty-plus hours) is not enough. Tutors should be supported continually—through consultations, focus groups, learning celebrations, as well as workshops, materials, and opportunities to practice and explore. Build relationships and communities in which tutors can be active members. Some programs have listservs that allow tutors to connect and ask questions, a newsletter, and monthly meetings, as well as conferences at which to learn more techniques. Two programs in New York City (those of Queens Borough Public Library and the New York Public Library) organized a conference for staff, learners, and tutors to come together from different literacy and ESOL programs to learn innovative techniques. Staff from these programs also attended local and national conferences on teaching English and on literacy. Also, remember that advanced-level students can make great tutors because they understand the learner's viewpoint.

Recruiting Students

Before you recruit students, reflect on how and what your program can offer different types of students. What resources do you have for tryout students (lists of educational television shows and books to check out); for short termers (GED preparation, driver's license preparation, TOEFL);

for long termers (conversation groups, one-to-one tutoring, and a social environment); for intermittent (drop-in groups, drop-in computer lab); and for mandatory (career exploration workshops, Internet classes)? Then, actively advertise these resources to potential students and other community agencies.

Recruitment Strategies

- Post flyers in communities (make them readable, colorful, clear—pilot them first).
- Run ads on radio, in newspapers, and on television; use multimedia approaches to attract diverse groups. Immigrants with low literacy skills are less likely to read newspapers, but would see an ad on TV or hear one on the radio.
- Make community-wide presentations; go to local community centers; use bilingual speech, if possible; bring library paraphernalia, pens, stationery, and logos from the program.
- Attend information and career fairs; find out where health, social service, and employment types of fairs are, and set up a table with important information immigrants might seek out.
- Use current and past learners to promote your programs. Program users often only give speeches about the library during times of crises. Give learners, especially long termers, opportunities to go to community-based organizations and give presentations about their experiences.
- Talk and network with other neighborhood professionals about their client base. Go to social and human service agencies; and ask them about clients that your program might help and how you can work together to support them as well as develop a dual referral system.

The last recruitment strategy is particularly important if you do not already have an awareness about the lives, goals, and needs of immigrant learners who might come to your program. Using these "short-cut" methods with other local agencies that have already built trusting relationships with local populations provides valuable information and supports your recruitment efforts (Sumerford 2005). Still, the best way to recruit learners is often through referrals by other learners and by word of mouth in the community.

A student staff member, Resonja Willougby, of Second Start, often went to neighboring agencies in Oakland and presented the program while answering questions and addressing concerns in a way that the audience understood.

She felt that this was a very successful strategy for spreading the word about the program and the importance of education.

Doing Literacy and ESOL Needs Assessments

Before designing your program, conduct literacy and ESOL needs assessments.[4] Use the array of tools discussed in previous chapters, such as surveys, community leader discussions, mapping, interviews, and community focus groups. Also, read up on national and local literacy research, and consult with local and national experts. Scan your community to learn about populations that other agencies are not serving. The information gleaned from an assessment should tell you about the rhythms of learners' lives—including their time allotments for participating in educational activities, their sense of trust, and whether they have made a habit of going to libraries. If learners cannot or will not come to the library, the program may need to come to them (Sumerford 2005). In your assessment include questions about learners' hidden obstacles to learning—barriers in their lives that do not readily surface in intake interviews. Remember, focus groups often make people feel more comfortable because they are not put on the spot. Use the findings to guide your programming and recruitment strategies.

Doing Intake Interviews

Literacy and ESOL needs assessments resemble intake interviews. But intakes are more personal and individualized. Intakes should happen right away, when people walk in the door, so that you do not lose them. Do not schedule appointments or make people wait. Get them in as soon as you can, and start them on some sort of learning activity. The intakes should solicit information for you, but more importantly, they should help learners feel comfortable, answer questions, plan a workable and realistic learning pathway, and become initiated into the community. During intakes, encourage students to talk about the barriers and supports in their lives, and begin to form working relationships. Tell them about the instruction and how it is geared toward the realities of their lives, focusing on topics that immigrants say are important such as health care, schooling, job seeking, driver education, and preparation for citizenship. During the intake, also ask whether there are other subjects they would like to learn about. This process helps you discover what kind of instruction they desire, all the while building a relationship. For example, new immigrants may tell you that they actually enjoy reading children's books. Because they like them, you can use them, at least initially. Other learners may feel patronized by using children's books. So you need to ask! Intakes can be done by bilingual staff, by students, or by the program head. If many students come at once, you can conduct intakes for groups, which saves time.

What does an intake interview look like? Do not turn this process into a governmental survey or an official registration. Your intake should be short, to the point, open ended, and friendly. It should serve as a conversation starter, not a turn-off. Ask these questions, or any others, that you think are important:

- Basic questions (official name and nickname, best contact phone, email, country of origin, reachable address, education level; remember even these can be sensitive, so ask them carefully)
- Why did you come to this program? How did you hear about it?
- What kinds of things can we help you with? (prompt with reading, listening, etc.)
- Have you attended any other programs in this community or elsewhere? For how long? Are you currently on a waiting list?
- How long have you studied English? What was that like?
- What type of instruction would you prefer? (name the kinds of instruction you offer: computers, books, tutoring, small groups, classes, and tell about each)
- What times are you available, and how often can you come?
- Would you like to speak to another student about our program? (offer information)
- Do you have any questions?

After the intake session, write down a few notes, attempting to identify their dominant learning pathway, and follow up with instruction and literacy activities based on your assessment.

What Type of Instruction?

You can offer many different types of instruction to new immigrant learners. *Self-study* learning, whether through book learning or on the computer, is useful for drop-in learning, and for learners on any of the learning pathways.

Pair tutoring can be useful for students learning specific skills; and it certainly helps to build relationships. It is often beneficial when the two people already know each other, and if they can attend the program together, at a nearby location, easily and regularly. Pair tutoring requires a certain level of commitment on the part of students and tutors. It may especially benefit students on the long-term pathway or, if there are time limitations, the short term.

You can also pair students together to practice the skills they have learned. Pair tutoring, once considered the most important form of instruction in volunteer literacy programs, is often costly in terms of training, staff time in creating matches, and can be fraught with logistical issues. Because it can be so effective, you should not rule it out. However, consider less time-consuming but beneficial instructional venues as well.

Small-group instruction, with tutors facilitating, is becoming more popular. This allows for learners to get to know one another and form a learning community. It may be also be peer based, consisting of students only. These groups can be bigger (up to ten) and loosely formed and for a limited time, or closed and intimate (three to five). This type of learning may be especially suited to students on the long-term pathway and mandatory pathway. But looser and more open-ended groups often work well for those on a short-term path.

Computer-assisted learning, whether self-directed, in pairs, or through classes, is popular in most library literacy programs these days; and this type of learning can be easily supplemented by tutoring, small groups, and classes. Professional community college teachers, on an in-house or off-site basis, teach classes focused specifically on building employment, grammar, or reading and writing skills. Workshops on these topics can also be conducted, so that those learners who cannot regularly attend classes can at least have exposure to opportunities and a chance to experiment with options. The Queens Borough Public Library, for example, has offered:

- Video discussion groups on a Saturday afternoons for immigrants to practice their English and make new friends
- Workshops on how to respond to emergencies and art workshops
- Specialty classes in conversation (such as the "say anything" group)
- Family literacy and English language learning
- TOEFL study
- Cultural reading
- Vocabulary
- GED
- Job training

Finally, computer-assisted curriculum can be diverse and can use different media, books, paraphernalia, and documents that learners bring in.

In accepting and educating new students, keep in mind not to limit your library literacy program to the conventional methods of federally funded adult education agencies, especially if you do not have enough resources, staff, and training. If this is the case for your library, consider how to provide programs through diverse strategies such as partnering or collaborating with other educational agencies in the community, using their resources, such as staff, as well as library users who can volunteer. Get training elsewhere in the community, write grants as collaborative ventures, and offer literacy and learning activities that match the needs of local contexts.

Staffing Issues

Staffing is one of the biggest issues (and challenges) you will encounter in setting up literacy programs (Sumerford 2005). When starting or improving a program, obtain assistance. Use listservs, local literacy agency consultants, and education and library conferences for information and support. You can use these resources to ask questions and get guidance. You can also visit other literacy programs (library and nonlibrary) to observe how they operate and to learn about innovative strategies for finding, keeping, and promoting literacy staff. Many libraries that run direct-instruction programs hire literacy educators who then hire and train assistants, volunteer tutors, and administrators. Be sure to avoid a disconnect between the library and literacy staff; each needs to understand the goal and importance of the programs and to discuss matters regularly with the others.

Staff turnover is one of the biggest problems literacy programs face, especially in areas with high salaries and costs of living (e.g., New York City). The Queens Borough Public Library's Adult Learning Center director did research on literacy salaries and campaigned for competitive salaries before hiring. Keep in mind that lower-level assistants' salaries are lower and less negotiable; their rate of turnover is higher; and because of their direct contact and frontline work with learners, turnover can be disruptive to learners.

Some library literacy programs have dealt with this problem in ingenious ways—by hiring more educated learners as tutors and helpers, by creating service-learning opportunities with the local colleges and universities, and by appointing long-term talented tutors, high-school technology assistants, and Americorps members.

Some literacy programs hire volunteers to do technical administrative work—including people from unemployment and welfare centers, as well as high-level students. Other programs have had success by hiring college and university students as interns. The New York Public Library's Centers for Reading and Writing hired college mentors to assist learners in small groups, on the computers, and in all areas of staffing. They worked part time, notably filling in the gaps left by assistant staff whose positions were cut or frozen because of budget shortfalls. The mentors used their positions to later step into staff positions, for which they were already trained.

Americorps workers have proven to be highly valuable, because they are in transition from college to graduate school or careers, and welcome experience in library work. In two library literacy programs (Redwood City's Project READ and at the Glenwood Branch of the Greensboro Public Library), they served as administrators, taught small groups and classes, conducted orientations, did on-the-spot counseling, and planned many different activities ranging from child care to field trips and learning celebrations. They often also speak several languages and thus can effectively bridge cultural differences in the library.

Service-learning students from universities can provide temporary assistance—for a quarter or a semester—in which they can conduct research for the program, look for grants and collaboratives, gather data and write reports, give the tutors support, teach specific subjects within a specific time frame, and co-teach with long-term tutors. However, it is inadvisable for them to teach alone, or under the auspices of being a bona fide tutor, because of their short-term availability, which discourages learners from staying on if they themselves do not feel well established. If they stay long enough, though, they can become tutors. High school students also can add breadth to a literacy program by assisting learners with computer activities and by getting to know them, both in the library and out in the community.

The following discussion focuses on innovative and promising library literacy and ESOL program specialties for new immigrants.

Conversation Groups

Conversation groups give opportunities for those immigrants who have little chance to speak and practice with people in their homes and workplaces to come out to a new place, learn or practice a new language, exchange information, and network. Conversation groups usually consist of four to ten learners who, with a trained facilitator, discuss topics of interest to them. The learners can be a mix of native-born and immigrants residents, or limited to only immigrants (who may speak the same or different languages). The topics for discussion are virtually limitless, as long as they are of interest to most, if not all, of the learners. Brainstorm and vote on topics either prior to the group's meeting or on the first day. A facilitator enforces the ground rules for communication and ensures an equality of viewpoints and turn taking. The facilitator also asks thought-provoking questions, makes valuable comments to get the conversation started and rolling, and encourages members to discuss and compare topics from their personal experiences.

Facilitating these conversations is an art and generally requires some training. One library (the Queens Borough Public Library's Adult Learning Centers) sent staff members to a conference to learn more about language learning, communication, and how to deal with group dynamics. The staff so appreciated the training that they came back and taught a workshop for tutors to get some practice. During that session, the staff gave tutors advice on how to handle conversation and distributed conversation checklists with guidelines for specific issues, including lulls (or not) in the conversation, the participation level, verbal cues, and the occurrence of sensitive subjects (such as disclosures and controversies).

The Glenwood Branch of the Greensboro Public Library offers conversation clubs loosely run by Americorps staff, which offer chances for cultural exchange between native-born and immigrant library users. They tell each other stories, share perspectives, focus on community problems, and make acquaintances. The facilitator sets the ground rules, calls on people, makes sure everyone's viewpoint is heard, and ensures that shy people, or those with less experience in articulating their ideas, have a voice. These conversations often lead to important discoveries between different cultures and provide participants with opportunities to make connections, especially when they are facilitated well. In one conversation group, run by a Senegalese Americorps volunteer, Moussa, the students sat on the floor, introducing their country on a map in an atlas. The learners asked questions of each other. A learner described her country, Colombia, by regions, pointing to the rural area where there is an interesting culture and making a distinction between that area and Bogotá, the cosmopolitan city where she is from. Another student from Colombia assisted her by explaining the roots of Afro-Caribbeans. After the group had moved on to discuss salt mining and marijuana, Moussa interrupted and announced that one of the students, who is from Togo, signaled to him that he has to leave. He said that the student was a big man from a small country. Everyone laughed.

Seattle's Talk Time is another model of a group conversation program for new immigrants. Housed at various locations within the Seattle public library system, the program provides an opportunity for immigrants of all ages to become more comfortable using English. It also offers an avenue for seniors, especially, to become more social. It not only breaks down isolation but also builds social connections and allows for cross-cultural exchange. Participants learn about cheap places to shop, about social services, and they share job information, too. For example, health may be discussed one week—including information about where to buy Chinese herbs, the names of the herbs, and using library books to find the names. During the ten-week period, each week's subject is different. Learners and tutors circulate at tables for discussion with volunteers, who facilitate the groups. With repeat exposure, many of the learners feel less intimidated by the library and begin to understand that it is there for them (Wong 2005).

Learner Leadership

Some library literacy programs offer opportunities for learners to gain skills in public speaking, leadership, and collaboration. These learners become leaders who bridge cultural differences between students and staff. One program (run at the Adult Learning Center at the Central branch of the Queens Borough Public Library) chose an immigrant student representative to do on-the-spot counseling and to check in with other students about how they were doing, help with their independent studying, lead peer study groups, devise learning celebrations, organize a student council, call students to encourage them to stay in the program, keep tabs on students not recently around, and give speeches at orientation times to potential students and tutors. This student representative, plus two others from two other sites, also assisted administrative assistants by doing odd jobs such as photocopying, greeting students, and helping them to register. The program staff focused on this student representative as a resource for filling in gaps and making up for their lack of tutors and staff, as well as for campaigning for more funds. The library also sent her to library literacy conferences to meet with other student leaders and develop leadership skills. All the while, this student benefited the program, other students, and herself.

Learner leaders can often obtain important information that the program staff might not otherwise get, even through doing needs assessments. Learner leaders can conduct student meetings, do research on other students, get more students involved in the program, and help students persist in their learning by being a role model. Through their political involvement they connect to learner-led movements, such as VALUE (http://www.value.org), which expands the boundaries of an equitable learning community by promoting adult literacy students' rights and voices. These learner leaders, of course, need training, resources, and comprehensive support, as well as credibility among other program staff, so that their work is fully appreciated and optimized at all levels.

Health Literacy Projects

The critical focus of health literacy helps to develop vital knowledge of our complex health care system as well as fosters knowledge about health care of different cultures. Learning activities can range from field trips, to getting practice in navigating the system, to looking at medical information online and in books, to having guest speakers from the community (doctors, nurses, midwives). Local experts can help students learn about community health resources, ask questions, and gain an advocate. It is essential to offer real-life information and practice, because most health literacy texts are commercial and contain general fact-finding technical information that does not focus on real problems of new immigrants in the American health care system.

Translation services are especially important for new immigrants who cannot read the materials that are sent to them, the prescription labels on medicine they buy, or appointment information. Have translators available in the library, as well as a referral list of good ones in the community.

Collect important health literacy and education resources that are high in quality and current to have them on hand for learners. Many learners need advocates to help broker the health industry obstacles they face. Learners who work in the health care field can assist other learners to navigate the system too. To maximize the impact of your health literacy program, collaborate with local clinics and community health experts to obtain current health information. Library staff may need training in current health care information from appropriate workshops and in conducting needs assessments on health care. One program, the Glenwood Branch library in Greensboro, North Carolina, held a class specifically for women and literacy (along with child care), and appointed a retired nurse as teacher in order to focus discussion on problems with health care. The teacher had significant knowledge of the system, and the learners benefited from her advocacy as well as from the information she shared.

Telling Stories in a Celebration of Learning

Opportunities for learners to share their unique experiences in a celebration of learning add richness to the library experience and encourages learners to feel that they belong. Sharing stories allows new immigrants to inform their compatriots, who have been in the United States longer, of the current status of their countries. One initiative (MetLife's Foundation *Reading America* project) has developed a *Reading America Toolkit* online (http://www.lff.org) to help libraries plan programs centered on interviewing and telling stories, because "population shifts are now happening so rapidly and over such a wide expanse of the nation that every public library needs to become skilled in reaching out to newcomers. . . . The libraries that [we] were lucky enough to work with led the way by building individual connections that can only spill over into greater communication throughout our communities" (Sonenberg 2005: 2).

Story celebrations also create opportunities for learners to express themselves and for more established community members—with whom learners might otherwise never come into contact—to hear about their lives. For instance, the New York Public Library's Centers for Reading and Writing focus their programs on students in small groups, writing their stories that are then edited by tutors and staff and bound into books. These books can be used for reading at future group meetings and for learners to check out of the library. The library even selects some to be read aloud in an annual event, "Symphony Space," by celebrities in New York. The authors of the stories, community members, and others all come together for this celebrated event, which is considered an outreach activity as well to recruit more support, tutors, and students. The Second Start program in Oakland sponsors celebrated authors (such as Ishmael Reed) to come to special events to read their work at the library or sometimes at the Oakland Museum.

Redwood City's Project READ program uses its annual learning celebration as a time to share food, have fun, and learn. The celebration brings in all types of learners, from different generations, and families. Each year there is a different theme for the celebration (such as the rain forest), arts and crafts activities, awards and certificates; and learners speak about their experiences. A local volunteer agency recruits some of the volunteers—for this event and for other celebrations—from its lists of people available to work. Several hundred community members typically attend this event, including members of the library board and city council, and the mayor.

When designing events for new immigrants, consider the special roles that everyone plays. Make sure to create collaborative opportunities for people in the community to get involved, using their talents and resources.

Civics Education and Citizenship

One of the major issues virtually all immigrants have to contend with is their legal status in the United States. Citizenship status connects to a panoply of other issues, including labor laws and rights to services. All of these matters are commonly combined under the topic of civics education, which focuses on the process of becoming a citizen and what it takes to pass the citizenship test (e.g., United States history). Some civics education focuses on the nuts and bolts of information (FAQs) about naturalization, whereas other types focus on culture and customs, and a few concentrate on teaching immigrants about their right to protest and social justice issues (Wallerstein and Auerbach 2004).

Citizenship is important to many immigrants who want the right to vote and want to be recognized as American. One refugee said that she sought citizenship because, "My husband is a citizen . . . [and] I love this country. I love this people, and I like the United States, and I don't want to come back to my country." She studied for the citizenship test and took it, despite being very nervous. The library staff member who supported her during this period cheered her on. During the test, the refugee remembered the words of her teachers and gained confidence to work through the questions. Even though she felt that the officer who gave her the test looked intimidating and "mean," she passed the test successfully.

For high-quality civics education, collaborate with local programs offering citizenship classes. For instruction (beyond simply teaching to the test), program staff should be knowledgeable about the most recent services in the community for immigrants, immigration trends, and changes in immigration policies as well as immigrant rights. Teachers and participants should also have quality materials (electronic and print) on civics education, including citizenship study guides in other languages. Conducting outreach to promote these services, collections, and programs attracts populations interested in civics education. As local, state, and federal governments become more invested in civics education for immigrants, more monies may be available for this purpose.

Bilingual and Native Language Literacy

Bilingual education (using both native language and English for instruction) has proved to be helpful in acculturating learners into the dominant society and in their learning a second language (Lewelling 1992). Because funding for bilingual education in schools and other programs has recently declined across states, communities are calling on libraries to fill the gaps left by these other organizations. Multilingual educational programs assist native-born English-speaking adults, too, because they will increasingly need to know at least one other language for employment, cultural, and social purposes. In addition, new immigrants often want mastery over a language other than English, such as Japanese, Tagalog, or Spanish, depending on where they live. The need for foreign language speakers is greater than ever before, especially in business and government (Malone et al. 2005).

The English-Plus movement aims to convey to all U.S. residents the right to become proficient in English *plus* at least one other language (Lewelling 1992). The movement also supports cultural competence measures, such as providing interpretive services in medical facilities including substance abuse centers, bilingual provisions of the Voting Rights Act, and the Court Interpreters Act. The purpose is to counteract what has been referred to as the English-only movement or official English (for more information, see the Center for Applied Linguistics website: http://www.cal.org/resources/digest/lewell01.html).

Also, remember that many ESOL adult learners do not have high literacy skills in their own languages, due to little schooling. Therefore, consider offering native language literacy programs as well as English classes. In particular, second- and third-generation immigrant adolescents, referred to as Generation 1.5, often have higher levels of oral proficiencies in their native language and in English than in first- and second-language literacy skills (Young 2005). Cultivate native language literacy (Gillespie 1994) for cultural preservation and transmission. Seattle Public Library sponsored a program in which different language groups met, obtained support from one another, exchanged information, and decided on group lessons (Villalpando 2005). The Greensboro Public Library sponsors Spanish-learning classes and conversation groups for English speakers, to which it invites the public and college students. Learners and staff can facilitate these learning opportunities through a collaborative effort with local colleges and ethnic associations. Learners often say that these bilingual and native language literacy activities increase their comfort levels and ease their transition into the library and the community.

Educational Television, Videos, and DVDs

Some learners respond best to multimedia approaches to learning. Consider using TV and video or DVD players as learning tools. TV 4-1-1 and other educational television programs such as CNN give learners a chance to see other learners read and succeed as well as develop skills. They can help learners to build confidence in learning. One learner at the Centers for Reading and Writing of the New York Public Library, David, said that the program he watched on TV 4-1-1 helped him to better define his goals. When he saw the main character succeeding, he said, "If she can do it I can do it too." Not surprisingly, David found out about the library's literacy program through seeing a television ad of a man trying to read. He also watched safety videos at his construction job, and at home he regularly watched public television to help with his reading and writing.

The TV 4-1-1 website (http://www.tv411.org/index.shtml) provides a viable option for independent home study or with a group in the library. Learners can watch videos alone or with others, learn vocabulary and math, or ESOL on their home or library computers.

In addition, many new immigrants use closed-caption television at home to learn English; think about capitalizing on this practice. If you decide to use education DVDs/videos or TV in the library, first get a willing group together, find a program that would be of interest to them, and use small clips to get a discussion going. The group can watch, then stop to talk, and then watch more. This approach makes the program more dynamic and interactive for everyone. It also breaks up the monotony of reading or writing.

Women's Literacy Groups

Because women are the biggest population in library literacy programs (Porter, Cuban, and Comings 2005; Spangenberg 1996), forming literacy and language learning groups specifically for them can increase your student population overall; and it contributes to their persistence. The group provides a way for immigrant women to come out of isolation, to socialize, to make new friends, to learn self-advocacy skills, to exchange information and news, and to receive support—all while learning literacy. For example, one learner said she appreciated her women's literacy group because of the deep level of support it offered her, especially in regard to some emotional problems she was having.

Curriculum content for these groups, of course, can be quite different from that of other groups; and the focus most likely will be on issues that women like to read and talk about. For example, the women's literacy organization WELEARN shares ideas for starting programs for women's book groups such as Women Leading Through Reading—a community-based initiative for women literacy learners (http://www.litwomen.org/welearn.html). Remember not all women think the same, so be sure to conduct a needs assessment for your group. Also keep in mind that without child care, you might find it hard to attract women immigrant learners. Offer it if you can, or think about times and days that women could come, for example, when their kids are not at home. These groups can also meet outside the library, to make it easier for women to attend.

INTERGENERATIONAL MENTORING

Because the library—unlike schools or senior centers—brings people of all ages together, you can build on this asset by offering programs of intergenerational mentorship. Teens can teach seniors English, and seniors may be able to teach teens their native country's language. Redwood City Library's Project READ, a literacy program, had a collaborative relationship with a local school in which Americorps volunteers enabled "at-risk" teens to read stories to elementary schoolchildren. The teens formed teaching relationships with the children, and while improving their own literacy and academic study skills as well as those of the children, they also gained a sense of greater self-worth. Such programs can also build on the family literacy programs already in place at many libraries (Estabrook and Lakner 2000). Intergenerational mentoring can take many forms: with adults reading to children, or children reading to adults, others with separate groups for adults and children, and still others providing homework help. Some simply foster enjoyment of reading (Knuth 1998). The family literacy coordinator of Oakland Public Library's Second Start program kept in touch with the many immigrant parent participants, some of whom attended the adult literacy program and others to whom she sent homework and reading packets. She also hosted programs with guest speakers who led literacy-related activities with all of the participants.

Another model is the Queens Borough Public Library Adult Learning Centers, which piloted a family literacy program for new immigrant caregivers and their children at the Flushing branch library. It offered all types of activities, and a videotape made of the program allowed the coordinator to assess strengths and weaknesses for the sake of future improvement. It was funded by external grants—a common way to secure funding for many of these family literacy projects.

Homework Help and Study Skills

After-school programs are becoming increasingly popular in communities. Libraries have always played an important after-school role, even when it was not formalized. In *Top of the Class*, a memoir by Korean sisters Kim Abboud and Jane Kim (Alex 2005), libraries perform an important function in helping parents push their children to achieve academically (in writing this book, the authors tried to disprove the typical assumption that Asians are "natural" honor students and need no assistance).

Consider offering after-school programming that other local agencies do not offer, tailored for teens and younger children. These might focus on test-taking skills, time management, ways to ask for additional help, and information on important resources (electronic or print) that improve the quality of completed assignments.

Study skills programs offer tutors and new learners a special opportunity to develop relationships across cultural and socioeconomic boundaries, without a large time commitment for either party. Tutors can teach immigrants about what written teacher feedback means and how to improve their writing in the context of U.S. academic culture. These programs, run by knowledgeable tutors who are familiar with school rules and regulations in addition to literacy training, also give immigrants an opportunity to learn advocacy skills for their children's schooling.

Three days a week, at four branch libraries in Seattle, volunteers (real estate agents, business owners, school administrators, newspaper reporters) assist immigrant teens with their homework assignments—in subjects ranging from biology to algebra. The volunteers make referrals, translate teacher comments, edit essays, and provide feedback on presentations. On the other days of the week, the students can use the library's online homework system, which is also available to students who cannot come to the library. Students can log on to the Online Homework Help system seven days a week to get assistance from specialists who are a paid pool of professionals from tutor.com. The system is offered in Spanish from 3:00 p.m. to 7:00 p.m. These sessions operate as chat rooms, with tutors using a computerized drawing board on which to make images, formulas, and diagrams (Lo 2005). Tutors also send students to other web links for more information.

Create manuals to help new immigrants learn about the schools' educational lingo. One library, for example, contracted with a school group to create a plain language manual on how public schools operate, with various web links and organizations listed, as well as educational terms (Osborne 2005). The manuals can be written in any language for use in programs.

Do not try to do it all yourself—collaborate with community colleges for tutors and the design of the program. Or consider working together with university schools of education (for both specialists and graduate students) and with mentoring organizations (such as Big Brothers Big Sisters). If you decide to go at it solo (involving only the library), remember that your staff will probably need training, available through various human service organizations and colleges.

Where to Start
- Talk to knowledgeable colleagues in other local agencies about how they started their study center.
- Go on a relevant listserv and ask for advice from colleagues.
- Check out web resources about study centers to find out what you will need.
- Seek out possible partners to help you (hint: schools!).

COMMUNITY ORGANIZING

Community organizing programs boost neighborhood sustainability, community and informational referrals, and conflict resolution, all of the things discussed in Chapter Six. These programs are akin to popular education programs, but focus on learning about community problems in a collective and then seeking out good types of solutions with other community members. The problems may be old or new, affecting new immigrant communities and native-born ones, and range from topics on housing to war.

Before getting started, check into some solid guides for community organizing and facilitation. These guides can help you collaborate with local community organizers to facilitate workshops and assemble materials. Begin with Larry Olds's *Popular Education News* website (http://www.popednews.org). Olds lists the following guides:

- *Stir It Up: Lessons in Community Organizing and Advocacy* (Sen and Klein, John Wiley, 2003)
- *Counting Our Victories: Popular Education and Community Organizing* (Nadeau, New Deal Productions, 1996)

- *Naming the Moment: Political Analysis for Action* (Barndt, Catalyst, 1989)

And see also:

- *Civic Participation and Community Action Sourcebook* (Nash, New England Literacy Resource Center, 1999)
- *Women's Education in the Global Economy* (Louie and Burnham, Women of Color Resource Center, 2000)

Part of the thrill and importance of community organizing is to engage in the endeavor with partners. Learn what their talents and resources are and how you can trade off. If no one in your collaboration team has any training, at least one person should take the time to get it. Attend a community organizing training at a popular education institute. Larry Olds, an old-timer community activist, recommends several major ones around the country.

Community Organizing Training
- Catalyst Centre: http://www.catalystcentre.ca/index.htm
- Highlander Research and Education Center: http://www.high landercenter.org
- Resource Center of the Americas: http://www.americas.org
- Growing Communities for Peace: http://www.humanrightsand peacestore.org
- IPEA: http://www.peopleseducation.org/
- Project South: (http://www.projectsouth.org
- Center for Popular Education and Participatory Research: http://www.gse.berkeley.edu/research/pepr/
- Pop Ed Links Directory: http://www.flora.org/mike/links/poped.html
- Centre for Popular Education: http://www.cpe.uts.edu.au/
- The Change Agency: http://www.thechangeagency.org/index.htm)

One popular education workshop in Oakland, California (2005), reported on in *Popular Education News* (Olds 2005) focused on immigrant and refugee rights. A collective of grassroots organizations focusing on working with the media, creating funding streams, supporting the politics of translation and interpretation, and providing advocacy, sponsored it. For its popular education curriculum, the collective used *The Bridge Project: Building a Race and Immigration Dialogue in the Global Economy—A Popular Education Resource for Immigrant and Refugee*

Community Organizer (Cho et al., *National Network for Immigrant and Refugee Rights*, 2004), a popular guide covering immigrant rights (http://www.nnirr.org/news/news_pub_archive.html).

The Highlander Research and Education Center, a well-known adult education center located in Tennessee, focuses on civil rights and human rights initiatives through community-based education. It is well known for its advocacy education around literacy; it offers numerous popular education workshops and training institutes on national and local issues.

Another good program, the Right Questions project in Sommerville, Massachusetts, teaches participants a questioning method that encompasses brainstorming, branching out, and prioritizing to make decisions that assist in self-advocacy for court cases and other legal contexts (http://www.rightquestion.org; *Change Agent* 2003; Wallerstein and Auerbach 2004).

Make sure to have plenty of information resources at hand for participants when you conduct community organizing projects or events. Collect listings of government agencies, in addition to immigrant rights materials and networks, so that people can build their knowledge of the issues. You might also have printed lists of useful websites, such as Skokie's "The New Immigrants: Resources for New Americans" or First Find (http://www.firstfind.org), which is targeted to low-level readers and can help immigrants obtain essential resources and materials (Osborne 2005).

How do you run a community organizing workshop? Bilingual outreach specialists can organize these groups and local and national experts facilitate them. The workshops cover whatever material or issues your community decides on. The goal is to build awareness and create solutions, as well as connect participants with local and national resources. A successful community organizing workshop was started in the 1990s in Arlington, Virginia, where the library launched Bilingual Outreach Centers in apartment complexes around town, to help immigrants adjust to a new life in a new culture and to connect them to the library (McMurrer and Terrill 2001).

Community organizing does not have to happen in isolated ways, or as one-session workshops. These groups can be linked to ESOL classes and smaller groups. For example, one nonlibrary program, English for Action (EFA), offered ESOL classes through a collaboration of neighborhood agencies and a local university (Brown University). The instruction was participatory, in that learners were involved in all aspects of their education, including community-based education workshops. In addition, six of the learners received stipends. The program went beyond promoting literacy to reporting on issues regarding immigrant rights, trash and recycling, rallying their city council representatives and senators, as well as tackling discrimination issues in the context of the police department (see http://www.rifoundation.org/matriarch/OnePiecePage.asp_Q_PageID_E_506_A_PageName_E_StrategyGrant 2004EnglishAction).

In short, your library can play different roles by sponsoring workshops; by providing facilitators; or by supplying space, resources, and materials.

ARTS AND CULTURAL EXPLORATION

Cultural programs also connect new immigrants to the library, supporting its role as a community center. As Susan Brandehoff, editor of *Whole Person* catalog, stated, "Libraries give their communities something less tangible, yet just as essential to a satisfying and productive life—nourishment for the spirit. . . . They stimulate us to make connections where we noticed none before—between our ancestors and ourselves, between one culture and another, between the community and the individual" (Robertson 2005: 2).

One example of a successful outreach program, that of the New York Public Library, serves the third largest Cambodian community in the United States (Cahalan 2001). Through research, a library literacy specialist learned about cultural traditions of the group and discovered what other agencies were serving this population. The head librarian and another staff member at the Fordham branch helped select materials on Cambodian culture for the program. Some of these resources were bilingual—ranging from cookbooks and poetry to publication on Khmer history and tourism. The librarians linked activities to Cambodian celebrations. They hosted a culturally authentic event with food, book exhibits, music, and dancing—a collaboration that involved many local enterprises. This project inspired the creation of more cultural programming for other ethnic groups in the Bronx and stimulated both the community and librarians. It was an effective means for bonding the Cambodian community with the library, fostering long-lasting relationships.

Most libraries are involved in cultural programs—86 percent, according to a survey in 1998 by the ALA Public Programs Office—to "entertain, enlighten, educate and involve adult and family audiences" and also to encourage dialogue and discussion of ideas (Robertson 2005: 3–4).

Apart from visibility in the general community, arts programming has secondary benefits, such as boosting circulation of materials, fostering networking and outreach among librarians and neighboring organizations, engaging diverse publics, and expanding the library's sphere of influence. Moreover, it may be easier to get funding for these, than for other types of programs—a good thing, because they are often expensive and labor intensive (Mehdi 2005; Robertson 2005; Rubin 1997).

Most librarians say they are excited about the potential of arts programs and view providing them as part of their role in the community. Because cooperative activities between public libraries and museums are now frequently funded by grants from the Institute for Museum and Library Studies, there is often an additional incentive to offer arts programming.

There are many options for expanding arts programming, including book and film discussions, bookmaking, theater, mask making, cultural fairs, traveling exhibits, craft and radio shows, live performances of music and dancing, poetry, and quilting. Programs can be conducted in another language, as in the Greensboro Public Library's "el dia de los libros" event, which featured poetry and performances for parents and teens. Cultural programs can be organized on a collaborative basis with other cultural agencies—for example, libraries can start to host museum exhibits, just as museums have long included library exhibits (Greenlee 2005; Sumerford 2005). Let's look at one of these: book and film discussion groups.

Book and Film Discussion Groups

Book groups take many different forms. If you have been assigned to running one on your own and do not know where to start, check out ALA's booklet *Let's Talk About It; One Community One Book*. Do not limit your discussion group to books only. Consider incorporating multimedia such as computers, film, and television. And consider following themes such as history or social issues (for example, Domestic Violence Awareness month, Black History month, Women's History month, Poetry month). Such groups can build all types of literacy skills and are fun (Constantino 1988).

The MetLife Foundation *Reading America* Program (sponsored by Libraries for the Future) and the Americans for Libraries Council conducted an intergenerational book and film discussion program with forty libraries participating as part of the Americans for Libraries Council. The main purpose of the program was to use the arts and literature as a "neutral ground to stimulate cross-cultural and cross-generational discussion," as well as to provide a place for teens and families to have meaningful conversations. Another major goal was to stimulate connections between new communities—the participating libraries were chosen because they would "jumpstart the conversations" in immigrant-dominated neighborhoods and help promote cultural exchange and adjustment (Sonenberg 2005).

The originators of the program discovered many challenges in building relationships with new populations. The challenges to reaching out to Somali families are examined in a report (MetLife Foundation *Reading America* Program 2004). Parents did not know whether the programs were "fun or educational"; many parents did not understand how to participate with their children. They had difficulties getting to the programs due to conflicting schedules and transportation problems; and they were not familiar with formal programs because they had no formal education.

In order to succeed with this group, the program needed to respond to the problems in the following ways:

- By strengthening the library–client relationship by building on trust and focusing on commitments rather than only on content
- By working closely with community partners for resources and contacts
- By asking about program needs to develop meaningful content
- By inviting entire families to attend, while providing some separate activities for children and for adults
- By stating explicit expectations and goals
- By scheduling class meetings at convenient times, accepting that there will be glitches; and celebrating "small wins"

Incorporating an intergenerational approach increases participants' learning. This can also help you, as a librarian, understand why, for example, a young Chinese man born in Texas prefers Eminem (the rapper) to traditional Chinese music. You will hear his viewpoint, and he will share it with his parents or somebody else in the group. Use all types of media (for example, audio books) that speak to both generations and help people adapt to life in America in supportive ways (Sonenberg 2005).

Conducting these groups as free-form discussions is essential in allowing all participants to feel comfortable, act casual, and hear more about views on contemporary problems in society. The Glenwood library's conversation club meets twice a week for all its community members to discuss problems and share in cultural exchange. Some people make lasting friendships and become personal sponsors of one another, helping each other in different ways in the community. The club is structured in that participants meet casually but regularly at the same time. For much younger children, consider holding story hours and sponsoring book giveaways. These events can be hosted in people's homes, in local community centers, and in ethnic associations' meeting places, for new immigrants who would not normally come to the library, but would come to a place they knew.

Checklist: Where Do I Start?

- Do research: Read whatever you can on book and film groups on the web. Ask patrons about their own book groups and how they are organized.
- Ask new immigrant patrons what books they would like to read and discuss with others. Ask about any other media they enjoy.
- Compile a list and test it out on a number of people, send it on list-servs to other librarians who can give you additions.
- Set your first date for a meeting (in the evening) and then make it flexible from then on, based on people's schedules.
- After your first successful meetings, start to advertise to recruit more participants.

TECHNOLOGY PROGRAMS TO ACCESS INFORMATION AND ENABLE LEARNING

Undoubtedly, public libraries are one of the few places in communities where people can go to use computers and access the Internet for free. It is therefore not surprising that members of low-income communities are more likely to rely exclusively on public libraries for this service than are people in higher-incomes communities (Gordon 2004).

Although more people are using—and owning—computers, societal disparities still exist, which is why a recent study funded by the Wallace Foundation focused on expanding the number of computers used in library literacy programs. These programs focused on increasing hardware, software, Internet connectivity, support, instruction, and independent learning. Findings later revealed that computer instruction among learners increased, on average. The Wallace Foundation—like some other private foundations (such as the Bill and Melinda Gates Foundation) and public agencies (funded by the Library Services and

Technology Act)—has focused in recent years on increasing computer usage for "21st century literacy skills" among low-income minorities who are often considered "the information have-nots." This includes new immigrants.

A Canadian study found that immigrant women most often use computers in a public space, the library being a favorite place because of the "professional help" offered. These women used computers for communicating with friends and family in their home countries as well as within the United States; and they were more likely than the national average to use the computer for career purposes (Bose n.d.).

Many Hispanics in the United States do not have regular access to computers or the Internet. A program director of the Central American Resource Center noted that computers are highly valued in Los Angeles, and immigrants see them as the wave of the future, but have little access. He observed one Central American woman for whom "the only time she had been exposed to a computer prior to coming to our class was when she was cleaning or dusting the computers at the place where she worked" (Bell 2004; Morris 2001).

In the future, members of new immigrant communities may come to the library specifically to use the Internet, to the point that they view the library solely as a "computer center," as Steve Sumerford noted (2005). Computers, however, should be considered only one of the many assets that library services provide; they can be used in tandem with other electronic and print media to boost many types of literacies. Set your computers next to book collections and audiotapes to encourage print literacy, too.

Design your computer space to accommodate the use of books and other types of print materials, as well as for electronic resources such as calculators and dictionaries. In addition, place computers together or make seats available for twin or group usage, especially for families (Cuesta 2005). One program, Project READ in Redwood City, allows learners and tutors to sit together at a computer, listening and responding through headphone sets to the software programs. This strengthens personal bonds as well as fosters learning. Although computers in libraries are set up for individuals, few of the stations provide privacy for users, and in prohibiting commercial transactions (at least at present), libraries make it difficult for their users to conduct business such as electronic banking. Libraries do, however, offer various off-site types of services, including the ATT language line, Webjunction, and LINCS, which help people access essential information in educational resources (Cuesta 2005).

New immigrant users may need more than skills to operate the computers or to achieve what is called technology literacy. Furthermore, they often want more. Your library can partner with other educational agencies to design learning through the library via a distance education program. ESOL labs are good candidates for such partnerships. And students do not have to attend distance education courses in the library or at set times, thanks to phone consulting and online tutoring (Osborne 2005); so they are good options for the homebound and full-time employed. A diverse array of curricula can be made available through distance education, including testing (for TOEFL, GED, and vocational assessments), diagnosis (assessing levels, goals, needs, interests, and skills), vocabulary and writing, and citizenship education skills. For example, Dave's ESOL café promotes sharing photographs, job searching, and learning slang terms (http://www.eslcafe.com/). With further mentoring, learners can use more resources to build on their skills— sharing stories, for example—and to foster their powers of expressive communication (http://www.literacy.net.org).

Most library literacy programs currently use computers (Estabrook and Lakner 2000; Spangenberg 1996) and are likely considered "rich" in the world of community-based organizations, which often have outdated equipment or lack computers entirely. Most library literacy programs also collaborate with other community-based agencies with the intent to build resources and expertise, and to become more visible. Your library can help build more literacy and learning opportunities for community members by sharing its computer and informational wealth—especially with community colleges, which generally need computers to support their long waiting lists for ESOL students.

Adult education teachers also often need technology skills and training. A study on adult education instructors (Carter and Titzel 2003) showed that they used technology regularly but did not feel proficient. They needed better access to up-to-date computers, tech support, and— clearly—higher-quality training, as well as time to learn and develop their skills. Your library can be a place where teachers receive professional development on technology from qualified librarians, instructors, or facilitators.

The Literacy in Libraries Across America (LILAA) initiative recommends a process for forming successful technology partnerships that is aligned with many of the processes detailed in this book. If a network or consortium is not already in place, take the steps needed to ensure the quality and diversity of collaborations. The first step that LILAA recommends is to chart gaps and assets in community agency technology.

This may mean approaching diverse local community-based agencies and asking what types and levels of computer learning they have. Before creating a partnership, assess whether the agencies' missions are compatible with the mission and goals of the library and of the project. Prepared brochures can help agencies to see what the library has to offer and to learn about the library in general. Select between five and ten organizations with mutual interests, and invite them, through their directors, to have a meeting. Repeat these steps to recruit new partners, when you need them. Once this process is begun, consider entering into a formal partnership (see Chapter Three).

What's next? The last chapter, Final Thoughts, discusses the importance of reflecting on and evaluating your programs and services, so your library is sure to be culturally competent and appreciated by new immigrant communities.

ENDNOTES

1. See Willard 2003; http://www.plainlanguagenetwork.org; http://www.plainlanguage.gov.

2. Cuban 1999.

3. Many of these findings are reported in the author's AERA papers and unpublished reports, 2003, as well as Porter, Cuban, and Comings 2005.

4. See American Library Association, *Tutor Trickle Down: Communicating with Literacy Tutors*, Literacy in Libraries Across America (LILAA). (Chicago: American Library Association, Office of Literacy Outreach Services [OLOS]), 2005. These and other how-to sheets, derived from the Literacy in Libraries Across America (LILAA) initiative, are available on the web and can assist libraries to start literacy programs; Dale Lipschultz, "Making Your Library Literacy-Ready," at http://www.ala.org/ala/olos/outreachresource/makingyourlibrary.htm; Buildliteracy.org, *Tool Kit—The Literacy Readiness Inventory (LRI)* (Chicago: American Library Association, 2005), http://www.buildliteracy.org; National Literacy Secretariat, *Tools to Help Make Your Services More Accessible: The Literacy Audit Kit* (Alberta, Canada: Human Resources Development Canada, 1997. See http://www.literacyalberta.ca/resource/auditkit/audktpg1.htm.

A Dynamic Future for Work with Immigrants

Libraries serve new immigrants because of their strong roles in local communities, and because they have always done so. But how can libraries and librarians do it even better? To make this happen, community assessment, as discussed in Chapters One and Two, is paramount. Thereafter, you must establish outreach as an integral part of library operations rather than being treated as a special project, as discussed in Chapter Three. This is what is called "institutionalization" of outreach. Moreover, as discussed in Chapters Three and Four, your library must ensure that conditions are set in place for this to occur. Community collaborations are essential to the process as well. Once these pieces are in place, you still need a solid base of resources. Yet—as Chapters Five and Six discuss fully—without policies and services, even the resources cannot be mobilized. Collections and programming, as discussed in the subsequent chapters, should accommodate the needs of new immigrants and demonstrate cultural responsiveness and attunement to unique community contexts.

Throughout this book, you have learned about various strategies for working with new immigrant communities, hand-in-hand with assessment, which can contribute to your success. Likewise, adhere to important principles and approaches as you begin your endeavors, with the prime one being proactive rather than reactive.

A PROACTIVE APPROACH TO WORKING WITH IMMIGRANTS

Be proactive in serving new immigrant communities and be creative. Like Steve Sumerford (of the Greensboro Public Library) says, "We have to find new ways to deliver services. The traditional path is not very satisfying, and not likely to be successful for those who have distrust, no time, and no tradition of library use—these are three strikes against the library. . . . The passive approach is not the right one for a population that is rapidly changing the face of America. We would miss a great opportunity" (2005).

The library offers immigrants a doorway through which they can enter into the American mainstream (Tjoumas 1995: 16) and become empowered. But widening a doorway is not enough. Your library needs to create new connections with its communities, especially when they are not well represented. Hediana Utarti, a project coordinator of a shelter for battered Asian immigrant and refugee women in San Francisco—those who have suffered from domestic violence—believes that the library can be a liberating force in many of these women's lives:

Public libraries are a savior for us; the libraries provide women access to the outside world that they otherwise would not have. Eighty percent of our clients are monolingual (non-English-speaking). When they arrived at the shelter, escaping from violence at home, their lives were essentially uprooted. Once they were rested, we would introduce them to the libraries and sign them up for membership. Here they are able to read newspapers and magazines and even videos in the language that they understand. . . . Public libraries play a big role in breaking the isolation that their batterers impose on them. Many batterers use the women's lack of English language proficiency to abuse them, by taking them everywhere including medical services, and not allowing them to take ESOL classes, or to meet English speaking people etc. . . . thus the women cannot communicate freely. By going to the public libraries, the women actually could access both English and non-English materials, which gives them power they never had. (Utarti 2006)

These community members walked through the doorway *because* the library attended to their needs, long before they asked. "'As long as there is respect and acknowledgment of connections, things continue working. When that stops, we all die,'" Gale Greenlee of the Glenwood Branch library in Greensboro, North Carolina, stresses, citing the Native American poet/novelist, Joy Harjo. She adds, "My library work is doing my part to build connections and keep things working" (Greenlee 2004).

A proactive approach means creating collaborations with other organizations in order to make the library feel more like a true community center and to gain the trust of new immigrant communities. Look at libraries from other countries as models for bringing in newcomers and making them feel connected to the community, through collaborative ventures. One Canadian library developed community collaborations to attract newcomers (Brown 2002) by cohosting Internet classes in the Khmer language with the Cambodian Association of Victoria, to bring in new potential library users. The library collaborated with other organizations to host business school classes and Vietnamese cultural programs, offer writing awards, arrange programs with the museum, and change the library's acquisition policies to create higher-quality collections.

In another case, a branch library in Denmark created a job center by partnering with an unemployment agency and the municipal social work department. A local health center is also on the premises, and coordination groups have been developed to link schools with the library, for using the Internet. These examples demonstrate how the proactive approach can nurture community connections, lifelong learning, and community collaborations for new immigrant communities.

Creating Communities to Address Change in Immigrants' Lives

Because new immigrants lives' change quickly as they adjust to their new lives in the United States—as they become citizens, move to new places, and transition into new jobs—you will want to address these transitions creatively, to help them feel that they belong in a wider cultural context. The longer a person resides in the United States, the more likely he or she is to become a citizen, learn English, and intermarry. Libraries can facilitate or soften the impact of these changes in ways similar to those of ethnic enclaves. These subcultures are still critically important for helping new immigrants acculturate, and your city or town may already have pockets or areas, such as a "little India" or "Manilatown." As a librarian, you can tap into these "small world lives" for important indigenous knowledge that will ease new immigrants' transitions into American life and create community.[1]

At the same time, because ethnic cultures also permeate mainstream popular culture and society—leading everyone to learn new ways in this "permanently unfinished country" (Rodriguez 1999)—the library needs to try creative approaches to addressing the needs, histories, and identities of new immigrants as they change in the diaspora. Creative approaches make it possible for the library to build communities for immigrants to acquire general skills and knowledge as they strive for both greater autonomy as well as connectedness. Libraries can help new immigrants to develop:[2]

- *Information literacy.* The ability and means to access, evaluate, and use information creatively, efficiently, and effectively in areas that can include searching for jobs in diverse sources
- *Socially responsible information.* The ability and means to acquire information that is critical to a democratic society—for example, information on citizenship as well as on asserting rights
- *Independent learning.* The ability and means to pursue information related to personal interests, and creative expressions of information, including art, poetry, and languages

How can you cultivate these skills and knowledge creatively with and for new immigrants? Involving new immigrants in conceptualizing and creating their own library services is important. Consider grassroots models such as the "barefoot librarian" (Yocklun 1988), which is sensitized to community needs because the librarian is an integral part of the community. This model, designed for developing countries' libraries, works as a good model for libraries in the United States because it focuses on librarians becoming part of the community and working alongside community members, using their indigenous knowledge as well as other resources to develop the community. The model emphasizes providing better services to rural areas, spending funds equitably (for example, creating committees that determine funding priorities), providing a first link in the information access chain (through getting information from the "street" out quickly), encouraging reading habits of its community members (through literacy programs), and providing materials and resources for many purposes and in the varied languages represented in the community. As representatives of their communities, community leaders may even be selected to lead and become trained as librarians. Independent learning, information literacy, and socially responsible information are exchanged in the process.

TRANSFORMING THE WHOLE LIBRARY
FOR CULTURAL COMPETENCE

A second principle for successful change is creating cultural competence in library management as well as staff members. Before you begin thinking about cultural competency training, consider who your staff is, and consider the hiring recruitment plan of your library. Is it structured so to attract ethnic minorities? Even if it is, there are numerous challenges. As Yolanda Cuesta puts it: "We don't do a good job in recruiting and mentoring people to enter the profession. We still attract the white middle class person. . . . We are still not seeing diversity." Some of the problem, she says, is practical and difficult to solve within the library itself—public library positions pay lower than at other institutions/organizations, low turnover and fewer vacancies exist, and city and counties do not tend to be proactive in diversity recruitment. We will come back to this pervasive problem. But let's consider an ideal scenario with a good representation of staff. Say you are in charge of cultural competency training. Where do you start?

First, make sure that all of the staff members are invited, not just a few. A key factor in successful cultural competence training is administrators who actively promote it as part of the whole organization rather than as part of staff training. To develop a culturally responsive library, you need to integrate diversity throughout the entire organization focusing on all that needs to change (Cuesta 2005).

In planning this training, ensure that it is not a quick-fix awareness workshop but something long lasting and comprehensive that involves and actively engages all participants. Establish a support system within the organization so staff training in cultural competence can be implemented at all levels. Make sure that staff members have opportunities to practice their newfound knowledge and skills. Administrators can further training through mentoring and networking programs, too. Remember, being "more responsive to minorities needs can bring a turnaround" (Cuesta 2004: 113; McCook and Geist 1993: 1).

Planning Your Cultural Competence Training

- Ask about the library's recruitment process and structure. What institutional barriers and environmental barriers are there to recruiting minorities?
- Invite the entire staff to cultural competence trainings.
- Seek the leadership of administrators who institutionalize it.
- Ensure that whatever training you decide to use is comprehensive and long lasting.
- Build a support system so the training can be implemented.
- Give trainees a chance to practice their skills and knowledge.
- Support further training through mentoring programs.
- Include consciousness building into your cultural competence training through discovering librarians' unique roots.

Building Consciousness Through Digging Up Your Roots

How do you make this turnaround happen? Look at your history and your library's past role in helping immigrants, roles that are part of your history of serving immigrant communities (Cuesta 2005). As discussed earlier, in the early part of the nineteenth century, librarians purposely developed libraries as "vibrant community centers" (Gottfried 2001: 146). For example, the Seward Park branch of the New York Public Library had a Mothers Club, which held Hanukkah and Purim parties; meetings in Yiddish; activities that focused on current events and stories; and speakers including theologians, poets, novelists, and playwrights; as well as field trips to museums and to city performances. A Yiddish-speaking librarian helped to bridge the communication and cultural gap between the community and the library.

This powerful tradition continues. Since the early 1990s and the fall of the Soviet Union, libraries have been serving many Russian immigrant communities, with the recognition that they come from a wide variety of ethnicities and speak a variety of languages (Kuharets 2001). The Donnell World Language Collection (in New York City) is an example. The librarian asks the community what they want and "grow[s] their book collection accordingly" (Kuharets 2001: 181). In focusing on Russian readership, the library provides diverse collections, with both classics and popular genre fiction. The library also hosts a literary evening, including dramatic recitals, music, and patron-assisted programs. The library's monthly newsletter advertises Russian radio shows and the Russian daily newspaper, with a passion for Russian culture. Go ahead, says Kuharets, "say, 'dobro pozhalovat' ('welcome') to the Russians in your community and celebrate their thirst for knowledge" (Kuharets 2001: 187). In designing future programming, gaze back at the roots of library history, and become retrained and literate in your own history.

When this conversion occurs, you can become a worldly wise "bridge" for transnational populations who are transforming their lives in sync with the library. "True and meaningful transformation occurs when people and organizations reframe the way they think about the world—their own internal world and the world about them" (McCook 2002: 328). Look first at your communities and how they view the world. The *Danville Community Encyclopedia* (Callahan 2003) contains "everyday knowledge" of this rural community that is critical to its continued existence (http://www.anna-callahan.com/encyclopedia.htm). The book looks like an encyclopedia of official knowledge and is organized as such (with alphabetical listings of words). But on opening it, you realize that the listed terms are not written by specialists, but community experts. It is a surprise when you open it up and see definitions of terms written in Plain Language, and with lots of description and stories. The topics, arranged from A to Z, range from Alto (Barbershop singing) to Zoning. This project allows all participants to become the "subjects" of their knowledge rather than the objects of it (Freire 1987) because the information comes from the ground up—from the community members—not top down. This compilation is the shared knowledge of community-based values and culture of Danville. It is a little like the popular encyclopedia website, Wikipedia (http://en.wikipedia. org/wiki/Main_Page) but it is based in a real place. Library and information studies schools should likewise nurture a culture of cultural competence. But there are many barriers to overcome; for example, barriers to recruiting students of color, including a lack of minority staff, the need for monetary incentives (scholarships, tuition waivers), lack of diverse curriculum, limited financial support, and a lack of a concerted recruitment effort. The library profession, as a result, is largely invisible to ethnic minorities. Although the reasons are both complex and multifaceted, the library community should research and deal with these barriers, rather than ignore them (McCook and Geist 1993: 2; Neely 2005).

As a result of this chronic neglect, many racial and ethnic minorities have few opportunities to study LIS, and attitudes among the dominant, white, middle-class group go unchallenged. No one gets a real education. Not surprisingly, white librarians have severely limited awareness of racism and discrimination. In a 1997 survey, Evan St. Lifer and Corinne Nelson found that although most whites thought attitudes and practices of racism and discrimination had improved, roughly 40 percent of librarians of color (Asians, African Americans, Latinos) reported that they had worsened; and a number of people even felt discriminated against at work (Neely 2005). Part of this trend among whites is due to the myths that exist and circulate—assumptions that minorities are homogeneous or the same as whites, that language issues are not important, and that people of color are interested only in certain services and careers. To destroy these myths, more than gestures needs to be done (Neely 2005; Wheeler 2005).

Why not redefine the library profession itself by attacking these institutional barriers, such as by revising admission requirements and fostering mentoring opportunities (Neely 2005; Roy 2005). These approaches could help open doors wider, in order to nurture many different types of relationships that should form in the library school community. Faculty in library schools could create opportunities for students to form communities that nurture cultural competence. These can consist of peer groups, conferences to meet other students, mentorships, service-learning and problem-based learning, and access to social support services on campus, as well as connections to other departments that have more minority groups. These opportunities should continue as minority librarians increasingly move into the public library field. Indirectly, these opportunities can cultivate diverse, significant outcomes for new immigrant patrons. The first thing they do is to sensitize new librarians to what new immigrants want from their libraries.

Focusing on What New Immigrant Communities Want

In 2005, a task force at the Seattle Public Library conducted a study of community outreach projects for various new immigrant communities. It discovered that the personal "attention" that users experienced at the library made them want to return. The task force also found that the library needed to do more promotion, have more translation services, and create more programs in life skills ("bread and butter" programs). It made recommendations for improving innovative services and programming, such as family planning, preschool information, theater, flamenco dancing, and story times in Vietnamese. In addition, the task force learned something important about itself: that outreach needed to be better integrated into the library fabric and that staff needed a sense of "ownership" over it (*Cultural Communities Report*, 2005: 8; Mehdi 2005). Library staff wanted to be involved in the early stages of planning and implementation; they felt that programs should be longer in duration and that child-care activities, regular workshops, homework help in other languages, and better communication about the programs should be offered. These many lessons emerged from an evaluation process (with surveys and interviews) conducted with community partners, library staff, and library users.

The Seattle Public Library intends to use these findings to create future programming that is focused, relevant, and has specific criteria that link them to community needs. Even so, critical questions remain about the quality of the assessments, implementing them, and linking them to outcomes; as Mehdi asks, "How well did we actually assess the communities? How frequently do we need to update them and what does updating look like? Is it just checking into key partners and set directions since we tested? And which communities? What would it take to serve particular groups, and what is their greatest need?" (Mehdi 2005).

Clearly, the library needs a framework to connect fragmented findings to larger outcomes for new immigrant communities. A case must be made that is more than simply asking, "Are we there [at our target] yet?" or "telling the story" of services[3] or—worse—listing narrowly conceived and measured "outputs," while hoping for the best results. In this age of accountability, too often the perception of evaluation as a panacea for library survival can be an overbearing activity, running amok with lots of data, little meaning, and interfering with actual delivery of services. In fact, it can become expensive cosmetic surgery that covers up deeper problems. Moreover, a vicious cycle occurs when rigid criteria determine both programming and outcomes.

You can maintain "promises" to your community by focusing on how the library is contributing to community development and renewal. These aims extend beyond the library's goals of improving services to improving the community as a whole. Such objectives may be articulated in library mission statements and in reports—anecdotes about the effects the library has had on a particular family's livelihood on the quality of a particular neighborhood, or on a particular individual's achievement. Even though outcomes such as these sometimes are hard to capture, they are crucial for making an argument that the library makes a difference—and therefore matters—in the lives of new immigrant communities. This is especially important in an era that has seen institutional support reduced for new immigrant groups. Simply put, the library needs to focus on important outcomes for its communities (Durrance and Fisher 2004). Outcomes are the things that people want and need—psychological, material, and social.

Your library can achieve all three through collaborations with other community organizations and the various resources they contribute. The library community, together with other organizations, must pursue outcomes. But before you decide on your intended outcomes, research what people want and need. Consider social capital categories as a starting place for learning comprehensive types of outcomes.[4] Consider how your library, in working with other community agencies, can increase new immigrants'

- Social network assets (relationships and interactions in neighborhoods). What kinds of networks exist for new immigrants in their neighborhoods and what social supports do they offer?
- Economic opportunity assets (employment, income, assets, debt). What types of job opportunities and career ladders are available to new immigrant communities in their neighborhoods and in the larger community?
- Neighborhood assets (neighborhood political power, resident satisfaction). What kinds of supports do new immigrants have that increase their political power?

• Family assets (adult caregiver assets, caregiver–child relationships, and well-being). What types of familial arrangements do new immigrant communities have that work well?

These assets can connect with other community agencies' agendas, and form the basis not only of missions but also of vision statements, goals, and objectives for libraries and communities (as discussed in Chapter Six). The entire community decides on these and focuses on its roles in improving these assets, to create more empowerment, the largest outcome of all!

One study (Durrance and Fisher 2004: 16) showed how libraries and librarians could help bridge the digital divide and build community. The research team examined services and outcomes for immigrant populations, after-school community technology programs for teens, community networks, information and referral services, ethnic programming, and health information services. The top for participants (discovered through qualitative methods) were attitude changes, increased ability to access information, personal efficacy, increases in skills, gains in learning and knowledge, and changes in social network and status.

In a real-life example of using asset-based inquiry to build positive outcomes for new immigrant communities, the Queens Borough Public Library's programs for new immigrants came to realize that Americanization was not a goal for them. One user said, "I came with my daughter to see a Korean music and dance performance. . . . I want my daughter to appreciate her native culture and this was an excellent opportunity for her to watch and learn" (Durrance and Fisher 2004: 19).

Use the following asset categories to research what people want (see Chapter One), and then to determine the kinds of *positive changes* the library can make in increasing the social capital of new immigrant communities. After you get responses, consider what your library can do by reflecting on:

• The kinds of activities that are needed to make this change
• Who would be affected
• Potential negative and positive effects

The idea to reflect on what kinds of deliberate, long-lasting, and positively received changes the library (with the community) can make.

Finally, when planning outcomes, be specific. For example, the Queens New Americans and Adult Learner Programs focused on *activities* (classes in coping skills, in ESOL small groups), the *people affected* (immigrant adult learners and their families), and both *negative and positive outcomes* (increased self-efficacy in navigating employment opportunities) (Durrance and Fisher 2004). But your outcomes may be more diffuse, scarcely identifiable, as well as hard to quantify. An example might be feeling more assertive or being more outspoken. These important "soft" outcomes need to be documented.

Once the assets, the changes, and the outcomes are known, the library can use these for marketing efforts, accountability, improved services and programs, as well as in resource allocations for the library; such as federal, state, and local grants (Durrance and Fisher 2004: 72). Once this happens, your efforts will have a ripple effect, penetrating the larger community—strengthening community networks, activities, relationships and coordination, capacity building, information sharing, and improved delivery services all over. In essence, your efforts may contribute to a community knowledge reservoir that fosters community renewal and locally based empowerment. But there is more.

An Enduring Identity

Consider what libraries can provide to communities. When they are culturally competent, they provide a *cultural commons*. What does this really mean?

A cultural "commons" means neighborhood revitalization—new immigrants forming social capital and fostering common values and community bonds when they participate in the library and community (McCook 2002: 326). Try to "plant the vision of a library democratically connected to its community" (Buschman 2003: 180). Librarians, like you, can further this value and create an active, reinvigorated citizenry. This vision, however, hinges on bringing new immigrants into the fold because they comprise an important part of this democracy.

Furthermore, it calls for fostering social belonging and creating a dynamic learning community for new immigrants. Taking a culturally responsive, collaborative approach to forming learning communities is essential because

Society is moving from an educational dissemination model to one of access-based, customer-driven needs. . . . This shift represents a move in learning from teacher-centered to learner-centered, and from organization-government and institutional needs to a focus on community-centered needs. (Humes et al. 1995)

Libraries need to protect—and promote—new immigrants' learning communities. This entails moving beyond a "customer-driven" focus and responding to needs that the community may not fully articulate. This means becoming safety nets, advocates, and agents for marginalized communities in society.

Becoming Safety Nets

In the early nineteenth century, librarian Ernestine Rose wrote, "A working woman, a Hungarian, had a sister detained at Ellis Island for some obscure technical reason. The public library was her refuge, for it is the most friendly agency with authority that her advisors could think of" (Rose 1917: 12–13). A century later, a Mexican user stated, "the library is a center for opportunity" (Luevano-Molina 2001: 54). As a public institution, the library is a second home. Visitors experience the personalized focus as care and respect. In this way, the library can foster relationships that are safe and welcoming. How does your library operate as a safety net for new immigrant communities?

Becoming an Agent for Marginalized Voices and Perspectives

Due to the disenfranchisement, segregation, and displacement of many new immigrants and communities of color, libraries must embrace their cultural citizenship roles of being culturally responsive and integrative and also of promoting social citizenship.[5] Social citizenship means the building and rebuilding of public institutions (health, education, and social services) so that its constituency can receive the various benefits of a democracy. This is especially important for reducing social exclusion and social distances between different economic groups in this country.

For example, although schools have become increasingly more segregated by race, ethnicity, and social class, there is a growing belief among the public, especially young adults, that desegregation has positive effects for everyone and that the federal government should ensure that integration occurs (Kozol 2005). Your public library can be a part of this effort. Social citizenship builds on the community discussion of the role of libraries and supports people in raising their awareness of social, political, and economic issues. Such discussion and exchange mean that libraries enhance democracy through fulfilling their public roles

(McCook 1997, 2002). It is also an opportunity for those who work in libraries to reflect on their own cultures and bring them into the community's discussions. These educative discussions can be extended to other public institutions, to create an advocacy network and, ultimately, social change.

How can you help make it happen? As a practitioner, get actively involved in creating and participating in local coalitions and consortiums with other community-based agencies and grassroots organizations. As an advocate, enter the political arena—of which you are already a part—to advocate with and for new immigrant communities, in local, state, national, and international policy making and legislating. This may require a complete revamping of your role, relationships, commitments, and interests, as well as for others involved in revolutionizing this culture.

"I Just Want to Be a Librarian!"

You may think, "I'm a librarian, *not* a politician!" Yet as you broaden your identity, you may think about yourself and your newfound knowledge in more complex ways, rather than in dichotomous terms: politician/librarian. In order to do your job better, you need to answer to the larger social forces in society that influence roles and relationships with those around you. You cannot stick your head in the ground and ignore the issues. You may also retort with: "But I don't get involved in politics—that's just not *me*." Again, find a way to get involved in the wider world in meaningful ways that motivates your very being, invigorates you, and builds on your strengths. Consider your unique contribution and build on this!

Education is key, for as Paolo Freire, through his partner and wife, Ana Maria Arujo, in *Pedagogy of Indignation*, wrote in 2004, "Education makes sense because women and men learn that through learning they can make and remake themselves, because women and men are able to take responsibility for themselves as beings capable of knowing. . . . Education makes sense because in order to be, women and men must keep on being" (Freire 2004: 15).

The library has been, and hopefully will always be, an important community-based sponsor for new immigrant communities. In turn, new immigrant communities will support libraries. Yet this can happen only when libraries are seen as culturally responsive community centers, interconnected with other community-based institutions, and as advocates that make immigrants feel they are "not alone."

ENDNOTES

1. See the following for information on adapting to "small worlds": Aguirre 2001: 76; Victoria A. Pendleton and Elfreda A. Chatman, "Small World Lives: Implications for the Public Library," *Library Trends* 46 (Spring 1988): 732–52; see also Robertson 2005: 7.

2. This is drawn from the University of Washington project on information literacy, see Mike Eisenberg, "Information Literacy and Social Action: Information Literacy for Students of Families in Transition" (Seattle: The Information School of the University of Washington, 2001) at http://www.ischool.washington.edu/lbruce/courses/Lectures/Social%20impactmaster.ppt.

3. Douglas Zweizig and others, *The Tell It! Manual: The Complete Program for Evaluating Library Performance* (Chicago: American Library Association, 1996); Douglas Zweizig, Debrah Wilcox-Johnson, and Jane Robbins, *Evaluation of Adult Library Literacy Programs: A Manual of Approaches and Procedures* (Madison: University of Wisconsin–Madison, School of Library and Information Studies, 1989).

4. See Durrance and Fisher 2004. See also Chapter One for community asset mapping.

5. Sparks 2001/2002; Kozol 2005; Aguirre 2001; Gloria Ladson-Billings, "Differing Concepts of Citizenship: Schools and Communities as Sites of Civic Development," in *Educating Citizens for Global Awareness* edited by Nel Noddings (New York: Teachers College Press, 2005).

Selected Bibliography

Abboud, Leila. "Public Libraries Court Immigrants and Thrive." Columbia News Service, May 8, 2002. Downloaded from the web on January 31, 2007. http://www.jrn.columbia.edu/studentwork/cns/2002-05-08/596.asp.

Adkins, Denice. "Quantitative Measures of Outreach Effectiveness." In *From Outreach to Equity: Innovative Models of Library Policy and Practice*, edited by Robin Osborne and Carla D. Hayden, 114–15. Chicago: American Library Association Office for Literacy and Outreach Services, 2004.

Adkins, M., D. Birman, and B. Sample. *Cultural Adjustment, Mental Health, and ESL*. Denver, CO: Spring Institute for International Studies, 1999.

Aguirre, Joan K. "'Passport to Promise': Public Libraries as Intellectual Spaces for Immigrant Students." In *Immigrant Politics and the Public Library* (Contributions in Librarianship and Information Science, No. 97), edited by Susan Luevano-Molina. Westport, CT: Greenwood Press, 2001.

Alfred, Mary. "Immigrants in America: Who Are They and Why Do They Come?" *Adult Learning* 12, no. 4 (Fall 2001/2002): 2–5.

Alire, Camila A., and Orlando Archibeque. *Serving Latino Communities: A How-to-Do-It Manual for Librarians*. New York: Neal-Schuman Publishers, 1998.

Allison, Michael, and Jude Kaye. *Strategic Planning for Nonprofit Organizations*. New York: John Wiley, 1997.

Alpi, Kristine, Jane Fisher, and Patricia Gallagher. "New York Online Access to Health (NOAH): New York Public Libraries Partner to Provide Quality Consumer Health Information in English and Spanish." In *Bridging Cultures: Ethnic Services in the Libraries of New York State*, edited by Irina A. Kuharets, B. A. Cahalan, and F. J. Gitner, 170–75. Albany, NY: New York Library Association Ethnic Services Roundtable, 2001.

American Libraries 26 (December 1995): 113–19. "12 Ways Libraries Are Good for the Country." Adapted, 2000.

American Libraries 28, no. 5 (May 1997). "To Read, to Write, to Understand."

American Library Association. "Libraries: An American Value." Chicago: American Library Association, 1999. Downloaded from the web on February 1, 2007. http://www.ala.org/ala/oif/statementspols/americanvalue/librariesamerican. htm.

American Library Association Office of Literacy Outreach. *Meeting Minutes 2004. Immigration and ESOL.* Downloaded from the web on February 1, 2007. http:// www.ala.org/ala/olos/aboutolos/commonliteracy/literacycteminutesmw04. htm.

Antin, Mary. *The Promised Land*, 2nd ed. [First Edition 1912]. Boston: Houghton Mifflin, 1969.

Anzaldua, Gloria, ed. *Making Face, Making Soul/Haciendo Caras: Creative and Critical Perspectives by Women of Color.* San Francisco: Aunt Lute Foundation Books, 1990.

Anzaldua, Gloria. "Tlilli, Tlapalli": The Path of the Red and Black Ink." In *Multicultural Literacy*, edited by R. Simmons and S. Walker, 29–40. St. Paul, MN: Greywolf Press, 1988.

Anzaldua, Gloria. *Borderlands/La Frontera: The New Mestiza.* San Francisco: Aunt Lute Foundation Books, 1987.

Arnold, John J. "Americanization and Libraries." *Illinois Libraries* (April 1919): 15–19.

Associated Press. "Hispanics Now One Seventh of U.S. Population." *MSNBC.* June 10, 2005. Downloaded from the web on February 1, 2007. http://www. msnbc.msn.com/id/8147476.

Bacon, David. "Communities Without Borders." *The Nation* (October 24, 2005): 15–22.

Banks, James, and Cherry Banks, eds. *Multicultural Education: Issues and Perspectives*, 5th ed. New York: John Wiley, 2004.

Barlow, Harriet, Karen Hering, and Stacy Mitchell. "Libraries, Liberty and the Pursuit of Public Information." *The Journal of the New Rules Project* (Winter 2001). Downloaded from the web February 1, 2007. http://www.newrules.org.

Barndt, Deborah. *Naming the Moment - Political Analysis for Action: A Manual for Community Groups.* Toronto: Jesuit Centre for Social Faith and Justice, 1989.

Barnett, Andy. *Libraries, Community, and Technology.* Jefferson, NC: McFarland, 2002.

Baumgartner, Lisa, and Sharan Merriam. *Multicultural Stories.* San Francisco: Jossey-Bass, 2000.

Beacon Hill News. "America's Migrant Workers" (October 26, 2005a). [From the Department of Labor's National Agricultural Workers' Survey, 2000].

Beacon Hill News. "Sowing the Seeds of a Political Movement" (November 16, 2005b).

Beaulieu, L. *Mapping the Assets of Your Community: A Key Component for Building a Local Capacity.* SRDC Series #227. Mississippi State, MS: Southern Rural Development Center, 2002.

Beck, N. R. "The Use of Library and Educational Facilities by Russian-Jewish Immigrants in New York City, 1880–1914: The Impact of Culture." In *The Quest for Social Justice II: The Morris Fromkin Memorial Lectures, 1981–1990*, edited by R. Aderman. Milwaukee: University of Wisconsin–Milwaukee, Golda Meier Library, 1992.

Bell, Melissa T. *Educating Immigrants—Trends and Alerts: Critical Information for State Decision-Makers.* Lexington, KY: The Council of State Governments, 2004.

Benton Foundation. *Buildings, Books, and Bytes: Libraries and Communities in the Digital Age.* Washington, D.C.: Benton Foundation, 1996. [Online version downloaded from the web on February 1, 2007]. http://www.benton.org/publibrary/kellogg/buildings.html.

Berelson, Bernard. *The Library's Public: A Report of the Public Library Inquiry.* New York: Columbia University Press, 1949.

Berger, Monica. *An Annotated Guide to Internet Resources on Immigration and Immigrants.* Downloaded from the web on February 1, 2007. http://home.earthlink.net/~monicaberger/immigration.html.

Bernstein, Nina. "Decline Is Seen in Immigration." *New York Times* (September 2005): A1–C22.

Betancourt, Ingrid, and Ina Rimpau. "The Multilingual Materials Acquisition Center." In *From Outreach to Equity: Innovative Models of Library Policy and Practice*, edited by Robin Osborne and Carla D. Hayden. Chicago: American Library Association Office for Outreach and Literacy, 2004.

Birge, L. E. *Serving Adult Learners.* Chicago: American Library Association, 1981.

Bischoff, Henry. *Immigration Issues.* Westport, CT: Greenwood Press, 2001.

Bledsoe, L. *Working Parts.* Seattle, WA: Seal Press, 1997.

Bose, Anu. "Online Activism for Women's Rights and Civic Participation." *Visible Minority Women and ICTs–MOIVMWC. Fact Sheets.* Downloaded from the web on February 1, 2007. http://womynsvoices.ca/en/node/98.

Brandt, Deborah. *Literacy in American Lives.* New York: Cambridge University Press, 2001.

Brown, Natalie. *Serving Diverse Communities: Findings from Four North American Public Libraries.* Margaret Ramsey Scholarship Report: 2. Service Development, City of Greater Dandenong Libraries, 2002.

Burge, E. "Adult Learners, Learning, and Public Libraries." *Library Trends* 31, no. 4 (1983).

Buschman, John. *Dismantling the Public Sphere: Situating and Sustaining Librarianship in the Age of the New Public Philosophy.* Westport, CT: Libraries Unlimited, 2003.

Buschman, John, and Michael Carbone. "A Critical Inquiry into Librarianship: Applications of the New Sociology of Education." *Library Quarterly* 61 (1991): 15–30.

Cahalan, Brigid A. "Connecting with the Khmer Community." In *Bridging Cultures: Ethnic Services in the Libraries of New York State*, edited by Irina A. Kuharets, B. A. Cahalan, and F. J. Gitner, 136–41. Albany: New York Library Association Ethnic Services Roundtable, 2001.

Callahan, Anna. *Danville Community Encyclopedia*. 2003. Downloaded from the web on February 1, 2007. http://www.anna-callahan.com.

Carlson, David B., Arabella Martinez, Sarah A. Curtis, Janet Coles, and Nicholas Valenzuela. *Adrift in a Sea of Change: California's Public Libraries Struggle to Meet the Information Needs of Multicultural Communities*. Sacramento: Center for Policy Development and the California State Library Foundation, 1990.

Carr, David. "Adult Learning and Library Helping." *Library Trends* 31, no. 4 (1983): 569–81.

Carr, John F. "The Library in Americanization Work." *Illinois Libraries* (October 1919): 60–61.

Carter, Jeff, and Judy Titzel. *Technology in Today's ABE Classroom*. Boston: World Education, July 2003.

Carton, Debbie Y. *Public Libraries and Cultural Diversity*. ERIC Digest. ED358871. Syracuse, NY: ERIC Clearinghouse on Information Resources, 1993.

Center for Immigration Studies on Assimilation, and Citizenship. Downloaded from the web on February 1, 2007. http://www.cis.org/topics/assimilation.html.

The Change Agent. Adult Education for Social Justice: News, Issues, and Ideas. Focus on Immigration 11 (September 2000); 15 (September 2002); 16 (March 2003).

Chatman, Elfreda. "Field Research: Methodological Themes." *Library and Information Science Research* 6 (1984): 425–38.

Ching Louie, Miriam, and Linda Burnham. *Women's Education in the Global Economy (WEDGE)*. Oakland, CA: Women of Color Resource Center, 2000.

Cho, Eunice H., Francisco Argüelles Paz a Puente, Miriam Ching Yoon Louie, and Sasha Khokha. *BRIDGE: Building a Race and Immigration Dialogue in the Global Economy—A Popular Education Resource for Immigrant and Refugee Community Organizers*. Berkeley: National Network for Immigrant and Refugee Rights, 2004.

Clarren, Rebecca. "The Green Motel." *Ms. Magazine* (September 29, 2005). Downloaded from the web on February 1, 2007. http://www.msmagazine.com/summer2005/greenmotel.asp.

Coalter, Fred. *Releasing the Potential of Cultural Services: The Case for Libraries*. Research Briefing. Edinburgh, Scotland: University of Edinburgh, Scotland, November 2001.

Cogell, Raquell, and Cindy A. Gruwell. *Diversity in Libraries: Academic Residency*. Westport, CT: Greenwood Press, 2001.

Cohen, David. "Recent Developments in Queens the Global Village: Forecasting the Future." In *Bridging Cultures: Ethnic Services in the Libraries of New York State*, edited by Irina A. Kuharets, B. A. Cahalan, and F. J. Gitner, 176–77. Albany: New York Library Association Ethnic Services Roundtable, 2001.

Coleman, Jean E. "The Social Responsibilties of Librarians Toward Literacy Education." In *Social Responsibilities of Librarians*, edited by Patricia Schuman. New York: Bowker, 1983.

Comings, John, Steve Reder, and Andrew Sum. *Building a Level Playing Field.* NCSALL Occasional paper. Cambridge: National Center for the Study of Adult Learning and Literacy, Harvard Graduate School of Education, December 2001.

Comings, John, Andrew Sum, and Johannes Uvin. *New Skills for a New Economy: Adult Education's Key Role in Sustaining Economic Growth.* Boston: Mass Inc., 2000.

Community Asset Mapping with Rural Schools and Communities. http://www. ael.org/rel/rural/pdf/mapping.pdf [EDVANTA site now].

Constantino, Rebecca, ed. *Literacy, Access, and Libraries Among the Language Minority Population.* London: Scarecrow Press, 1988.

Cook, Wanda D. *Adult Literacy Education in the United States.* Newark, NJ: International Reading Association, 1977.

Corona Research. *Denver Public Library Focus Group Findings.* Report. Denver, CO: Prepared for the Denver Public Library by Corona Research, Inc., April 1, 2005.

Cuban, Larry, and Heather Kirkpatrick. "Computers Make Kids Smarter, Right?" *Technos* 7, no. 2 (Summer 1998), 26–31.

Cuban, Sondra. "'So Lucky to Be Like That': Two Case Studies of Women Learners Persisting in a Hawai'i Literacy Program." *Adult Basic Education* (March 2003): 19–43.

Cuban, Sondra. *"Before Days": Women in a Library Literacy Program in Hilo, Hawai'i Talk Story.* Unpublished dissertation, University of Wisconsin–Madison, 1999.

Cuesta, Yolanda. Personal communication, October 17, 2005.

Cuesta, Yolanda. "Developing Outreach Skills in Library Staff." In *From Outreach to Equity: Innovative Models of Library Policy and Practice*, edited by Robin Osborne and Carla D. Hayden, 112–13. Chicago: American Library Association Office for Literacy and Outreach Services, 2004.

Cumming, A. "Access to Literacy for Language Minority Adults." ERIC Digest. ED350886. Columbus, OH: ERIC, 1992.

Dain, Phyllis. "Ambivalence and Paradox: The Social Bonds of the Public Library." *Library Journal* 100 (1975): 261–66.

D'Elia, George. *The Roles of the Public Library in Society. The Results of the National Survey. Final Report.* Evanston, IL: Urban Libraries Council, 1993.

D'Elia, George, and Eleanor Jo Rodger. "The Roles of the Public Library in the Community: The Results of a Gallup Poll of Community Opinion Leaders." *Public Libraries* 34 (March–April 1995): 94–101.

Denver Public Library. *Valdez-Perry Branch. A Community Analysis: Recommendations.* Downloaded from the web on February 1, 2007. http://skyways.lib. ks.us/pathway/ca_report.html.

Dervin, Brenda. "Communication Gaps and Inequities: Moving Toward a Reconceptualization." In *Progress in Communication Sciences*, edited by B. Dervin. Norwood, NJ: Ablex, 1980.

Dervin, Brenda. *Communicating with, Not to, the Urban Poor.* Columbus, OH: ERIC, 1977.

Dewdney, Patricia, and Roma Harris. "Community Information Needs: The Case of Wife Assault." *Library and Information Science Research* 14 (1992): 5–29.

Dodge, Christopher. "Knowledge for Sale: Are America's Public Libraries on the Verge of Losing Their Way?" *Utne Reader* (July/August 2005). [Online version downloaded from the web on February 1, 2007]. http://www.utne.com/pub/2005_130/promo/11706-1.html.

Drago-Severson, E., et al. "The Power of a Cohort and of Collaborative Groups." *Focus on Basics* 5 B (2001): 15–22.

Du Mont, Rosemary. *Reform and Reaction: The Big City Public Library in American Life.* Westport, CT: Greenwood Press, 1977.

Durrance, Joan. "Community Information Services—An Innovation at the Beginning of Its Second Decade." In *Advances in Librarianship* 13 (1984): 119–27.

Durrance, Joan, and Karen Fisher. *How Libraries and Librarians Help: A Guide to Identifying User-Based Outcomes.* Chicago: American Library Association, 2004.

Edelman, M. "The Political Language of the Helping Professions." *Politics and Society* 4 (1974): 295–310.

Eisenberg, Mike. *Information Literacy and Social Action: Information Literacy for Students of Families in Transition.* Seattle, WA: Information School of the University of Washington, 2001.

Ellingson, Jo Ann. "21st Century Literacy: Libraries Must Lead." *American Libraries* 29, no. 11 (December 1998): 52–53.

Elturk, Ghada. "Diversity and Cultural Competency." *Colorado Libraries* (December 1, 2003). Posted on Webjunction, June 1, 2004. Downloaded from web on December 5, 2005. http://webjunction.org/do/DisplayContent; jsessionid=425CD830E30AE7D1B27989EA544AA2CA?id=1525.

Escatiola, Evelyn. "Anti-Immigrant Literature: A Selected Bibliography." In *Immigrant Politics and the Public Library* (Contributions in Librarianship and Information Science, No. 97) edited by Susan Luevano-Molina, 161–82. Westport, CT: Greenwood Press, 2001.

Essman, Elliot. *Life in the USA, 2005.* Downloaded from web on Feburary 1, 2007. http://www.lifeintheusa.com/index.html.

Estabrook, Leigh, and Edward Lakner. *Literacy Programs for Adults in Public Libraries: A Survey Report.* Prepared for the LWRD. Champaign, IL: The Library Research Center, Graduate School of Library and Information Science, University of Illinois, 2000.

Fain, Elaine. "Books for New Citizens: Public Libraries and Americanization Programs, 1900–1925." In *The Quest for Social Justice II: The Morris Fromkin*

Memorial Lectures, 1981–1990, edited by R. Aderman. Milwaukee, WI: Golda Meier Library, University of Wisconsin–Milwaukee, 1992.

Feagin, J. R. *Racist America: Roots, Current Realities, and Future Reparations.* New York: Routledge, 2005.

Fingeret, Hannah, and C. Drennon. *Literacy for Life: Adult Learners, New Practices.* New York: Teachers College Press, 1997.

Fitzpatrick, Mary. "Library Services for Immigrants." Paper. Downloaded from the web on February 1, 2007. http://www.pages.drexel.edu/~mf34/Rol.htm.

Foerstel, Herbert. "Secrecy in Science, Panel II, Remarks." Speech delivered at MIT, Cambridge, MA, March 29, 1999.

Freire, Paolo. *Pedagogy of Indignation.* Boulder, CO: Paradigm Publishers, 2004.

Freire, Paolo. *Literacy: Reading the Word and the World.* South Hadley, MA: Bergin, 1987.

Gans, Herbert J. "The American Kaleidoscope, Then and Now." In *Reinventing the Melting Pot: The New Immigrants and What It Means to Be American*, edited by Tamar Jacoby, 33–46. New York: Basic Books, 2004.

Garrison, Dee. *Apostles of Culture: The Public Librarian and American Society, 1876–1920.* New York: Free Press, 1979.

Gee, James. *What Video Games Have to Teach Us About Learning and Literacy.* New York: Macmillan, 2003.

Gillespie, Marilyn. *Native Language Literacy Instruction for Adults. Patterns, Issues and Promises.* Washington, D.C.: Center for Applied Linguistics, 1994.

Giroux, Henry. *Border Crossings: Cultural Workers and the Politics of Education.* New York: Routledge, 1992.

Gitner, Fred J., and Wai Sze Chan. "Community Analysis for the Twenty-First Century: The New Americans Program Model." In *Bridging Cultures: Ethnic Services in the Libraries of New York State*, edited by Irina A. Kuharets, B. A. Cahalan, and F. J. Gitner, 122–30. Albany: New York Library Association Ethnic Services Roundtable, 2001.

Glazer, Nathan. "Assimilation Today: Is One Identity Enough?" In *Reinventing the Melting Pot: The New Immigrants and What It Means to Be American*, edited by Tamar Jacoby, 61–74. New York: Basic Books, 2004.

Godin, Joanne. *A World of Information: Creating Multicultural Collections and Programs in Canadian Public Libraries.* Ottawa: National Library of Canada, 1994.

Gollop, Claudia J. "Health Information-Seeking Behavior and Older African–American Women." *Bulletin of the Medical Library Association* 85, no. 2 (1997): 141–46.

Gordon, Andrew. *Toward Equality of Access: The Role of Public Libraries in Addressing the Digital Divide.* Seattle: Gates Foundation, 2004.

Gottfried, Harriet. "'I Lift My Lamp': The New York Public Library Serves Immigrants." In *Bridging Cultures: Ethnic Services in the Libraries of New York State,* edited by Irina A. Kuharets, B. A. Cahalan, and F. J. Gitner, 145–51. Albany: New York Library Association Ethnic Services Roundtable, 2001.

Gray, William S., and R. Munroe. *The Reading Interests and Habits of Adults.* New York: Macmillan, 1929.

Greene, Linda S. "Learning by Doing: Outreach Training in a Branch Library." In *From Outreach to Equity: Innovative Models of Library Policy and Practice,* edited by Robin Osborne and Carla D. Hayden, 123–24. Chicago: American Library Association Office for Literacy and Outreach Services, 2004.

Greenlee, Gale. Personal communication, November 9, 2005.

Greenlee, Gale. "The Middle of Everywhere." Libraryjournal.com (March 15, 2004). Downloaded from the web on February 1, 2007. http://www.library journal.com/article/CA385868.html.

Gunselman, Cheryl. "'Illumino' for All: Opening the Library Association of Portland to the Public, 1900–1903." *Libraries and Culture* 36, no. 3 (Summer 2001): 432–64.

Gupta, Kavita. *A Practical Guide to Needs Assessment.* San Francisco: Jossey-Bass/Pfeiffer, 1999.

Hall, Tracie. Personal communication, June 8, 2005.

Hannah, P. *People Make It Happen.* Metuchen NJ: Scarecrow Press, 1978.

Harris, Michael. "State, Class and Cultural Reproduction: Toward a Theory of Library Service in the United States." In *Advances in Librarianship* 14 (1986): 211–52.

Harris, Michael. "The Purpose of the American Public Library: A Revisionist Interpretation of History." *Library Journal* 98 (September 1973): 2509–14.

Hayes, Elisabeth. "Women, Videogaming, and Learning: Beyond the Stereotypes." *Techtrends,* forthcoming.

Hernstein, R. J., and C. Murray. *The Bell Curve: Intelligence and Class Structure in American Life.* New York: The Free Press, 1994.

Humes, Barbara A., and others. *Public Libraries and Community-Based Education: Making the Connection for Lifelong Learning.* Vol. 1. Proceedings of a Conference Sponsored by the National Institute on Postsecondary Education, Libraries, and Lifelong Learning. Washington, D.C., April 12–13, 1995.

Isserlis, Janet. "Trauma and the Adult English Language Learner." ERIC Digest. ED444397. Columbus, OH: ERIC, 2000.

Jacobs, Deborah. Personal communication, December 5, 2004.

Jacoby, Tamar. "Defining Assimilation for the 21st Century: The New Immigrants, a Progress Report." In *Reinventing the Melting Pot: The New Immigrants and What It Means to Be American,* edited by Tamar Jacoby. New York: Basic Books, 2004a.

Jacoby, Tamar. "What It Means to Be American in the 21st Century." In *Reinventing the Melting Pot: The New Immigrants and What It Means to Be American,* edited by Tamar Jacoby, 3–32. New York: Basic Books, 2004b.

Jeng, Ling H. "Some Basic Issues of Diversity: A Contextual Inquiry." In *Immigrant Politics and the Public Library* (Contributions in Librarianship and Information Science, No. 97), edited by Susan Luevano-Molina, 151–60. Westport CT: Greenwood Press, 2001.

Jensen, Robert. "The Myth of the Neutral Librarian." *Progressive Librarian* 24 (Winter 2004). Downloaded from the web on February 1, 2007. http://www.libr.org/PL/24_Jensen.html.

Jones, DeEtta. "Evolving Issues: Racism, Affirmative Action, and Diversity." In *Unfinished Business: Race, Equity, and Diversity in Library and Information Science Education*, edited by Maurice B. Wheeler, 43–55. Lanham, MD: Scarecrow Press, 2005.

Jones, Plummer A. *Still Struggling for Equality: American Public Library Services with Minorities*. Westport, CT: Libraries Unlimited, 2004.

Jones, Plummer A. *Libraries, Immigrants, and the American Experience*. Westport, CT: Greenwood Press, 1999.

Jones, Plummer. *American Public Library Service to the Immigrant Community, 1876–1948*. Unpublished doctoral dissertation, University of North Carolina, Chapel Hill, NC, 1991.

Kao, Bernice. "Training Staff for Job Service Outreach." In *From Outreach to Equity: Innovative Models of Library Policy and Practice*, edited by Robin Osborne and Carla D. Hayden, 118–19. Chicago: American Library Association Office for Outreach and Literacy, 2004.

Karetsky, Stephen. *Reading Research and Librarianship: A History and Analysis*. Westport, CT: Greenwood Press, 1982.

Karp, Jane. "Library Elderly Outreach Project." In *From Outreach to Equity: Innovative Models of Library Policy and Practice*, edited by Robin Osborne and Carla D. Hayden, 7–8. Chicago: American Library Association Office for Literacy and Outreach Services, 2004.

Kerka, Sandra. "Community Asset Mapping." *Trends and Issues Alert No. 47*. ERIC Educational Resources Information Center. Columbus, OH: Clearinghouse on Adult Career and Vocational Education (ACVE), 2003a.

Kerka, Sandra. "Intergenerational Learning and Social Capital." Educational Resources Information Center. ERIC Digest No. 244. Columbus, OH: Clearinghouse on Adult Career and Vocational Education, 2003b.

Knowles, Malcolm. "The Future Role of Libraries in Adult Education." *The Southeastern Librarian* 12 (1975): 43–46.

Knox, Alan. "Counseling and Information Needs of Adult Learners." *Library Trends* (Spring 1983), 555–67.

Knuth, Rebecca. "Family Literacy: A Critical Role for Libraries Worldwide." In *Libraries: Global Reach–Local Touch*, edited by Kathleen de la Peña McCook, Barbara J. Ford, and Kate Lippincott, 219–33. Chicago: American Library Association, 1998.

Kozol, Jonathan. "Overcoming Apartheid." *The Nation* 281, no. 21 (December 19, 2005): 26–30.

Kretzmann, J., and S. Rans. *The Engaged Library*. Evanston, IL: Urban Libraries Council, 2005.

Kristi, Carol. "Library, City Help Immigrants." *American Libraries* 28, no.10 (1997): 23.

Kuharets, Irina A. "Serving the Russian Readership Going Beyond the Facts." In *Bridging Cultures: Ethnic Services in the Libraries of New York State*, edited by Irina A. Kuharets, B. A. Cahalan, and F. J. Gitner, 179–87. Albany: New York Library Association Ethnic Services Roundtable, 2001.

Kulthau, Carol. "Inside the Search Process: Information-Seeking from the User's Perspective." *Journal of the American Society for Information Science* 42, no. 5 (1991): 361–71.

Larsen, Jens, Deborah Jacobs, and Ton van Vlimmeren. *Cultural Diversity: How Public Libraries Can Serve the Diversity in the Community*. Gütersloh: Bertelsmann Stiftung Gütersloh, 2004.

Larsen, Jens, Deborah Jacobs, and Ton van Vlimmeren. "Cultural Diversity: How Public Libraries Can Serve the Diversity in the Community." Paper presented at ALIA 2004, Challenging Ideas. December 2003. Retrieved on January 31, 2007 from http://conferences.alia.org.au/alia2004/pdfs/vlimmeren.t. paper.pdf.

Lawson, Rhea B. "Outreach Inside the Library." In *From Outreach to Equity: Innovative Models of Library Policy and Practice*, edited by Robin Osborne and Carla D. Hayden, 27–29. Chicago: American Library Association Office for Literacy and Outreach Services, 2004.

Lee, Ming-Yeh, and Vanessa Sheared. "Socialization and Immigrant Students' Learning in Adult Education Programs." In *Learning and Sociocultural Contexts: Implications for Adults, Community, and Workplace Education: New Directions for Adult and Continuing Education*, No. 96, edited by Mary Alfred, 27–36. New York: John Wiley, 2003.

Levinson, D., and M. Ember. (Eds.). *American Immigrant Cultures*. New York: MacMillan, 1997.

Lewelling, Vickie W. "English-Plus." ED350884. Washington, D.C.: ERIC Clearinghouse on Languages and Linguistics, 1992.

Lieschoff, S. C. *Practitioner Toolkit: Working with Adult English Language Learners*. Washington, D.C.: National Center for ESL Literacy Education at the Center for Applied Linguistics. U.S. Department of Education, Office of Vocational and Adult Education, December 2004.

Lipsman, Claire K. *The Disadvantaged and Library Effectiveness*. Chicago: American Library Association, 1972.

Lo, Carol. "Got the Homework Blues? Our Libraries Have Great, Free Help." *Beacon Hill News: South District Journal* (November 30, 2005): 6.

Lobo, Arun P., and Joseph J. Salvo. *The Newest New Yorkers 2000. Briefing Booklet. Immigrant New York in the New Millenium*. New York: New York Department of City Planning, Population Division, 2004.

Lovell, George. *Human Rights in Changing Contexts*. University of Washington Fall Lecture series, October 18, 2005.

Luevano-Molina, Susan. "Introduction: New Immigrants, Neo-Nativism, and the Public Library." In *Immigrant Politics and the Public Library* (Contributions in Librarianship and Information Science, No. 97), edited by Susan Luevano-Molina, 1–13. Westport, CT: Greenwood Press, 2001.

Luttrell, Wendy. "Taking Care of Literacy: One Feminist's Critique." *Educational Policy* 10, no. 3 (1996): 342–65.

Lyman, Helen. *Library Materials in Service to the Adult New Reader.* Chicago: American Library Association, 1973.

Lyman, Helen. *Literacy and the Nation's Libraries.* Chicago: American Library Association, 1977a.

Lyman, Helen. *Reading and the Adult New Reader.* Chicago: American Library Association, 1977b.

MacDonald, Barbara A., and Patricia A. Scollay. "The Focus on Family in Adult Literacy Improvement." American Education Research Association, New Orleans, LA, April 1–6, 2002.

Mager, Robert F. *Making Instruction Work.* Belmont, CA: Lake Publishing, 1988.

Malone, Margaret E., Benjamin Rifkin, Donna Christian, and Dora E. Johnson. "Attaining High Levels of Proficiency: Challenges for Foreign Language Education in the United States." Digest based on a paper presented at the Conference on Global Challenges and U.S. Higher Education. Duke University (January 23–25, 2003) and the Center for Applied Linguistics, 2005.

Manglitz, E., J. Johnson-Bailey, and R. Cervero. "Struggles of Hope: How White Adult Educators Challenge Racism." *Teachers College Record* 107, no. 6 (June 2005): 1245–74.

Marshall, John D. *Place of Learning, Place of Dreams: A History of the Seattle Public Library.* Seattle: Seattle Public Library Foundation and the University of Washington Press, 2004.

Martin, L. *Baltimore Reaches Out.* Baltimore: Enoch Pratt Free Library, 1967.

Martinez, R. *The New Americans.* New York: New Press, 2004.

McCook, Kathleen de la Peña. Personal communication, August 9, 2005.

McCook, Kathleen de la Peña. "Rocks in the whirlpool: Equity of access and the American Library Association." Commissioned for the American Library Association, Chicago. "Key Action Area: Equity of Access," 2002. Retrieved from the web on January 31, 2007. http://www.ala.org/ala/ourassociation/governingdocs/keyactionareas/equityaction/rockswhirlpool.htm.

McCook, Kathleen de la Peña. "Introduction." *Library Trends* 49, no. 1 (2000a): 1–5.

McCook, Kathleen de la Peña. *A Place at the Table: Participating in Community Building.* Chicago: American Library Association, 2000b.

McCook, Kathleen de la Peña. "Librarians as Culture Keepers and Information Providers." In *Libraries: Global Reach—Local Touch,* edited by Kathleen de la Peña McCook, Barbara J. Ford, and Kate Lippincott, 1–5. Chicago: American Library Association, 1998.

McCook, Kathleen de la Peña. "The Search for New Metaphors—Buildings, Books, and Bytes: Perspectives on the Benton Foundation Report on Libraries in the Digital Age." *Library Trends* 46, no. 1 (Summer 1997). Downloaded from the web on February 1, 2007. http://www.findarticles.com/p/articles/mi_m1387/is_n1_v46/ai_19969812.

McCook, Kathleen de la Peña, and Peggy Barber. "Public Policy as a Factor Influencing Adult Lifelong Learning, Adult Literacy and Public Libraries." Background Paper for USF Seminar in Adult Lifelong Learning and Literacy, Summer 2001. Downloaded from the web on February 1, 2007. http://www.cas.usf.edu/lis/literacy.htm.

McCook, Kathleen de la Peña, and Paula Geist. "Diversity Deferred: Where Are the Minority Librarians?" *Library Journal* 18 (November 1, 1993): 1–3.

McDonald, Barbara. *Literacy Activities in Public Libraries: A Report of the Study of Services to Adults.* Chicago: American Library Association, 1966.

McGinnis, Leslie. "A Place in the World: Building a Learner-Centered Participatory Literacy Program." In *Literacy and Libraries: Learning from Case Studies,* edited by GraceAnne A. DeCandido, 16–29. Chicago: American Library Association Office of Literacy and Outreach Services, 2001.

McKnight, John, and John Kretzmann. *Building Communities from the Inside Out: A Path Toward Finding and Mobilizing a Community's Assets.* Evanston, IL: Institute for Policy Research, Northwestern University, 1993.

McLean, S. "Sisterfriends @ Your Library: Marketing and Building Support for Programs." In *From Outreach to Equity: Innovative Models of Library Policy and Practice,* edited by Robin Osborne and Carla D. Hayden, 94–95. Chicago: American Library Association Office for Literacy and Outreach Services, 2004.

McMurrer, Eileen, and Lynda Terrill. "Library Literacy Programs for English Language Learners." ERIC Digest. ED459629. Washington, D.C.: National Clearinghouse for ESL Literacy Education, 2001.

Meadows, Jan. "Services Outside Library Walls." In *From Outreach to Equity: Innovative Models of Library Policy and Practice,* edited by Robin Osborne and Carla D. Hayden, 1–6. Chicago: American Library Association Office for Literacy and Outreach Services, 2004.

Mehdi, Yazmin. Personal communication, October 27, 2005.

Melcher, John, Joanne Keith, Marsha McDowell, and Penny Foster-Fishman. *Best Practice Briefs.* Outreach Partnerships at Michigan State University. No. 4, 1998.

MetLife Foundation *Reading America* Program. "The Somali Family Part Two." Presentation of an Intergenerational Book and Film Discussion, sponsored by the Libraries for the Future, 2004.

Metoyer-Duran, Cheryl. "Cross-Cultural Research in Ethnolinguistic Communities: Methodological Considerations." *Public Libraries* (January/February 1993a): 18–25.

Metoyer-Duran, Cheryl. *Gatekeepers in Ethnolinguistic Communities.* Norwood, NJ: Ablex, 1993b.

Middle American News. "American Libraries Foreignized to Help Aliens." Downloaded from the web on February 1, 2007. http://www.manews.org/10libraries.html.

Milam, Daniel. *Public Library Services to New Americans: Speeding Transitions to Learning, Work and Life in the U.S.* Evanston, IL: Urban Libraries Council, 2003.

Mitchell, B. M., and R. E. Salsbury. *Encyclopedia of Multicultural Education.* Westport, CT: Greenwood Press, 1999.

Monroe, Margaret. "The Evolution of Literacy Programs in the Context of Library Adult Education." *Library Trends* (Fall 1986): 197–205.

Morris, Cicely. "Interview with Marvin Andrade. The Central American Resource Center. Teaching to Change LA (TCLA)." 2001. Downloaded from the web on February 1, 2007. http://www.tcla.gseis.ucla.edu/divide/community/lausd_andrade.html

Morrison, James L. "Environmental Scanning." In *A Primer for New Institutional Researchers*, edited by M. A. Whitely, J. D. Porter, and R. H. Fenske, 86–99. Tallahassee, FL: Association for Institutional Research, 1992.

Mullins, Barbara K. "The Cultural Repertoire of Adult Learning." *Adult Learning* 11, no. 1 (2000): 3–5.

Nadeau, Denise. *Counting Our Victories: Popular Education and Organizing.* Toronto: The Catalyst Centre, 1996.

Nash, Andy. *Civic Participation and Community Action Sourcebook.* Boston: New England Literacy Research Center, 1999.

National Center for Education Statistics (NCES). *Programs for Adults in Public Library Outlets.* NCES 2003-101. Washington, D.C.: U.S. Department of Education. ED Pubs, Office of Educational Research and Improvement, 2002.

National Center for the Study of Adult Learning and Literacy (NCSALL). *What Every Library Should Have: Important Resources on Literacy For Libraries.* Boston: World Education, December 2004.

National Center for the Study of Adult Learning and Literacy (NCSALL). *Learner Persistence in Adult Basic Education, Study Circle Guide.* Boston: World Education, December 2003.

Nauratil, Marsha. *Public Libraries and Non-Traditional Clienteles: The Politics of Special Services.* Westport, CT: Greenwood Press, 1985.

NBLC. *Library Work for Immigrants: A Handbook.* The Hague: NBLC, 1990.

Nee, Victor, and Richard Alba. "Toward a New Definition." In *Reinventing the Melting Pot: The New Immigrants and What It Means to Be American*, edited by Tamar Jacoby, 87–98. New York: Basic Books, 2004.

Neely, Teresa Y. "Minority Student Recruitment in LIS Education: New Profiles for Success." In *Unfinished Business: Race, Equity, and Diversity in Library and Information Science Education*, edited by Maurice Wheeler, 93–117. Lanham, MD: Scarecrow Press, 2005.

Neely, Teresa, and Kuang-Hwei (Janet) Lee-Smeltzer, Eds. *Diversity Now: People, Collections, and Services in Academic Libraries.* Selected Papers from the Big 12 Plus Libraries Consortium Diversity Conference. New York: Haworth, 2002.

Nelson, Sandra. *The New Planning for Results: A Streamlined Approach.* Chicago: American Library Association, 2001.

Nieto, Sonia. *The Light in Their Eyes: Creating Multicultural Learning Communities.* New York: Teachers College Press, 1999.

Noddings, Nel. *Caring, a Feminine Approach to Ethics and Moral Education.* Berkeley: University of California Press, 1984.

Norton, Bonny. *Identity and Language Learning: Gender Ethnicity and Social Change.* London: Pearson Education Limited, 2000.

O'Brien, Dinah S. "Outreach Starts at the Top: Advice from a Library Director." In *From Outreach to Equity: Innovative Models of Library Policy and Practice,* edited by Robin Osborne and Carla D. Hayden, 96–103. Chicago: American Library Association Office for Literacy and Outreach Services, 2004.

O'Connor, Maureen. "Advocacy and Outreach: A Natural Connection." In *From Outreach to Equity: Innovative Models of Library Policy and Practice,* edited by Robin Osborne and Carla D. Hayden, 90–93. Chicago: American Library Association Office for Literacy and Outreach Services, 2004.

Ogbu, J. "Literacy and Schooling in Subordinate Cultures: The Case of Black Americans." In *Literacy in Historical Perspective,* edited by Daniel Resnick. Washington, D.C.: Library of Congress, 1983.

Olds, Larry. *Popular Education News.* Activism [October 2005]. Minneapolis. Downloaded from the web on February 1, 2007. http://www.popednews.org/popular_education_news%20Oct%2005.htm.

Olds, Larry. *Popular Education News.* Community Organizing. [September 2005]. Downloaded from the web on February 1, 2007. http://www.popednews.org/popular_education_news%20Sep%2005.htm.

Orange, Satia, and Robin Osborne. "Introduction." In *From Outreach to Equity: Innovative Models of Library Policy and Practice,* edited by Robin Osborne and Carla D. Hayden, xi–xvii. Chicago: American Library Association Office for Literacy and Outreach Services, 2004.

Orlando, Angela. "How Do Americans View Immigrants?" *Change Agent* 20 (March 2005): 37.

Osborne, Robin. Personal communication, November 5, 2005.

Osterman, Karen F. "Students' Needs for Belonging in the School Community." *Review of Educational Research* 70, no. 3 (Fall 2000): 323–67.

Owens, Major. "The War on Poverty and Outreach." In *Activism in American Librarianship 1962–1973* (Contributions in Librarianship and Information Science, No. 58), edited by Mary Lee Bundy and Frederick Stielow, 73–82. Westport, CT: Greenwood Press, 1987.

Owens, Major. "A Model Library for Community Action." In *Social Responsibilities of Librarians,* edited by Patricia Schumann. New York: Bowker, 1983.

Padilla, Amadado M. *Public Library Services for Immigrant Populations in California.* A Report to the State Librarian of California. California State Library Foundation. Sacramento, CA, January 1991.

Pateman, John. *Developing a Needs-Based Library Service.* Leicester: NIACE Lifelines in Adult Learning, 2003.

Patterson, Thomas. "'Idea Stores': London's New Libraries." *Library Journal* (May 1, 2001): 48–49.

Paulson, Amanda. "Gateway to a New Country." *Christian Science Monitor* (April 13, 2004): 11. Downloaded from the web on February 1, 2007. http://www.csmonitor.com/2004/0413/p11s01-legn.html.

Porter, Kristin, Sondra Cuban, and John Comings. "One Day I Will Make It": A Study of Adult Student Persistence in Library Literacy Programs. New York: MDRC, 2005.

Portes, Alejandro. "For the Second Generation, One Step at a Time." In *Reinventing the Melting Pot: The New Immigrants and What It Means to Be American*, edited by Tamar Jacoby, 155–66. New York: Basic Books, 2004.

Public Library Association Standards Committee. *Minimum Standards for Public Library Systems*. Chicago: American Library Association, 1967.

Pulver, Isaac, and Joan Clark. "World Language Collections: Mining Demographic Data." In *From Outreach to Equity: Innovative Models of Library Policy and Practice*, edited by Robin Osborne and Carla D. Hayden, 106–8. Chicago: American Library Association Office for Literacy and Outreach Services, 2004.

Quezada, Shelley. Personal communication, July 22, 2005.

Quezada, Shelly. "Multicultural Reader's Advisory." Unpublished PowerPoint presentation to the Massachusetts Board of Library Commissioners, March 11, 2003.

Quezada, Shelly. "Mainstreaming Library Services to Multicultural Populations: The Evolving Tapestry." *Wilson Library Bulletin* (February 1992): 28–29.

Quezada, Shelly. "The Role of Libraries in Providing Services to Adults Learning English." ERIC Digest. ED334868 91. Washington, D.C.: National Clearinghouse on Literacy Education, 1991.

Rao, Deepa. "The 'Somali Invasion.'" *The Change Agent* 20 (March 2005): 38–41.

Reforma Executive Board. "Resolution in Support of Immigrants Rights to Free Public Library Access." Approved by American Library Association Council, June 28, 2005.

Reiss, Roberta. "Libraries and Literacy: Making New Connections." In *From Outreach to Equity: Innovative Models of Library Policy and Practice*, edited by Robin Osborne and Carla D. Hayden, 102–3. Chicago: American Library Association Office for Literacy and Outreach Services, 2004.

Rhode Island Foundation. "Current Grantees. English for Action. Project." Downloaded from the web on February 1, 2007. http://www.rifoundation.org/matriarch/OnePiecePage.asp_Q_PageID_E_325_A_PageName_E_stratgrantEFA.

Rhode Island, State of. Office of Library and Information Services. "Tip Sheet to Assist Libraries with Minimum Standards for Rhode Island Public Libraries." Downloaded from the web on February 1, 2007. http://www.olis.ri.gov/pubs/plstandards/tip_43.php.

Rice, Robin. "SC 16. The USA PATRIOT Act and American Libraries." *Information for Social Change Journal*. Downloaded from the web on February 1, 2007. http://www.libr.org/ISC/articles/16-Rice.html.

Rinku, Sen, and Kim Klein. *Stir It Up: Lessons in Community Organizing and Advocacy*. San Francisco: Jossey-Bass, 2003.

Roberts, Faye C. "Hiring for Outreach." In *From Outreach to Equity: Innovative Models of Library Policy and Practice*, edited by Robin Osborne and Carla D. Hayden, 116–18. Chicago: American Library Association Office for Literacy and Outreach Services, 2004.

Robertson, Deborah A. *Cultural Programming for Libraries' Linking Libraries, Communities, and Culture*. Chicago: American Library Association, 2005.

Rockhill, Kathleen. "Literacy as Threat/Desire: Longing to be SOMEBODY." *TESL-Talk* 20, no. 2 (1990): 89–110.

Rodriguez, Gregory. "Mexican-Americans and the Mestizo Melting Pot." In *Reinventing the Melting Pot: The New Immigrants and What It Means to Be American*, edited by Tamar Jacoby, 125–38. New York: Basic Books, 2004.

Rodriguez, Gregory. *From Newcomers to New Americans: The Successful Integration of Immigrants into American Society*. Washington, D.C.: National Immigration Forum, 1999.

Rong, Xue L., and Frank Brown. "The Effects of Immigrant Generation and Ethnicity on Educational Attainment Among Young African and Carribean Blacks in the United States." *Harvard Educational Review* 71, no. 3 (Fall 2001): 536–65.

Rose, Ernestine. *Bridging the Gulf: Work with Russian Jews and Other Newcomers. Seward Park Branch New York Public Library*. New York: Immigrant Publication Society, 1917.

Roy, Lorienne. "Creating Opportunities and Opening Doors: Recruiting and Mentoring Students of Color." In *Unfinished Business: Race, Equity, and Diversity in Library and Information Science Education*, edited by Maurice B. Wheeler, 131–46. Lanham, MD: Scarecrow Press, 2005.

Rubin, Rhea Joyce. *Humanities: A How-to-Do-It Manual for Librarians*. New York: Neal-Schuman Publishers, 1997.

Sataline, Suzanne. "English Language Classes in Short Supply." *Boston.com* (August 15, 2002).

Seager, Andrew. *Learning from Public Library Literacy Programs*. Portsmouth, MA: RMC Corporation, 1993.

Seattle Public Library. "Cultural Communities Program Evaluation." [Unpublished draft report by the Multicultural Task Force 6F3CE.doc]. June 30, 2005.

Seidman, I. E. *Interviewing as Qualitative Research: A Guide for Researchers in Education and Social Sciences*. New York: Teachers College Press, 1991.

Sherill, Lee L. *The Affective Response of Ethnic Minority Readers to Indigenous Ghetto Literature: A Measurement*. Doctoral dissertation, University of Wisconsin–Madison, 1972.

Shriver, Mercedes. "Case Study: What's Really Involved in Public Library Services to Immigrants." University of Michigan School of Information, Class SI 667, Issues in Public Libraries, 2002. Downloaded from the web on December 5, 2005. http://www.si.umich.edu/libhelp/immigrants.htm.

Singleton, Kate. "Health Literacy and Adult English Language Learners." ERIC/ NCLE Digest, 2002. Downloaded from the web on February 1, 2007. http:// www.cal.org/caela/esl_resources/digests/healthlit.html.

Sisco, B., and D. Whitson. "Libraries: The People's University." In *Education Through Community Organizations* (New Directions for Adult and Continuing Education, No. 47), edited by Michael Galbraith, 21–28. San Francisco: Jossey-Bass, 1990.

Sleeter, Christine E., and C. A. Grant. "An Analysis of Multicultural Education in the United States." *Harvard Educational Review* 57, no. 4 (1987): 421–43.

Smith, Esther G. "The Literacy Education Gap: The Involvement of Public Libraries in Literacy Education." *Library and Information Science Research* 6 (1984): 75–94.

Sonenberg, Nina. "Telling Their Own Stories." *American Libraries* 36, no. 4 (April 2005): 72–74.

Spangenberg, Gail. *Even Anchors Need Lifelines: Public Libraries in Adult Literacy.* New York: Spangenberg Learning Resources and the Center for the Book, 1996.

Sparhawk, Sally, and Marian Schickling. *Strategic Needs Analysis.* Info-Line: Practical Guidelines for Training and Development Professionals. Alexandria, VA: American Society for Training and Development (ASTD), 1994.

Sparks, Barbara. "A Sociocultural Approach to Planning Programs for Immigrant Learners." *Adult Learning* 12/13, no. 4 (Fall 2001/2002): 22–25.

Spencer, Michael. "Libraries and Liberties: A Transcript of Jim Lehrer's News Hour." June 18, 2003. Downloaded from the web on February 1, 2007. http://www.pbs.org/newshour/bb/law/jan-june03/library_6-18.html.

Spradley, James P. *The Ethnographic Interview.* New York: Holt, Rinehart and Winston, 1979.

Squire, Kurt, and Constance Steinkuehler. "Meet the Gamers." *Library Journal. com* (April 2005).

Steinberg, Stephen. "The Melting Pot and the Color Line." In *Reinventing the Melting Pot: The New Immigrants and What It Means to Be American,* edited by Tamar Jacoby, 235–48. New York: Basic Books, 2004.

Sticht, Thomas. "Persistence in English as a Second Language (ESL) Programs: Research Using the Method of Natural Variations." [AAACE-NLA] January 31, 2005.

Strand, Kerry, Nicholas Cutforth, Randy Stoeker, Sam Marullo, and Patrick Donohoe. *Community-Based Research and Higher Education.* San Francisco: Jossey-Bass, 2003.

Strong, Gary. "Teaching Adult Literacy in a Multicultural Environment." In *Literacy and Libraries: Learning from Case Studies,* edited by GraceAnne DeCandido, 110–15. Chicago: American Library Association, 2001.

Suarez-Orozco, Marcelo M. "The Need for Strangers: Proposition 187 and the Immigration Malaise." In *Immigrant Politics and the Public Library*

(Contributions in Librarianship and Information Science, No. 97), edited by Susan Luevano-Molina, 17–30. Westport, CT: Greenwood Press, 2001a.

Suarez-Orozco, Marcelo M. "Globalization, Immigration, and Education: The Research." *Harvard Educational Review* 71, no. 3 (Fall 2001b): 345–65.

Sumerford, Steve. Personal communication, October 12, 2005.

Sumerford, Steve. "Creating a Community of Readers to Fight Functional Illiteracy." In *From Outreach to Equity: Innovative Models of Library Policy and Practice,* edited by Robin Osborne and Carla D. Hayden, 97–105. Chicago: American Library Association Office for Literacy and Outreach Services, 2004a.

Sumerford, Steve. "Libraries as Community Builders: The Greensboro Experience." In *From Outreach to Equity: Innovative Models of Library Policy and Practice*, edited by Robin Osborne and Carla D. Hayden, 39–41. Chicago: American Library Association Office for Outreach and Literacy, 2004b.

Sykes, Vivian. "Perspectives on Cultural Diversity." In *Cultural Diversity in Libraries*, edited by Donald Riggs and Patricia Tarin. New York: Neal-Schuman Publishers, 1994.

Tandler, Adriana A. "New Americans Program: Outreach Through Partnerships." In *From Outreach to Equity: Innovative Models of Library Policy and Practice*, edited by Robin Osborne and Carla D. Hayden, 104–5. Chicago: American Library Association Office for Literacy and Outreach Services, 2004.

Taylor, Deborah. "Community Youth Corps: Teens as Library Resources." In *From Outreach to Equity: Innovative Models of Library Policy and Practice*, edited by Robin Osborne and Carla D. Hayden, 45–47. Chicago: American Library Association Office for Literacy and Outreach Services, 2004.

Taylor, Pamela. "Countdown to Culturally Responsive Teaching." PowerPoint presentation at Seattle University, 2004.

Tecker Consultants. "The Public Library Association: Strategic Plan." Downloaded from the web on February 1, 2007. http://www.ala.org/ala/pla/plaorg/plastrategicplan/stratplan.pdf [See also updated plan]: http://www.ala.org/ala/pla/plaorg/plastrategicplan/plastrategic.htm.

Thernstrom, Stephen. "Rediscovering the Melting Pot—Still Going Strong." In *Reinventing the Melting Pot: The New Immigrants and What It Means to Be American*, edited by Tamar Jacoby, 47–60. New York: Basic Books, 2004.

Tinto, V. C. "Taking Learning Seriously." Speech given at Seattle University, Convocation Day, September 18, 2005.

Tjoumas, Renee. "Opening Doors to New Immigrants: Queens Borough Public Library's Coping Skills Component." *Public Library Quarterly* 14, no. 4 (1995): 5–19.

"Travelin' Librarian." Michael Gorman Response in the *Denver Post*. Editorial section August 18, 2005. Downloaded from the web on December 15, 2005. http://www.travelinlibrarian.info/2005_08_01_archive.html.

Trejo, Fujibayashi, and Mary Kaye Trejo. "The Library as a Port of Entry." *American Libraries* (November 1988): 890–92.

Trejo, Ninfa A. "Impact of Proposition 187 on Public Libraries and Elementary Education in Tucson, Arizona." In *Immigrant Politics and the Public Library*

(Contributions in Librarianship and Information Science, No. 97), edited by Susan Luevano-Molina, 89–100. Westport, CT: Greenwood Press, 2001.

Tumulty, Karen. "Should They Stay or Should They Go?" *Time* 167, no. 15 (2006): 30–39.

Utarti, Hediana. Personal communication, September 15, 2006.

Vang, Vang. "Public Library Services to the Hmong-American Community: Much Room for Improvement." Paper, n.d. http://libres.curtin.edu.au/libres14n1/March%2004_Ess%20%20Op_VangNov20_03.htm.

Villalpando, Maru. Personal communication, October 19, 2005.

Virgilio, Damone. "Infobus: Serving Immigrant and Refugee Populations." In *From Outreach to Equity: Innovative Models of Library Policy and Practice*, edited by Robin Osborne and Carla D. Hayden, 9–11. Chicago: American Library Association Office for Outreach and Literacy, 2004.

Wagner, Pat. "Outreach as Friendship in a Peer-Based Community." In *From Outreach to Equity: Innovative Models of Library Policy and Practice,* edited by Robin Osborne and Carla D. Hayden, 128–29. Chicago: American Library Association Office for Outreach and Literacy, 2004.

Waldinger, Roger. "The 21st Century: An Entirely New Story." In *Reinventing the Melting Pot: The New Immigrants and What It Means to Be American*, edited by Tamar Jacoby, 75–86 New York: Basic Books, 2004.

Waldinger, Roger. *Strangers at the Gates: New Immigrants in Urban America.* Berkeley: University of California Press, 2001.

Wallerstein, Nina, and Elsa Auerbach. *Problem-Posing at Work: Popular Educators Guide.* Edmonton, Alberta, Canada: Grassroots Press, 2004.

Waples, Douglas, and Ralph Tyler. *What People Want to Read About: A Study of Group Interests and Survey Problems in Adult Reading.* Chicago: American Library Association, 1931.

Walters, S. (1992). *A How-to-Do-It Manual for Librarians.* New York: Neal-Schuman, 1992.

Weaver, R. "Another Divide: Low Literacy Adults and the New Technology." In *Literacy and Libraries: Learning from Case Studies*, edited by GraceAnne A. DeCandido, 141–45. Chicago, IL: American Library Association Office of Literacy and Outreach Services, 2001.

Webjunction. "Spanish Language Outreach Program." October 5, 2004. Downloaded from the web on February 1, 2007. http://www.webjunction.org/do/DisplayContent?id=7780.

Weibel, Kathleen. *The Evolution of Library Outreach 1960-75 and Its Effect on Reader Services.* Champaign, IL: Graduate School of Library and Information Studies, University of Illinois, 1982.

Wheeler, Maurice B., ed. *Unfinished Business: Race, Equity, and Diversity in Library and Information Science Education.* Lanham, MD: Scarecrow Press, 2005.

Wiegand, Wayne. "The Politics of Cultural Authority." *American Libraries* (January 1998): 80–82.

Wiegand, Wayne. *"An Active Instrument Of Propaganda": The American Public Library During World War I.* Westport, CT: Greenwood Press, 1989.

Wiegand, Wayne. "The Socialization of Library and Information Science Students: Reflections on a Century of Formal Education for Librarianship." *Library Trends* 34 (1986): 383–99.

Willard, Archie. "Plain English Is for Everyone." *The Change Agent* 16 (March 2003): 21.

Williams, Alex. "Item: Sisters Think Parents Did OK." *New York Times* (October 16, 2005): Section 9.

Wolmuth, Sonia, and Kathleen de la Peña McCook. "Equity of Access: Igniting a Passion for Change." *WebJunction*, June 1, 2004. Downloaded from the web on February 1, 2007. http://webjunction.org/do/PrinterFriendlyConte nt?id=5507.

Wong, Emily. Personal communication, August 6, 2005.

2004 Yearbook of Immigration Statistics. Washington, D.C.: U.S. Government Printing Office, 2006.

2002 Yearbook of Immigration Statistics. Washington, D.C.: U.S. Government Printing Office, 2003.

Yoklun, John. "The Barefoot Librarian: A Model for Developing Countries?" *Libraries Alone: An International Journal* 1, no. 1 (Spring 1988): 13–20.

Young, Sarah. "Adolescent Learners in Adult ESL Classes." Center for Adult English Language Acquisition (CAELA), Center for Applied Linguisitics. Brief. October 2005.

Zhang, Xiwen. "The Practice and Politics of Public Library Services to Asian Immigrants and Mexican Immigrants at the Santa Ana Public Library: An Urban Ethnography." In *Immigrant Politics and the Public Library* (Contributions in Librarianship and Information Science, No. 97), edited by Susan Luevano-Molina, 43–63. Westport, CT: Greenwood Press, 2001.

Zhou, Min. "Assimilation the American Way." In *Reinventing the Melting Pot: The New Immigrants and What It Means to Be American*, edited by Tamar Jacoby, 139–54. New York: Basic Books, 2004.

Zinn, Howard. *You Can't Be Neutral on a Moving Train: A Personal History of Our Times.* Boston: Beacon Press, 1994.

Zipkowitz, Fay. "Introduction: Library Services to Unserved Populations." *The Reference Librarian*, no. 53 (1996): 1–4.

Zweizig, Douglas. "How Firm a Foundation?" *Library Trends* 46, no. 1 (1997).

Zweizig, Douglas. "With Our Eye on the User: Needed Research for Information and Referral in the Public Library." *Drexel Library Quarterly* 12, no. 1 and 2 (1976): 48–58.

Index

ABOUT THE AUTHOR

SONDRA CUBAN is a lecturer in the Department of Educational Research at Lancaster University, England. A former ESOL and ABE teacher, she also worked as a librarian in Hawai'i. A grandchild of immigrants from Poland and Russia, Sondra remembers visiting the library in a suburban Cleveland neighborhood with her grandmother, Anne (Shmigelsky) Smith, who borrowed mystery books and read them voraciously in her apartment after she retired from her job as a secretary for a social service agency. As a former librarian and educator, Sondra is passionately committed to the powerful role that libraries can play as advocates for new immigrant communities.